*In memory of Layden Stroud*

*1926–2010*

*U.S. Navy Corpsman*

*Second World War*

*And, in gratitude, to*

*Bruce Merrill and Bruce Parham*

# The Fires of Patriotism

# The Fires *of* Patriotism

## *Alaskans in the Days of the First World War 1910–1920*

Preston Jones

Photographs and illustrations
edited by Neal Holland

University of Alaska Press
*Fairbanks*

University of Alaska Press
P.O. Box 756240
Fairbanks, AK 99775-6240

ISBN 978-1-60223-205-1

Library of Congress Cataloging-in-Publication Data

Jones, Preston, 1966–
The fires of patriotism : Alaskans in the days of the First World War 1910–1920 / Preston Jones ; photographs and illustrations edited by Neal Holland.
pages cm
Includes index.
ISBN 978-1-60223-205-1 (pbk. : alk. paper) — ISBN 978-1-60223-206-8 (electronic book)
1. World War, 1914-1918—Alaska. 2. Alaska—History—1867–1959. I. Title.
D570.87.A5J66 2013
940.3'798—dc23
2012040552

Cover design by Dixon Jones

Cover illustration: Soldiers march in Nome. Archives, University of Alaska Fairbanks, UAF-1980–68–257.

This publication was printed on acid-free paper that meets the minimum requirements for ANSI / NISO Z39.48–1992 (R2002) (Permanence of Paper for Printed Library Materials).

# CONTENTS


*Timeline* *ix*

*Preface and Acknowledgments* *xi*

1. The Alaskans 1

2. The War before the War 27

3. Over Here—Words 45

4. Over Here—Deeds 63

5. Organizing 91

6. Aftermath 123

Appendix I: Primary Sources 139

Appendix II: Alaska in 1918: A Letter from Governor Strong 163

*Endnotes* 167

*Bibliography* 181

*Index* 187

# TIMELINE

## 1912

U.S. Congress passes Second Organic Act. Alaska gains its own legislature, though Congress retains significant control over matters such as fish and game, gambling, divorce, and the incorporation of towns. Alaska's judges are appointed by the U.S. president.

## 1913

The Alaska legislature's first bill gives women in the territory the right to vote. (Women do not gain complete suffrage throughout the United States until 1920.)

J. F. A. Strong (Democrat) sworn in as governor of Alaska.

Territorial legislature passes legislation related to compulsory education and an eight-hour workday on public projects.

## 1914

Congress votes to build a railroad in Alaska from Seward to Fairbanks.

Anchorage and Nenana founded.

First World War begins in Europe (August).

## 1915

*Lusitania* is sunk by a German submarine (May). Nearly two thousand people die, nearly 130 of them Americans.

## 1916

Alaskans choose, via an advisory vote, to put the prohibition of alcohol into place. (U.S. Congress passes the Alaska "Bone Dry" Law in early 1918.)

Woodrow Wilson elected for a second term as U.S. president.

## 1917

Germany begins unrestricted submarine warfare, including against U.S. ships en route to Britain.

Alaska Agricultural College and School of Mines (future University of Alaska Fairbanks) founded.

The Zimmermann Telegram, a German cable that offers a military agreement with Mexico in case of war with the United States, is intercepted by the British and passed on to the U.S. government.

United States declares war on Germany (April 6).

United States declares war on Austria-Hungary (December).

## 1918

Governor Strong, discovered not to be a U.S. citizen, loses his office.

Thomas Riggs is appointed governor of Alaska.

First World War ends in German defeat (November).

# PREFACE AND ACKNOWLEDGMENTS

This book aims to tell a story that has not been told before: the story of Alaska society during the era of the First World War. The author has previously published some pages on the war as experienced in Nome and Anchorage. This book benefits from that work but goes well beyond it.

While these pages were being written, Steven C. Levi published *The Great Red Scare in World War One Alaska: Elite Panic, Government Hysteria, Suppression of Civil Liberties, Union-Breaking, and Germanophobia* (2010). That book and this one are quite different. Where, in the words of a back-cover blurb, Levi aims to describe the "terrible period" that foreshadows the United States' "drift into permanent emergency paranoia" since the terrorist attacks of 2001 on American soil, this book offers a point of view but no overt political agenda. Another difference is that while this book focuses on the First World War, it also aims to capture the social history of an era and to place Alaska's experience of the war in a broad social, national, and international context.

A third point is that *The Great Red Scare in World War One Alaska* makes some claims that cannot be sustained. Levi writes, for example, of noncitizens being "interned" in Alaska during the war and asks, "What of the enemy aliens who were not interned?"[1] It is a pointless question because, while some in Alaska called for an internment policy in the territory, no such policy was put into place.[2] Elsewhere Levi writes of Alaskans seeing "more and more military might appearing in their community" during the First World War.[3] But the military presence in Alaska, weak before the conflict, was weaker afterwards. Levi writes that during the war the "United States government was gravely concerned that the territory of Alaska might fall into enemy hands."[4] If action points to truth, then the opposite is the case. Before the war, during the war, and afterwards, the U.S. government did not look seriously to Alaska's defense. The Panama Canal, among other assets, was deemed more important. For a final example, Levi writes that, during the war, anyone who was "noticeably foreign was un-American which was, by logical implication, pro-German."[5] As the following pages show, this claim is simply wrong. Some foreign-born Alaskans faced problems; a few confronted serious problems. This was not the case for the majority. Having offered these few thoughts on *The Great Red Scare in Alaska*, I will argue with it no further.

It is not difficult to understand why Alaska's general experience during the First World War has received little coverage in historical writing up to now. Where the Second World War transformed Alaska, its grim predecessor initiated a time of economic sluggishness. Before the war, which the United States entered in April 1917, hopes for Alaska's development were high. Construction of the Alaska Railroad began in 1915, and with that work sprang up two new towns, Anchorage and Nenana. For Alaskans, this was a sign of prosperity to come.

When the United States declared war against Germany in 1917, Alaskans hoped that their territory's resources would take a central place in the nation's calculations. Given Alaska's wealth, this hope was reasonable. "When the United States entered World War I," one historian writes, "the need for coal and fuel across the nation propelled Alaska into the limelight."[6] But that light soon dimmed because, given the lack of infrastructure in the territory, Alaska's coal and other resources could not be quickly or easily transported Outside.

Such was Alaska's fix: its distance from the nation's decision-making centers had made it easy to forget. Thus, the territory went without infrastructure, and now that its resources were needed, they could not be easily accessed. This led to another shifting of the federal government's eyes from Alaska. A *Miami Herald* headline in the spring of 1918 made the point: "Work on the Alaskan Road Being Delayed." Washington, D.C., would not again focus on Alaska in any sustained way until the next world war.

This perceived lack of interest was not reciprocated, for Alaskans contributed significantly to the war cause. "Alaska has led the nation in the number of [military] inductions in proportion to population," a 1918 memo distributed to the territory's authorities noted.[7] But this, in addition to the loss of laborers who left the territory to work in war-related industries, meant an almost crippling loss of manpower. Writing in the early 1920s, historian Jeannette Nichols reflected on Alaska's public life. She noted that Alaska's population was declining instead of multiplying. Alaska's "industries, instead of expanding, have suffered a severe slump." And this, she observed, was the result of the Great War. "That conflict drained Alaska of her younger pioneers and discouraged investment in the north."[8] In a real sense, then, the economic depression that descended on the United States and the industrialized world in late 1929 began twelve years earlier in Alaska. Perhaps the theme of Alaska and the Great War has not been attractive to historians because it seemed that there was not much to say.

This book suggests that there is something to say. At one level, the Alaska experience during the First World War was similar to that in, say, Arkansas, Maine, or California. Certain themes held nationwide. The general tone and temper of Alaska public life—to the extent that this can be determined from available sources—was generally the same as it was throughout the United States. But there was an Alaska difference. Considering the special rigors that came with life in sparsely settled Alaska, Governor Strong wrote to a correspondent from Illinois that conditions in the territory were "*absolutely different* from those in the well settled states."[9] Focusing on place and diet, the writer John Underwood observed that Alaskans eat "moose steaks for breakfast and roast or baked moose meat for dinner," appealing at once to the mixed images of wild and romance that Alaska still evokes.[10]

Subtitled *An Empire in the Making*, Underwood's thick tome focused on Alaska's fantastic natural wealth and promise. "The glory of the North is dawning," he wrote, "its infinite wonders are gradually unfolding."[11] Alaska, one-fifth the size of the United States and more than double the size of the German Empire, had "room for millions" and was capable of producing food sufficient to supply a Euro-American population of more than seven million. (Underwood was writing in 1912. A century later Alaska's population stood at just under seven hundred thousand.) "It may sound like a wild dream," he wrote, but he saw the day coming when Europe's immigrants would decide to forgo the "polluted atmosphere of the sweat-shops" in eastern cities and would instead make their way through the Panama Canal, up the West Coast, and into Alaska ports with the aim of "rearing their families, building their schools, and evolving a race of robust, intelligent citizens." On a per capita basis, he noted, each white Alaskan was worth in trade nearly five Hawaiians and four hundred Filipinos. And where China was an "old country," Alaska was a "coming country."[12]

This points us to another Alaska difference, and another meaning of the word *empire*. In 1917 Alaska was more than forty years from statehood. As far as informed Americans at that time were concerned, Alaska was an element of the young American Empire. As one naval strategist whose work was read by at least a few authorities in Anchorage noted, either "acquisitiveness or destiny" had presented the United States with an empire that included Alaska.[13] The territory was different from Guam, Hawaii, and the Philippines, yet in some ways more like those imperial holdings than Florida or Michigan. So to consider Alaska society during the First World War is to consider a society that was truly American but also set apart—by distance, but also by a broader outlook on the world. The Siberia Natives who sometimes walked the streets of Nome reminded Alaskans they lived not only *in* a frontier but *on* a frontier—the decidedly unsettled frontier of the Pacific Rim. Longtime Alaskans were Americans, yes, but Americans apart—geographically and also, in some ways, psychologically.

While this study gathers and organizes material into narrative form, a key goal is to let Alaskans speak for themselves. Thus, excerpts from letters written by Alaskans are reproduced following chapters 1–5, and numerous documents from the era of the First World War, mostly newspaper articles, have been collected in the appendices. In addition to allowing readers to read the words of people who lived in Alaska during the war, many of the excerpts display the literary quality of Alaska's early newspapers, most of which were produced for people whom we now call "blue collar." These documents contribute detail where the book's narrative operates at a higher level of generality.

A word on sources. In my earlier work on Nome and Anchorage, I uncovered some archival materials related to the First World War. I draw on those sources, as well as on the diary of Alaska congressional delegate James Wickersham and the correspondence of Governors John Strong and Thomas Riggs. I also consulted the *Alaska Railroad Record*, a government publication. These sources alone account for perhaps fifteen hundred pages of source material. In addition, I have drawn heavily from newspapers published in all parts of Alaska.

As this study is concerned primarily with public culture, its judicious, critical use of newspapers does not pose a problem. It is true that newspaper editorial voices do not speak for everyone in a community, but it is also true that Alaska's community newspapers relied on locals for financial support and could not alienate a large number of readers. Since community smallness made for reportorial accountability, stories about local events can be taken as generally accurate, if inevitably lacking in nuance and complication.

During the war, Alaska's newspapers effectively became compendiums of news (mostly local and Alaskan), opinion, private correspondence made public, and government information. Official speeches were reprinted in the newspapers. Much material that otherwise would be lost is preserved in the newspapers. Many letters sent home to Alaska from soldiers would be unknown had they not been published in newspapers. I am especially gratified to have been able to bring to light again a remarkable and informative letter written by Molly Smith, from Valdez, who served in France as a nurse with the Red Cross.

The many thousands of dense newspaper pages reviewed for this study amount to treasure troves comprising items related to business, schools, churches, family news, the coming and going of visitors, and so on. It would be a mistake to think of early-twentieth-century newspapers as we think of them in the twenty-first century. Alaska's newspapers of the First World War era acted as community diaries.

I have limited most endnotes to sources quoted. Throughout the narrative, and in the excerpts of original texts, I have corrected typos, added or deleted some punctuation, and updated spelling and phraseology—for example, changing "partisanism" to "partisanship." Most of the titles of the documents in the appendix are original, though I have edited or created a few.

I am grateful to Elisabeth Dabney, formerly of the University of Alaska Press, for her help and encouragement early in the process. I am grateful to Rachel Fudge and Sue Mitchell for their admirable work on the manuscript. I thank Joan Braddock and James Engelhardt, at the UAP, for picking up where Elisabeth left off and for patiently seeing this book through the process. I also thank: Kerry Feldman, of the University of Alaska Anchorage, for critical comments on various manuscripts; Catherine Harbor, my assistant, for transcribing the letters that follow the book's chapters and also many of the documents in the appendix; Simone Schroder, of my university, for procuring numerous books and documents via interlibrary loan; Chip Pollard, Ed Ericson, Rick Froman, Galen Johnson, and Cary Balzer, administrators at my university, for making research funds available; and Neal Holland, for his editing of the photographs and newspaper images included in these pages.

For their help, I am also grateful to a few people at the Alaska State Library in Juneau: James Simard, director of historical collections; Becky Orford, interlibrary loan librarian; and Freya Anderson, head of information services. Thanks also to Richard H. Van Cleave of the museum at Ketchikan, as well as to the helpful, though unnamed, archivist at the museum in Seward who sent some documents to me via old-fashioned mail. Tatyana Stepanova at the Alaska State Archives kindly provided me with the most complete list available on Alaskans who served in the military during the First World War.

The manuscript's second round of reviewers, Claus-M. Naske and John Stewart, provided very helpful suggestions. Mr. Stewart also made available to me a short manuscript of his on Alaska and the First World War. I thank him. As for the first-round reviewers, I do not know who they are, but I am grateful for their helpful comments.

A special word of thanks goes to Steven Haycox, Bruce Merrell, and Bruce Parham, all of whom retired from full-time work in Alaska history while this book was being contemplated and written. I thank them for their years of labor and for the example they set.

I thank the following students in a U.S. history class of mine who read and critiqued various chapters of the manuscript: Sam Boehning, Victoria Cook, Katie Douglas, Danielle Hancock, Josh Tures, and Autumn Weese.

And, finally, a word to the family of Layden Stroud, who made many of the photographs included in this book available to me. The photos were taken in France during the First World War by Layden's father-in-law, Emmett Lemuel Graham. Aside from a small public showing at my university, the photos have not been previously available to the public. Layden passed away as this book was being written. I thank his family for sharing such a good man with the world.

Preston Jones
John Brown University
Siloam Springs, Arkansas

# CHAPTER ONE

# The Alaskans

## Alaska and the City

While many Americans living in the southern states during the Civil War experienced a degree of battle-related deprivation and hardship unknown to other American communities, the Great War was the first American conflict to enlist all of the nation's resources. Where an older, wealthy, and childless resident of central Maine could live through the Civil War era almost oblivious to news of the hostilities, this was not possible during the brief but intense period between the United States' declaration of war against Germany in early April 1917 and Germany's suit for peace in November of the following year. The war seemed to touch every aspect of American society. As we shall see, even Americans' efficiency in the privacy of their own homes became a topic of wartime commentary. This was all the more striking because of the great indifference many Americans displayed toward the European war through its first three years.

In the decade before the war, the United States' chief preoccupations were with problems linked to urbanization, industrialization, and immigration. That fact alone points to how life in Alaska was set apart from the broader American experience—geographically, of course, but also culturally and socially. Even communities in rural states had increasingly easy access to large cities via railroad. This was not the case in Alaska. Life in what was then a territory (Alaska did not become a U.S. state until 1959) offered particular rigors. Success in the face of Alaska's rigors spurred the idea that Alaskans comprised an especially sturdy type of person. The "ordinary Alaskan," wrote Frank Foster of McCarthy, "is physically superior to most city bred men."[1]

Still, Alaska communities were identifiably American. This point was made in the numerous commentaries from Alaskans and visitors to the territory, which aimed to show the extent to which Alaska life did not really differ from life Outside. It was true, an observer wrote in 1912, that the residents of Nome spent months at a time in frosty darkness and experienced a degree of civic isolation unknown in any town Outside. But Nomeites knew how to occupy themselves, and their "entertainments are not by any means of the crude character that would be expected." The town's women were "just as well gowned," and its men were "just as carefully groomed as though they were in attendance at an inaugural ball at the National capital."[2]

For many living Outside, cities were associated with pathology—excessive drinking, crime, squalor, and the loosening of moral culture. But cities were also associated with economic efficiency and the creation of wealth and opportunities. Alaska newspapers regularly carried stories touching both themes. But, for Alaskans, the ups and downs of urban life were mostly abstractions. Yes, Alaska was tied economically to Seattle, and many Alaskans had experienced city life; and, yes, Alaskans sometimes missed the Outside's easy access to electricity, bustling streets, theaters, streetcars, and the other amenities that tended to pamper the "appetite of civilization." But Alaskans had also seen the Outside's "distress ... worry ... oppression, [and] ... heart-breaking poverty." And so, as one writer put it, "with a deep and abiding disgust for the selfishness, shallowness, and meanness of it all," the Alaskan turned away from the corrupt realm of tall buildings and toward "his beloved Northland."[3]

Yet Alaska writers regularly expressed a desire for more people, more settlements, and more development—more of what modern America had to offer. Governor John Strong echoed a general sentiment when he noted that Alaska could not and would not be developed until a comprehensive system of roads was laid.[4] Many Alaskans wanted cities, and questions about whatever problems such population growth might lead to were rarely considered.

Once the United States entered the First World War, there were some expressions of relief that Alaska was far removed from the dangers facing American cities on the East Coast. A year into the war, Fairbanks's *Alaska Citizen* noted that small communities seemed to be better able to respond to the war's burdens than cities were. But the hope that Alaska would soon sprout its own urban centers persisted.

Nenana in 1917. Anchorage Museum, AMRC-aec-j60

Work on Alaska's first and only substantial railroad, which would connect Seward and Fairbanks and would lead to the establishment of Anchorage and Nenana, began in 1915. Like the turn-of-the-century gold rushes, this project spurred competitive sparring over which of Alaska's settlements would prosper and become the territory's "metropolis." During the gold rush, Skagway's boosters had called their town a "city of destiny" and derided Juneau as a "dyspeptic dwarf."[5] Residents of the soon-dead settlement of Dyea prophesied that their community of 150 businesses would become the "seaport of the gold fields, the greatest outfitting center in America, a mining point of importance—the metropolis, in fact, of the northern wonderland."[6] On the Seward Peninsula, Teller, which would never thrive, was looked to as an up-and-coming "Queen city of the ice," while an Alaska poet wondered, with conscious overstatement, whether the "burg of Nome will rival Rome."[7] Soon after the Great War, the English travel writer Charlotte Cameron wrote of Fairbanks as the future "Metropolis of Alaska." As for Nenana, it seemed "primitive" but "rich in possibilities," given its place along the new railroad. It was a place of friendly, literate people and hosted the "nice, clean, and comfortable" Cooney Hotel.[8] The survival of the young town of Anchorage seemed "probable," though few without vested interests in its success saw much in

Juneau, circa 1917. University of Alaska Fairbanks, UAF-1989-166-159-Print

the place to brag about.[9] Anchorageites described their community as "a prospective commercial center of importance."[10]

As for Juneau, the territory's capital, businessman Sanford Mackeever predicted a future population of one hundred thousand—about seventy thousand shy of what it would be one hundred years later. And the *Seward Gateway* foresaw that by 1920 the population along the train route would "probably serve a population of tens of thousands," a prediction that would be fulfilled in the 1940s.[11] The U.S. secretary of the interior, Franklin Lane, looked forward to Alaska providing a home to "millions."[12] Charles Tuttle, author of *Alaska: Its Meaning to the World* (1914), predicted the rise of a "great commercial city" on Prince William Sound that, with Seattle, would rival the regional power and influence of New York, Boston, and Philadelphia.[13]

Some Alaskans had gone to the territory because they were worried about or disenchanted by the problems and challenges that came with cities and industrialization. But Alaskans also fretted about the problems and challenges that came with not having cities and the industry associated with them.

## Americans New and Old

In 1870, the United States' population stood at about forty million. By 1917, that number had risen to about 103 million, thanks in part to the highest levels of immigration seen in the country at that point. About half of these immigrants lived in cities like New York and Chicago. These cities now hosted large neighborhoods where English was not widely used and where poverty and the problems stemming from it prevailed in some cases.

Some immigrants went to Alaska. Indeed, nearly forty percent of the Alaska men who registered for military service in 1917 were foreign born.[14] Some of the newcomers who went to Anchorage were named Tasaki, Tanaka, Kamada, Yokota, and Kemota. The patriarch of Nome's prominent Lomen family was an immigrant from Norway. A Russian Jew named Z. J. Loussac settled first in Juneau and later in Anchorage, where he became a community pillar. A list of names from Skagway in the year 1917 provides a sense of the ethnic variety of Alaska's towns: Abrahams, Bender, Fowler, Toyozumi, and Wurzbacher. The town's *Daily Alaskan* referred to itself as a "cosmopolitan" place.[15] That term also applied to Nenana, home to Sam Geroff, Jack Hohoff, Harry Gasaloff, and Kyuzabura Saito.

While there were no organized settlement homes and few community social programs arranged for their benefit, few of Alaska's immigrants experienced

*Nenana Daily News*, January 4, 1918

hostility on account of their accent, skin tone, or place of birth. The simple reason for this was that early-twentieth-century Alaska always needed more people. The territory could hardly afford wasteful public prejudice when all capable hands were needed. It is true that there were occasional expressions of ill will, such as when foreign-born Alaska Railroad workers were collectively belittled in a newspaper editorial as "Jesus Patagaschsky and his friends,"[16] or when Mexicans were called "greasers" and Montenegrins, or Greeks and Canadians were brushed off as more interested in playing pool than building up Alaska.[17] But by far the greater story was civility among Alaskans of different backgrounds. When Hamma Haddad of Syria petitioned in Anchorage for American citizenship, George Abraham and Frank Walsh spoke for his moral character. And William Kimura, the son of Japanese parents, remembered late in life that his childhood friends in Anchorage had been Finnish, Swedish, German, Italian, Russian, and Native. There never was anything in Alaska comparable to the keen anti-Japanese sentiment that broke out in parts of the American and Canadian west coasts.[18]

As we will see, after the declaration of war in April 1917, Germans especially, but also Austrians and immigrants from other enemy nations, would come under scrutiny for signs of disloyalty. Some would face hostility, and at least one death was shrouded in ambiguity. Soon after the United States entered the war, a miner in La Touche, himself an immigrant, wrote about a friend who "nerly went insen" and "tore his heir and cursd the Germans" and "hasent spoken A word to a German."[19] But in well-settled areas, personal interethnic animosity was unusual.

It is certainly true that Alaskans shared the human preoccupation with racial and ethnic difference that was not tempered, as in later times, by an interest in interracial sensitivity. In one case, "Mrs. John Bean" was held up as a model pioneer—"the first white woman to bear a thoroughbred white child in interior Alaska."[20] And social events that would be starkly unacceptable a century later made for simple entertainment. A "Darktown" minstrel show organized in McCarthy falls into this category. And some of the language used to describe Alaska Natives—"dusky children of the wilds," "brunette children of the mossy glades," "dusky maids"—was dismissive and derogatory. [21]

## Natives

Writers' reflections on Alaska Natives were often complimentary, though sometimes backhanded. Southeastern Alaska Native women were sharp and shrewd bargainers, John Underwood wrote, even if they lacked basic economic knowledge. Natives were clever, but they were also simple-minded and "much afraid of anything which they do not understand." While the "Alaska Indians" retained "the savage ideas of workmanship in their carvings," they excelled at copying designs made by professionals Outside. In Nome, Underwood saw a picture of President Taft reproduced expertly on a walrus tusk. Considering Japan's rise as a nation, substantially as a result of its appropriation of western military and economic methods, Underwood wondered if the Alaska Natives' "efficiency at copying" lent strength to a theory that Alaska's first inhabitants had originated in Japan.[22]

Obviously, the territory's Natives had been Alaskans long before immigrants from New York, California, Argentina, and eastern Europe assumed that identity. As was true throughout the Americas, Australasia, and parts of Africa, the descendants of Alaska's first immigrants had been confronted with the se of European civilization since the early modern period. For many Alaska Natives, the Russian colonial presence was distant and of little significance. From the American purchase of Alaska in 1867, the Yankee presence combined with the influx of immigrants was increasingly difficult, and finally impossible, to avoid.

It is possible to speak in general terms about Euro-Alaska society in the First World War era. Nome's public culture differed from Anchorage's, for example, but not very much. When talking about Alaska Natives, however, generalizations are more difficult to make. The term "Alaska Native" refers to different groups speaking about twenty languages and, in some cases, separated by hundreds of miles. Given this diversity, we will focus here on relations between Natives and non-Natives.

For decades, the approach to discussions of interactions between the descendants of Alaska's first human settlers and its later American immigrants has been shaped by the rubric of victim and victimizer. There is a reason for this. The arrival in Alaska of tens of thousands of non-Natives—and their weapons, diseases, passion for gold and other natural resources, and ready supply of alcohol—brought psychological disequilibrium, social destruction, and sometimes death to Native communities. At the same time, it is important to see that Natives were not only on the receiving end of things. They were also active agents, and many non-Native Alaskans admired and adopted elements of Native culture. Natives influenced how some Alaskans dressed, talked, studied, traveled, decorated their homes, and presented themselves to the outside world.

We gain some insight into the complicated relationship between Natives and non-Natives in the correspondence of Governor John Strong. In the fall of 1917, he received a letter asking if the state of Washington could be reimbursed for the cost of educating an Alaska Eskimo who was blind. "I regret to say," the governor responded, that the law allowed payment "only for white children and, as the case mentioned by you is an Indian or Eskimo child, the law will not cover it." Strong's response reads cold and bureaucratic, but the governor offered an additional thought. He suggested that the child might be sent to a hospital in Juneau where the U.S. Bureau of Education would pick up costs.[23] Regulations bound but did not prevent him from seeking another solution. And while in later decades there would be justifiable critique of demeaning policies related to Native education, there is no reason to doubt what Strong wrote to Ralph Young, of the Alaska Native Brotherhood, about his interest in contributing to the "betterment of the native people of Alaska."[24] (We see Strong's relative broad-mindedness at work in a different context. At a time when feelings against Chinese were high Outside, the governor wrote warmly of his Chinese cook and steward of five years as "honest, competent, loyal, always dependable" and "entirely deserving.")[25]

The governor more directly took up the case of a ten-year-old Native girl who was fatherless and whose mother was "dissolute." Writing to the superintendent of the Sheldon Jackson School in Sitka, he asked to be informed "at as early a moment as possible" whether it was possible for the girl to be admitted to the school.[26] And in a private letter to Ella Carr of Klukwan, in Alaska's Panhandle, Strong rued the fact that abuse of Native children was often hard to prove and prosecute as there were so many "designing men" who intimidated and manipulated witnesses. He wrote of his "sincere desire to assist... in the uplift of natives and the enforcement of the law at all times."[27]

Using the language typical of his day, which at a later time would seem quite patronizing, Strong wrote to the Native Presbyterian Church congratulating it on its work in "helping the native peoples to understand themselves, [and] to think and to act as members of a higher civilization." The Natives of southwest Alaska, he continued,

> are among the most intelligent and industrious of the race, and the progress which they are making toward higher ideals speaks more loudly than any mere words, and illustrates forcefully what they are capable of becoming. When a primitive people emerge from almost absolute barbarism to an efficient state of civilization within a generation, the lesson to be learned

> therefrom is obvious. It shows unmistakably that they have within them the qualities which enable them to rise from the stepping stone of their dead selves to higher things.[28]

This was in mid-November 1917. After a few more months of war news, Strong might have agreed with others who wondered if Europeans were not, after all, the greater brutes. When had Natives ever slaughtered one another as the advanced nations were now doing? William T. Lopp, the chief of the Education Bureau's Alaska division, saw this point. In his commentary on Natives who were fashioning and selling ivory and furs to raise funds for the Red Cross, Lopp noted that the "peaceful Eskimo is sacrificing for the savage white man."[29] And during the war, Strong praised Natives' contributions to the Red Cross. The "Indians of Alaska are to be congratulated upon the interest and intelligence they are displaying in this great conflict."[30] Later, Governor Riggs, too, learned of Natives' contributions to the Red Cross. Riggs also learned that many Inuit "signified their willingness to go to the [battle] Front if needed."[31]

Certainly Natives were sometimes spoken of in crass terms—as "slant-eyed" people who spoke "gibberish."[32] It is also true that segregation sometimes prevailed; such was the case at Ketchikan's skating rink and at many churches in the territory.[33] But it should be noticed, for example, that in 1917 Nomeites were invited to the Easter service at the Eskimo Methodist Church.[34] And the ubiquitous references in archival materials, newspapers, and memoirs to marriage and intimate relations between Native women and non-Native men point to an obvious breach of segregationist sentiment. One Alaska pioneer publicly hymned his love for the "Eskimo girl" with whom he had produced "fruitage"—presumably children.[35]

Evidence from Nome tells another part of the story, however. Some of the community's residents were irritated by Natives loitering around town, and a twenty-acre voluntary reservation was set up twenty miles to the town's west. Still, Natives were a constant presence. The Catholic Church provided a heated trading room for Native use, and Natives patronized Nome's stores such as the Lomen brothers' pharmacy. In turn, the Lomens, loyal Republicans, displayed Native art in their store's windows, to the applause of the socialist *Industrial Worker.*

Soon after the city was founded, some Nomeites began to dress like Natives, especially in the winter. This was not necessary, as a perusal of newspaper advertisements from Nome's merchants makes plain. Nomeites could have kept warm through winter dressed like urban Canadians or Minnesotans. Instead, they dressed like Natives because they liked Native clothing, recognized its usefulness, and appreciated the skill of the Natives who had made such attractive and useful apparel. Nomeites also liked the way the annexation of part of Native culture helped to set them apart from other Americans—a continuing staple of Alaska marketing to the Outside.

In the early twentieth century, we also find James Wickersham, a federal judge and future congressional delegate for Alaska, studying Native culture, decorating his sleeping quarters with Native art, and presenting a scholarly paper on Native culture to a literary society. We find Native and non-Native children playing together. We find Elizabeth Wood, a fervent photographer of family life, writing of her son and three Native boys as "four of a kind."[36] And we find Alaska high school students writing and reciting essays on Native culture. Through the first decades of the twentieth century, almost every edition of the *Aurora*, Nome High School's annual, included thoughtful articles on Natives.

Native education was a major American preoccupation closely tied to beliefs about the merits of modern civilization—beliefs that reading, writing, and the ability to act intelligently in an increasingly complicated global economy were vital to the pursuit of good lives. In 1917, a writer for the *Overland Monthly* observed that the system of education set up for Natives in Alaska was superior to what many Americans had in the States. The schools, the writer noted, were devoted to preparing Native youth for the modern world; they emphasized instruction in cleanliness, nutrition, ethics, and civics. Both girls and boys voted for school officers. "The entire scheme of educating the Alaska Natives is to make them into self-supporting citizens, that when they leave school they may build up their social status and do their part in developing the territory of Alaska."[37] The impressive work of the Tlingit William Paul—founder of the Alaska Native Brotherhood, attorney, Alaska legislator, officer in the federal Bureau of Indian Affairs, and promoter of Native civil rights—is unimaginable apart from the formal, western education he received.

Education was not directed only at reforming Native cultures along western lines. It was also intended to serve as a safeguard against the depredations of unscrupulous non-Natives who traded in weapons, alcohol, and venereal disease. Commentary in newspapers, memoirs, and other sources directed against self-serving "whites" is easy to find. As early as February 1900, Nome's *Gold Digger* observed that American drink, greed, and debauchery had corrupted too many Natives. Several years later, another editorial expressed its pity for the "poor Eskimo" who was learning the "white man's" ways.[38] In an essay written in 1915, high school senior Helen Kreps wrote that before

> the coming of the white men to Alaska the Eskimo were a simple, honest, affectionate people. Stealing was so entirely unknown to them that after the arrival of the white strangers they were very much surprised to find that their boats and nets which they had left on the shore had disappeared.[39]

Thus, Natives were sometimes seen as being in some ways better than the new immigrants. A Fairbanks writer claimed that Native women were physically superior to the "wiry" white women of the Interior. And Native women were known to have saved the lives of more than a few white men who were too "lazy" to care for themselves.[40]

Certainly at times there was an old-time "noble savage" mythology at work in such reflections. From the vantage point of industrialized society, supposedly simple, indigenous cultures were, and are, easily romanticized. But there is no reason to disbelieve the myriad statements Alaskans made about the corruption the newcomers introduced into Native societies.

Inevitably, the record of Native and non-Native relations was mixed. Native involvement in the American economy—in canneries, for example—could lead to higher standards of living, but it might also involve exploitation. (In a few cases, Chinese immigrant cannery workers faced violence from Natives jealous of their positions.)

Interracial mixing could lead to culture-sharing and cross-cultural amicability. On the Seward Peninsula, a young Carl Lomen wrote detailed notes on Native languages in his diary. During July 4 celebrations in Anchorage, Natives beat non-Natives in picnic competitions. But mingling also led to disease, "psychological indigence," and language loss.[41]

Often, "education" really did mean education—reading, writing, and arithmetic. At other times, the cause of education was trumped by lesser concerns such as the proper use of forks and spoons. And sometimes the interests of civilization—the development of civic trust and moral habits conducive to prosperity—were trumped by the actions of self-serving non-Natives who took advantage of their relative technological and cultural power. "Unscrupulous white men," John Underwood noted, "have a tendency to degrade the natives."[42]

Numerous observers would praise Native contributions to the American effort in the First World War. "The Alaska aborigine is one of the best and most patriotic citizens in existence," one commentary declared. "The Alaska native has shown that he is behind the government heart and soul, and the war has demonstrated that the American patriot is of no particular race or color."[43]

## A Temperate, Imperfect Society

The general evenhandedness that marked Alaska's settled communities sprang from a spirit of equanimity forged by the relative difficulty of life in the territory. Commenting on Alaska's churches, travel writers and passers-through noted the Alaskans' easy-going, interdenominational temperament. The British writer Charlotte Cameron took an interest in Robert Divin, a Presbyterian minister in Nenana whose son liked jazz and the foxtrot. As for the town itself, the fact that people went to the movies on Sunday and later to evening worship services pointed to a "broad-minded spirit" that Cameron found refreshing.[44]

Alaska's towns offered church options. If you lived in Fairbanks, you might have attended Episcopal, Catholic, Methodist, Presbyterian, or Christian Science services.[45] Skagway's Seventh-Day Adventists were keen to advocate for Saturday as the proper day of worship. In dense, almost scholarly essays published in newspapers throughout the territory, the Christian Scientists upheld Mary Baker Eddy as an esteemed prophet.[46] St. Philip's Episcopal Church in Wrangell, meanwhile, offered a sermon series titled "Man's Place in Nature" with the aim of unifying biblical reflection and evolutionary theory.[47] Such an effort must have made some locals uneasy, but theological disagreement seemed rarely to spill into public life.

Unusual among Alaska's newspapers in the era of the First World War, Juneau's *Daily Alaska Dispatch* revealed an editorial page preoccupation with theological reflection, though this, too, was offered in an open spirit. The paper did obliquely criticize residents who did not go to church, the assumption being that church attendance strengthened a town's moral culture. As for which church to attend, the *Dispatch* suggested that any would do. No church was perfect, the paper noted, but the benefits of communal worship were great. "[W]e all know this would be a much better world if every person attended church and carried into the practice of his daily life the precepts taught there."[48]

Certainly differences of opinion existed and debates were joined. One-third of Alaska's voters did not approve of the territory's "Bone Dry" prohibition law that went into effect at the beginning of 1918, just when mobilization for the war overseas was reaching high gear. Early on, the prohibition of alcohol seemed to be a great success. In March, Governor Strong wrote to Ernest Cherrington of the Anti-Saloon League recounting the legislation's triumph. Since January, the governor wrote, the "decrease in the number of arrests for drunkenness and all other crimes, and in pauperism, is almost marvelous to the observer." In the

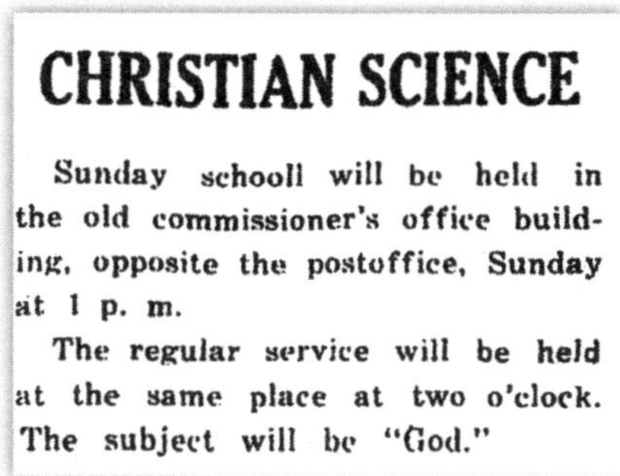

**CHRISTIAN SCIENCE**

Sunday schooll will be held in the old commissioner's office building, opposite the postoffice, Sunday at 1 p. m.

The regular service will be held at the same place at two o'clock. The subject will be "God."

*Nenana Daily News*, January 4, 1918

year's first two months, there had been just one arrest in Juneau, as opposed to fifty-two in the same period the year before. When "no intoxicating liquor can be had," Strong predicted, "there will be little use for Federal jails in Alaska."[49] He could not know how persistent and creative bootleggers and their thirsty clients would be—as seen, for instance, in the exploits of black marketers in Anchorage who soon would ferry their products through underground tunnels.

More in public view was the sometimes sharp tone of political combat. In early 1918, Strong wrote to a friend about feeling exhausted by the demands of his job, particularly in a time of war. But he saved his strongest words for Alaska's "political hacks" and "highbinders." Chief among them was the newspaper editor and future governor John Troy, whom Strong described as a prince of political "pork, and pelf and privilege in behalf of the Prussian autocracy of Alaska."[50] (Earlier in life, Strong himself had been a combative newspaper editor in Nome.)

Come wartime, dressing an adversary in the enemy's clothing was a tempting tactic. Cornelia Hatcher of Juneau attacked all of Alaska's Democratic Party leadership as a pack of "Huns" (one of several derogatory terms for Germans), and she predicted that in the next election "the Democratic Hun submarine…will come to the surface with her upper works shot to pieces, and her pirate crew will take to the life-raft."[51]

Captain John Hunt, working in Governor Strong's office, wrote a lengthy memo to authorities in the federal government about the scorn being heaped on the governor in the pages of Troy's *Alaska Daily Empire*, suggesting that the criticism brought the law and its agents into public contempt. Hunt hoped to shut the newspaper down with claims that broadsides against the governor were harming the wartime military draft. Hunt did not add that the keenest criticism directed against Governor Strong centered on allegations that the governor was not an American citizen—he had been born and raised in New Brunswick, Canada—and that Strong had no legal right to serve as Alaska's executive officer. The charge was correct. Alaskans soon learned that Strong had abandoned his Canadian wife and children and illegally married another woman in the United States. President Wilson removed him from office.

Congressional delegate James Wickersham faced a fiercer assault. In the late summer of 1919, after speaking with soldiers stationed at Fort Liscum at Valdez, he was physically attacked by political adversaries Hal and Tom Selby, father and son residents of the town. The attack left Wickersham temporarily unable to chew. He took liquid meals and noted in his diary that Tom Selby was twenty-two years old and "has just had a year's training in the Army."[52] As for the military men stationed at the fort, Wickersham wrote that they were "pleased at my humiliation & publicly express their feelings."[53]

So Alaska was not a paradise free of the complications linked to the human condition. Court records from the early twentieth century reveal an endless string of lawsuits and divorce cases. Of the first one hundred civil cases brought to Anchorage's court between 1915 and 1917, thirty involved divorce. For example, Olga McCullough wanted to divorce her husband because "during their married life [he] used the plaintiff cruelly and inhumanely by addressing her in violent, offensive, profane, and obscene language, privately and in the presence of strangers."[54]

Alaska's towns were generally secure, but care had to be taken. It was not true, as the English travel writer Charlotte Cameron claimed, that there were "no crooks or evil people in this sparsely populated land."[55] In May of 1915, a single notice from Ketchikan reported that A. E. Austin had shot a girl in the leg; that a man named Maldano had stabbed someone; that Ramon Gomez and Joe Sousa had been indicted for burglary; and that Harry Sushnick had been charged with assaulting a Native girl.[56] Governor Strong acknowledged that Alaska's remote regions were a kind of legal "no man's land" where miners and travelers were left to their own defense.[57]

Sometimes the desire for civic order led to personal infringements, such as when a U.S. marshal in Haines ordered a woman to leave town, despite the fact that she had married, settled down, and left behind a dissolute past. But Governor Strong advised the woman that no person who kept the law and led a decent life could be kicked out of a town, and he encouraged her to continue in the ways of sobriety and virtue.[58] Strong's seriousness about the moral order, his own sad ethical story notwithstanding, was driven home in a letter to the mayor of Petersburg. The governor inquired unhappily about reported violations of anti-alcohol laws and stories of disorderly women "who flaunt themselves in public and solicit trade more or less openly at all times."[59]

As noted above, town promoters sometimes attacked their counterparts in other settlements. In 1917, Seward was publicly reviled as a "dirty little cur" and its residents as a contemptible and "disgruntled clique."[60] Distance from the stress of big city life could not, by itself, relieve the strains of personal despair. Alaska congressional delegate James Wickersham wrote in his diary about a certain Jimmy Ryan who committed suicide with a revolver. "Poor Jimmy went to Nome in '98," the delegate wrote, "and never found the rainbow's end."[61]

The conclusion to all this is that Alaska was no utopia, no paradise, no destination for seekers of civic perfection or personal tranquility. Problems, and some genuine evil, were inevitable. Despite all this, it remained true that an easygoing spirit generally marked Alaska society. When Thomas DeVane of Ruby denounced the town newspaper's editor for being critical of U.S. policy after the country had declared war on Germany, he was careful to say that he did not suspect the editor's loyalty to the nation itself. The editor, DeVane suggested, had "perhaps unthinkingly" offended many of his readers.[62] A traveler wrote of "a bon camaraderie in Alaska that I have found nowhere else in the world. Perhaps it is of a brand not to be found except in the far spaces of the universe!"[63] The expression was excessive, but it echoed a common theme.

Alaska *was* a place where a person could start anew. Given the dearth of women in Alaska's Interior and its newer towns, one observer said, a woman "who has sinned in the past" but who "is now respectable, is respected by others."[64] She could come to Alaska and begin again.

This culture of evenhandedness sprang from experience with the difficulties of life in the territory. "[E]mpire building in Alaska is a good deal like missionary work," wrote a lawyer from Fairbanks. "The best that one can get is the worst of it."[65] Most Alaskans had little spare energy for self-defeating public animosity. But at the same time, life was not so difficult that Alaskans became highly stressed and turned on one another, as in, for example, the deadly race riots of 1919 in Chicago and Elaine, Arkansas.

## Learning

In the First World War era, public culture in Alaska differed from civic life Outside. Alaska's most pressing problem, a lack of economic infrastructure, did not

*Daily Alaska Dispatch* (Juneau), May 8, 1915

stem from urbanization or industrialization and the attentions of politicians. Alaska's economic challenge sprang from these things' absence. This absence reflected the fact that Alaska, being so far away from key decision-making centers Outside, was obscure.

Alaskans wanted to erase that obscurity. They worked hard to create in their communities a life that was comfortable for themselves and recognizable to guests from Outside. Visitors were often surprised at how normal Alaska's towns seemed. A guest in Nenana commented on the number of shops and the availability of canned goods, chocolate, and ice cream sodas. "[L]ife in Alaska is much like life elsewhere."[66]

In one respect, perhaps, Alaska towns seem to have been generally more sophisticated than Outside communities of similar size. Journalists described Alaskans as unusually literate and well informed. An article in *McClure's Maga-*

*zine* claimed that, thanks partly to the long winters, Alaskans read more books and newspapers than other Americans.[67] Charlotte Cameron saw the same thing: Alaska's long winters "prove a stimulus to the acquirement of knowledge."[68] Another visitor described the territory's miners as "good geologists" with a solid grasp of natural science.[69] John Underwood noted that "virtually all the Alaska centers of population have literary and debating societies, and there are many well-filled libraries in different parts of the territory."[70]

A review of Alaska newspapers supports these observations. Not many Alaskans were sincere Marxists, but the territory's socialist papers provided excerpts from the *Communist Manifesto* and other communist classics. On the other side of the theoretical divide stood Adam Smith, a founding theorist of capitalism, whose lofty work was lengthily excerpted at least once in Juneau's *Daily Alaska Dispatch*.[71] Alaskans had regular access to articles that made passing reference to classical and biblical characters under the assumption that no explanations were needed. Ruby's *Record-Citizen*, for example, noted in March 1917 that Germany seemed committed to the grim destruction of other nations, "even if, like the thwarted Samson, she pulls down upon the world the pillars of the Philistine temple and dies under its crashing walls."[72] Editors assumed their readers shared a common literary heritage.

The overall quality of Alaska's early-twentieth-century newspapers points to an impressive system of education. Alaska schools faced the challenge of high turnover among teachers, many of whom were single women who left the classroom upon getting married. Yet, as the school at Nome shows, a solid education could be acquired.

As was common Outside, Latin was near the core of high school studies. In Nome, student Alfred Lomen wrote that he appreciated the study of Latin for the way it developed the mind. Nome's young people also studied mathematics, French, German, physics, chemistry, history, civics, physical geography, bookkeeping, and physiology. They studied English and its history, learning not only to read Chaucer but to emulate his fourteenth-century style: "At Nome there wendes to high scole any day/Full twenty scolers in a compaignye."[73]

Many of Nome's students excelled academically, and they went on to colleges and universities at a rate that is impressive even by early-twenty-first-century standards. Each of Nome's three high school graduates of 1908 planned to continue their education. Of the twenty-three alumni listed in the 1914 edition of the school's yearbook, the *Aurora*, ten had gone to, or had already graduated from, a postsecondary educational institution—preponderantly the University of California, Berkeley and the University of Washington. Given the norms of the day, it was more notable that seven of these ten alumni were women. The *Aurora* could say with justification that Nome high school prepared students for the rigors of college.

The same was true of the school in Anchorage, which, with just over two hundred students in 1917, already hosted the largest student body in Alaska. In 1925, seven boys and four girls graduated from Anchorage's school. Four of the boys and all of the girls planned to attend university.

## Americans Apart

Alaskans wanted to re-create mainstream American society, but at the same time they knew that their life in Alaska was unique. They lived between the desire to be unique and the desire to stay within the lines of commonplace America. On the one side was Alaska, a dream realm of "unconquerable yearning" whose wintertime ambiance made it possible "to have a more Christmassy Christmas time."[74] On the other side, some Alaskans resisted the idea that life in the territory was mysteriously different from life elsewhere. They shook their heads at—even felt offended by—Americans who thought of Alaska as a perennially ice-locked world of wild frontiersmen.

One reason such beliefs persisted Outside was that, from the visitor's point of view, life in Alaska really was unusually challenging. Given the profound darkness of winter, the inescapable light of summer, the swarming mosquitoes, and the distance from American centers of power and influence, there is little wonder that passers-through referred to Alaskans as "hardy," "indomitable," unusually resourceful people who had "fought against great odds and conquered."[75] And there was the complicating fact that Alaskans themselves promoted and even celebrated this heroic image. It remained true one hundred years later, after all, that Alaskan status partly depended on how many hard winters one had passed on the North American continent's last frontier.

By 1915, Alaskans living in Juneau were sufficiently far removed from the hardships of nature to romanticize it. A poem published there placed the weak Alaska newcomer—the "chechaco"—next to the leathered and grizzled pioneer, leaving it to insects to make the difference.

*The mosquitoes were thick, [the chechaco's] hide was thin,*
*'Twas easy to puncture the chechaco's skin.*
*With the pioneer the mosquito had a tussle,*
*For all he had to work on was nerve and muscle.*[76]

It was fun reading for the comfortable resident of the Alaska capital who had just returned from purchasing a suit at the Irving Company.

Many Alaskans liked the mystique that came with living close to the wild. They liked to believe that the trials of living in the high north made the hardships experienced Outside seem like "mere trifles."[77] And the experience of life in Alaska, even though temporary, evinced a measure of lasting devotion. Once the United States entered the war, a Presbyterian missionary who had been busy working among railroad workers offered his services "for the country and Alaska."[78] James Willis, who at the time of military registration was working in Washington, D.C., wrote to Alaska's governor to say that he wanted his name to be listed not with men from the East but with his fellow Alaskans.[79] H.D. Reynolds, living in New York, also considered Alaska his true "homeland," and he offered to form an Alaska Loyal Legion for one-time Alaskans living on the East Coast, though it appears that the organization never took hold.[80]

While prizing their distinct place in American society, Alaskans also wanted its mainstream benefits. Alaska announced itself as a "guiding star" that would "lead the world to a knowledge of the truth concerning the vast domain of the Newer Northwest." The short-lived *Boston Alaskan* plucked both chords, advertising Alaska equally to the economically and romantically minded: "Wealth is in Alaska; health is in Alaska; all that conduces to prosperity and happiness is in Alaska."[81]

## Uncle Sam

Related to this tension is another: the embrace of a rugged individualist outlook combined with a desire for government largesse. This often-unnoticed paradox found its way into a single sentence in Seward's *Alaska Evening Post*, which noted that Alaska was pulling up her own bootstraps and "working out her own destiny" thanks in large measure to the infusion of resources the new "government railroad" brought to the territory.[82]

Readers devoted to small government will be distressed by the degree of open dependence on government that existed in early-twentieth-century Alaska. Consider the case of Anchorage, born and raised by Uncle Sam. Even before the new city had taken rudimentary shape, the *Knik News* published information about the "government railway scheme," the "government mess house," a "government agricultural experiment station," a "government school teacher," and a government hospital.[83] By the summer of 1915, long and tedious articles with titles like "Regulations Governing the Disposal of the Lots in the New Government Townsite" were published in the *Cook Inlet Pioneer.*[84] Government officials decided where the new city would be founded, how many lots would be available for sale, and for what minimum price (twenty-five dollars). Anchorage's early settlers looked to government to provide livable wages. Government agents received high praise for their energy and capable direction.

A shortage of drinking water in Anchorage in the winter of 1915 was the government's problem to solve, as was the task of combating mosquitoes. The government installed a sewer system and sought to provide model housing to railroad employees—living quarters that would serve as "object lessons of possibilities of what the best practical methods of housing, feeding, and sanitary conditions should be."[85] Residents could criticize the government sewer system, but final decisions were not the people's to make.

Alaskans soon learned that government involvement also meant red tape and inefficient bureaucracy. In 1915, the U.S. secretary of the interior wrote an article for the *North American Review* titled "Freeing Alaska from Red-Tape." The writer criticized the "interlocked, overlapped, cumbersome, and confusing" government activity in Alaska. He listed more than twenty federal agencies with some kind of entangling oversight in the territory.[86]

But there was no question that government action led to development. We have noted that Nenana, like Anchorage, owed its existence to government operations. However enterprising Alaskans might have been, the territory's distance from the lower states put its development substantially beyond individuals' abilities. This was obvious.

It was equally obvious that Alaska's resources were vast and could contribute mightily to the economic power of the United States. This was observed when the Nome gold rush of 1898 helped to end political advocacy for the use of silver as U.S. currency. Twenty years later, Alaskans spoke of the wealth to be made from copper. As Seward's *Alaska Evening Post* reported, four million dollars' worth of that metal had been exported from the territory in 1914. The next year, the figure had risen to $5 million. In fiscal year 1917, the number rose to $25 million. The latter amount alone repaid the U.S. Treasury the $7.2 million cost of purchasing the territory from Russian in 1867.

Given Alaska's natural wealth and contributions to the United States, the apparently low level of government activity was difficult to understand. As the *Post* put it, "Considering the amount of money the United States has invested in Alaska, the returns made by [the] territory are almost phenomenal."[87] Important people Outside did not fail to see Alaska's significance. In his 1906 message to Congress, President Theodore Roosevelt called for the development of Alaska, linking it directly to the development of commerce on the increasingly important Pacific Rim. "When properly developed," the president said, Alaska would "become in large degree a land of homes"—that is, a well-settled part of the American commonwealth.[88] But the road to proper development never went far.

The feeling that Alaskans contributed greatly to the American economy even while the federal government treated Alaskans with indifference helped to account for an enduring Alaska myth—the story of "Seward's Folly." According to the tale, when Secretary of State William Seward orchestrated the purchase of Alaska from Russia in 1867, he was widely ridiculed. Critics supposedly shouted that the $7.2 million the U.S. government paid for such a huge and frosty wasteland was wasted. In the words of one historian, Seward's enthusiasm "was not shared by his ignorant or uninformed countrymen, who jeered at 'Seward's Folly,' 'Seward's Icebox,' 'Frigidia,' and 'Walrussia.'"[89] Another history text added to this list, saying that during discussions of the purchase, the halls of Congress "reverberated" with creative epithets such as "Icebergia" and "Polaria."[90] Early in the twenty-first century an Alaska political memoirist inflated the story further, producing the customary reference to "Seward's Folly" and then noting that Seward had been a person of uncommon good sense with the unhappy experience of working among dimwits. "Seward withstood the mocking and disdain," the former Alaska governor wrote, "because of his vision for Alaska." He was vindicated, but not until "decades later."[91]

The trouble with this evolving story is that there is little evidence to support it. It is true that two U.S. senators voted against the Alaska Purchase in April 1867, but the thirty-seven who voted for it point to substantial agreement. It is true that some members of the House of Representatives stated their strong determination not to vote for the appropriation that would actually make the purchase possible, though the final vote in July 1868 of 113 in favor to 48 opposed also indicates strong support for the acquisition.

A review of dozens of American newspapers published at the time of the Alaska Purchase reveals general support for the transaction, especially in California. There was a small amount of negative commentary. One New Jersey newspaper belittled the former Russian turf as the stuff of mere icebergs and snowdrifts—"not of much value."[92] The *New York Tribune* claimed that ninety-nine percent of Alaska was "useless," and the *World*, also of New York, observed that Russia had sold the United States a "sucked orange."[93]

Overwhelmingly, though, editors and writers could see that the vast new American territory was well worth $7.2 million even if detailed knowledge about Alaska's resources was lacking. "There will be excursion trips to Alaska," a California newspaper noted in the summer of 1867, "and the new copper and gold mines of that almost unknown country will unfold their wealth to thousands of hardy and enterprising men." In turn, these adventurers would help to lay the "foundation of a new Commonwealth."[94] Near the end of 1867, *Flake's Bulletin* of Galveston, Texas, declared itself "continually surprised" by the growing news of Alaska's resources.[95]

By the time of the First World War, it had become Alaska dogma that Americans Outside were almost completely ignorant of Alaska's wealth. This may have been true to the extent that most people are unaware of things beyond their immediate spheres of interest. But it was not true, and never had been, that knowledge about Alaska's resources was unavailable. Between 1911 and 1917, Florida's *Miami Herald Record* alone published nearly 650 articles that at least mentioned Alaska.

Knowledge about Alaska's wealth was not lacking, but government action based on that knowledge certainly seemed to be. Alaskans were bewildered that a government possessing so rich an asset could appear to be indifferent to its development. And it was hard for Alaskans not to feel angry when their portion of government attention seemed meager when compared to Uncle Sam's purported doting on Puerto Rico, Hawaii, and the Philippines. In the eyes of the U.S. Congress, an angry Alaskan wrote, "one brown Filipino is better than fifty thousand white Alaskans."[96]

That Uncle Sam took his Alaskans for granted was another popular theme. In 1900, Sam C. Dunham published the much-reproduced poem "Alaska to Uncle Sam," in which the territory complains:

*Sitting on my greatest glacier,*
*With my feet in Bering Sea,*
*I am thinking, cold and lonely,*
*Of the way [Uncle Sam's] treated me.*[97]

Other Alaskans spoke of the territory as America's unwanted "stepdaughter."[98]

Thus, current feeling was read back into history. By the time of the Great War, the idea grew up among Alaskans that the federal government had always been against the territory. Only bright-eyed Seward had seen things clearly, and they laughed him to scorn! The overwhelming support for Seward's scheme in Congress was forgotten, and a short-lived minority opposition to the Alaska Purchase was remade into strong claims about the way things had always been. The "Seward's Folly" myth was born, appearing for the first time in Outside newspapers in 1913, the year before the Great War began.

Around the same time, some leading Alaskans, including delegate James Wickersham, were calling for statehood. Alaskans wanted their place at the American table.

Alaskans were Americans of a different kind. Ruby's *Record-Citizen* called itself "intensely pro-American" but also "Alaskan to the core." Following Governor Strong's fall, the paper did not support the appointment of Thomas Riggs as Alaska's governor, partly on the grounds that he was "not an Alaskan," had "never pioneered in Alaska," and therefore was not fit to confront the territory's problems.[99] Around the same time, "Alaska for Alaskans" gained currency as a slogan directed against self-serving "carpetbaggers" from Seattle.[100]

When the United States declared war against Germany in April 1917, feelings of national patriotism and duty would trump all other concerns. But a sense of Alaska difference would abide. Alaskans would put their nation's interests first, all the time hoping that their interest—Alaska's interest—would become a national interest.

*Wrangell Sentinel*, April 5, 1917

# LETTER FROM FRANCE (I)

*Coe Allen of Douglas enlisted in the army soon after the United States declared war against Germany in April 1917. He sent the following letter to James Garner, a watchman at the wharf in Douglas. A copy of the letter appeared in the* Anchorage Weekly Times *on January 31, 1918.*

We are nicely located here [in France] at present and I have had an opportunity to visit some small villages near here and see how the country people live. They seem very pleasant, and I was surprised to find them so husky. The country people in this part of France do not live on their own land as in the states, but live in small unkempt villages and walk or ride to and from their fields. They live under the same roof with their stock—all enter by the same big door near the center of the building, but, of course, stay in different compartments.

The villagers wear wooden shoes over felt ones, and leave the wooden shoes at the doorstep when they enter the house. The children are very smart and assist us in our efforts to learn something of the French language. There are very few young folks in the villages, and the old people and children carry nearly all of the ordinary work.

The railroad stations here were deserted except for a few workmen. In England we saw many more people who do not seem nearly so busy.

In spite of the fact that France has been at war more than three years, I have yet to see a person in actual want, so good seems to be the system of distribution here. Of course, many people here live on a pittance which would be considered entirely inadequate in the states.

Nearly everyone here drinks wine instead of water, and though we have traveled several hundred miles here, I have yet to see a drunken Frenchman. Foreigners, however, are not so moderate.

We have had very little sunshine here, but I am told the weather in spring and summer is of the best. Prices here are high on many things but on others very cheap, i.e. a shave can be had for 6 cents, haircut, 12 cents, shampoo, 12 cents; board is somewhat cheaper than in the states and living must be very cheap in peace times.

American soldiers in France. Stroud Collection

CHAPTER TWO

# The War Before the War

## An Empire in the Making

The American flag came to Alaska amidst wars, rumors of wars, and international jockeying for power and territory. A look at the map might have suggested that the British Empire, of which Canada was an important part, would want Alaska for itself. That could not be. Britons and Russians had fought one another in the Crimean War of the mid-1850s, and Russia was hardly interested in handing rich territory to its recent enemy, let alone giving Britain easy access to Siberia across the Bering Strait.

When Senator Charles Sumner of Massachusetts made his case for the American purchase of Alaska in 1867, he emphasized the acquisition's international implications.[1] The Aleutian chain, he noted, stretched almost to Japan, a recently awakened nation with which the advanced countries were eager to trade. Trade with China also beckoned. Sumner cited the distance between Alaska and Hong Kong, and the Sandwich Islands—the name Hawaii went by at the time. Everyone was "looking to the Orient," Sumner said, "as in the time of Columbus."[2] As in the days of Columbus, the most powerful nations were still locked in economic competition. If the United States did not acquire Alaska, some other power would.

Knowledgeable Americans approved of the Alaska Purchase in light of its economic and international possibilities. Even before the purchase, articles appeared that conceptually linked Alaska to sought-for gold fields in Siberia and to the promotion of a telegraph that would tie America to Asia, by way of Alaska and Siberia.

Some hoped that the addition of Alaska to the American commonwealth would spur a spirit of acquisition leading to other transnational deals—the purchase of Baja California from Mexico; of Borneo from the English and the Dutch; of Samana Bay from the Dominican Republic; and of northern Canada from the Hudson Bay Company. None of these transactions were realized. Among the territorial gains that did come to pass were the purchase of St. Thomas in the Caribbean from Denmark in 1917 and the annexation of Hawaii in 1898. The U.S. victory in the Spanish-American War of 1898 led to American control of Puerto Rico, Guam, and the Philippines.

Alaska was bought with trade expansion in mind; its acquistion would add to American-controlled turf and American prestige. Of course, the addition of new territory brought new defense responsibilities. Editorial writers studied maps looking for possible sites for a naval base in the Aleutian chain "for the protecting of our whaling and other fishing interests."[3]

Many saw that the Alaska Purchase had literally and figuratively expanded America's horizons. There was no doubt in the minds of astute observers that Alaska's entry into the American fold signaled the country's heightened status in the western hemisphere. For one thing, the Alaska Purchase jeopardized Britain's North American holdings. As the San Francisco *Evening Bulletin* observed, the "extension of our flag to the northernmost point of the continent…will deal a fatal blow to British interests in the North Pacific."[4] The London *Times* took it for granted that the primary motivation behind the purchase was the United States' desire to expand its rule. "The aspiration of the United States to absorb the whole of North America is no secret."[5]

Inside and outside the United States, the Alaska Purchase was interpreted as the act of a country on the move—a nation gaining in wealth, power, and influence. In November 1867, residents of New Orleans peered into one aspect of this new American wealth in the form of the cod fisheries recently discovered in "our new Russian-American possessions." Almost eight hundred tons of cod had been harvested thus far, the *Times Picayune* noted, "with the probability of twice this amount…before the end of the season."[6] In the next month, word arrived in New Orleans of "auriferous sands" in Alaska that suggested riches greater than what had been seen in the great gold rushes of Australia and California.[7]

## Natives

The people already living in Alaska when the United States took over in 1867 would learn something about imperialism. In the first chapter we noted the mixed record of Native and non-Native relations in Alaska in the time of the First World War. In some cases, relations were cordial, cooperative, and romantic; in others, they were bitter and deadly. Such interactions were as complicated as the people who participated in them.

Lester Henderson, Alaska's commissioner of education in the war era, discussed one complication in a territory more than twice the size of Texas and inhabited by tens of thousands of people. In commenting on the local control that prevailed in Alaska's schools, Henderson wrote that some schools were segregated and others were not. In the 1919–1920 school year at Nome, for example, seventeen students with one Native parent studied alongside students of no Native heritage. In Wrangell the figure stood at twenty-one; in Tanana at sixteen. The school at Douglas hosted five students with Native parents who studied alongside peers without Native family members.

On the other hand, of the sixty-six schools Henderson reported on, fourteen had no students of Native background. "Full blood Alaska natives are received in some schools without protest," he wrote, but in other schools Natives were allowed "under protest," and in still others they were excluded entirely. It is worth noting that if in some jurisdictions there was felt a need for "protest" against Native inclusion, then that meant that others argued for inclusion. And "[s]trange as it may seem," Henderson continued, "some mixed-blood schools strongly protest against admission of full blood natives."[8]

There is no question that the rapid advent of thousands of non-Natives, many of them single men—and many of these from eastern European societies with no history of paying even lip service to civil liberties—took a toll on Native society. Lands were trampled, fish overharvested, traditional ideas and beliefs undermined and overturned, and traditional authorities debased. Alcohol addiction and venereal disease, with other social pathogens, entered Native communities.

At the same time, many Natives desired American products and opportunities, and they found that "their material culture had economic value in the white marketplace." Tourists to Alaska "gave Indians money in order to acquire items of Indian manufacture, and the Indians then paid the money to white traders in order to acquire items of American and European manufacture." Eliza Ruhama Scidmore, a traveler to Alaska, wrote that the "Tlingit's aim [is] to dress and live as the white man, and he fills his home with beds, tables, chairs, clocks, lamps, stoves, and kitchen utensils, and even buys silk gowns for his wife. He is no longer picturesque, distinctive, or aboriginal."[9] For some, these kinds of observations signaled progress; for others, they signaled cultural collapse. The plaint of Kah-du-shan, a clan leader from Wrangell, is poignant. "We are not fish," he told Alaska governor John Brady in 1898.

> We like to live like other people live.... [W]e are very poor now. The time will come when we will not have anything left. The money and everything else in this country will be the property of the white man, and our people will have nothing. We... [ask] you to write to the chief at Washington [the president] and to let him know our complaint. We also ask him to return our creeks and the hunting grounds that white people have taken away from us.[10]

All around the world, indigenous peoples confronted similar hardships stemming from imperial powers' quest for territory, wealth, and international prestige.

## A Violent Era

Early-twentieth-century histories of Alaska often place the territory in a context of international competition. John Latané, a professor at Washington and Lee University, published *America as a World Power* (1907), which included a chapter on the United States' dispute with Canada over the Alaska–British Columbia boundary. Decided in the United States' favor, with the help of the British, this historical event has dropped from American history textbooks, although not from schoolbooks in Canada, where the episode is remembered as an example of the American republic's pushiness. Sandwiched between chapters on U.S. action in Cuba and Panama, where an American-built canal connecting the Atlantic and Pacific Oceans opened in 1914, Latané placed Alaska in a context of international striving.

According to the prevailing theory of the day, a nation's growth in power necessarily came at the expense of others. "Great Britain has abandoned the Pacific; we are about to enter it," said the author of an article titled "The Imperial Future of the United States." Made in 1913, the claim was premature; Britain's presence in the Pacific would be significant into 1940. But the scholar was correct that the balance of military and economic power in the world was shifting from Europe to the Pacific, a process still under way one hundred years later. What the United

States needed was to "rise to a larger view of our responsibilities" and to "place an adequate fleet in the Pacific and an adequate army on our threatened [west] coast."[11] Stretching as it did into Asia, Alaska figured into such thinking. Another author wrote grandly of Alaska as more than a mere "land of promise" but as a "new empire of destiny"—indeed, as the very "key to the new prosperity now dawning on the United States."[12]

These kinds of reflections show us why it would be difficult for the United States to stay out of the war that erupted in Europe in 1914. In that year, and for the next two years, Americans wanted to think that their world was still that of George Washington and Thomas Jefferson, who famously advised the nation to promote international trade while also avoiding "entangling alliances" with them. Or, as the revolutionary philosopher Thomas Paine put it, Europe was America's "market for trade," but Americans should "form no partial connection" with any country.[13] The goal was to trade with the world while remaining unmarked by the world's military problems.

The goal was unattainable. Since the end of the Civil War in 1865, American forces had seen small-scale combat in Korea, Samoa, and China. Americans experienced greater battle against the Spanish Empire in the Caribbean and Pacific. The brief Spanish-American War was followed by an insurgent conflict in the Philippines. Then came fighting in Haiti and the Dominican Republic, and the United States adopted the role of international policeman in Latin America. Americans might have been isolationist in sentiment, but their country had long since emerged as a global presence.[14] The Alaska Purchase symbolizes this phenomenon, and, in that way, it is indirectly linked to the circumstances that would draw the nation into the First World War.

The Great War was the result of decades of international competition and rivalry. For years, Alaskans had been able to track global news. In 1899, for instance, Juneau's *Weekly Mining Record* reported on Germany's growing military power. That country's army, the paper said, now outmanned France's by a million. Sixteen years later, Alaskans learned that Germany had triggered war in Europe because that country felt itself "entitled by her achievements to a greater place in the world and to wider markets for her commercial activities."[15] As for Great Britain, her globe-girdling imperial reach was old news, as many Alaskans who lived close to British Columbia or the Yukon were often reminded.

The United States, too, had sought international economic opportunities and built an empire, of which Alaska was a part. But the United States and its empire were far from Europe and its problems. Most Alaskans, like most Americans, wanted the nation to stay clear of Europe's bloodbath. As we shall see, there were some eager Alaskans who slipped across the Canadian border to fight with the British, but these became heroic in Alaskan eyes only after the United States joined the conflict.

## For Noninvolvement

In the minds of Alaska editorialists, there were myriad reasons for the United States to stay out of the European conflict. One of these was war's basic insanity—what one psychiatrist called "bellicose psychosis," a key symptom of which was "ingenious, inflamed, and persistent lying," such as one reportedly found in government bulletins regularly produced by the embattled nations.[16]

Alaskans did not want to be crazy.

Aside from the appalling carnage of the war, there was psychological and spiritual devastation, described in a striking article in Juneau's *Daily Alaska Dispatch*. In the piece, a German officer admitted to weeping after a battle, stating his belief that "the tears shed by men on the battlefields are the typical expression of a mute tragedy of the soul."[17] The officer alluded to the shock that came with seeing comrades disappear under incoming artillery fire.

Alaskans did not want to get mangled or suffer what would soon be called "shell shock."

Then there was the fact that war was often immoral and in conflict with basic Sunday-school teachings. One commentator asserted that every "instinct of imperialism and the wars it causes is in constant friction with the rules of Christ."[18] True, it took a certain kind of courage to fight, but refusing to fight called for a higher, nobler strength. "If the people of the leading nations possessed as much moral as they do physical courage, there would be no war."[19]

Alaskans wanted to be morally courageous. To assist them, Juneau's *Daily Alaska Dispatch* offered spiritual reflections:

> There are enough praying souls in America to call down a truce on every battle front if once they felt the agony of Christ's intercession. That our country is as yet free from the madness of strife should the more move us to importunate and increasing petition that God will make his voice to be everywhere heard again on land and sea.[20]

There was also the fact that modern warfare, with its sophisticated armaments, was so expensive. According to a report from April 1915, the conflict was costing Britain four million dollars a day.

Alaskans did not want to see their nation's wealth squandered.

There was, moreover, the reality that munitions makers and other business interests profited from combat. For some, war was good business. It was time that workers, who always seemed to suffer the most in conflicts, "quit killing each other for the sake of commercialism or the private ambitions of those in responsible positions."[21]

Alaskans wanted to stand up for the average man.

Then there was the observation that neither side in Europe's struggle held the moral high ground. It was true, as we shall see, that Germany was responsible for the deaths of civilians at sea. But it was also true that Britain's blockade of the German coast was causing starvation among civilians. Both nations' actions at sea harmed American commerce. Germany was the greater offender, but Alaskans did not want to side with any of the Old World's powers.

Such arguments were important, but we should not press them too hard. Few Alaskans were eager for their nation to go to war, but fewer of them had detailed, clearly articulated reasons for not wanting to get involved. Europeans had been killing one another from ancient times, preoccupied Alaskans were heard saying, and if they wanted to keep it up, it was their problem.

## To War

On February 2, 1917, Alaska's delegate to Congress, James Wickersham, wrote in his diary that relations between the United States and Germany were on the point of cracking. He felt "oppressed" by President Wilson's threat to break diplomatic relations with Germany; he believed that "it is our duty to *keep out of the struggle*." He added that the American people "stand to lose much if we go in."[22]

As the hours went by, U.S. entry into the war appeared increasingly inevitable. On February 4, Wickersham recorded the U.S. government's formal breaking of relations with Germany. The president had been "diplomatically correct," Wickersham thought. Thanks to the German submarine menace, U.S. merchant ships were unable to travel the seas freely. But Wickersham also recorded his fear of the deadly consequences to come.

Germany's reason for sinking noncombat ships is clear: munitions and other goods of use to Britain were being transported in them. The United States claimed to be neutral, but from the German point of view, American policy clearly favored Britain. Germany stated openly that it would sink cruise ships en route to Britain; the German embassy in the United States published notices in American newspapers warning Americans against sailing across the Atlantic.

The problem had begun a couple years before. On March 28, 1915, the British ship *Falaba* was sunk by a German submarine, with the loss of more than one hundred passengers and crew. Four days later a German U-boat torpedoed and damaged the *Gulflight*, an American ship, with three lives lost. In August, the British cruise liner *Arabic* sank due to a German submarine attack. Forty of the 429 on board did not survive, among them two Americans.

The most devastating submarine attack had come several months before. On May 7, the British ship *Lusitania* went down, torpedoed, off the coast of Ireland. Of the nearly twelve hundred who died, nearly 130 were Americans.

Textbooks sometimes make it seem like the distance from the sinking of the *Lusitania* to Congress's declaration of war was the matter of a short step. But the events were separated in time by almost two years, and American reactions to the *Lusitania*'s downing were mixed. It was well known that the German government had used newspaper notices to warn Americans not to get on the ship. It was also known, or widely (and correctly) suspected, that British steamships carried American-made munitions in their hulls. New York's collector of customs noted that the *Lusitania* was carrying large quantities of brass, copper, "180 cases of military goods," almost 1,300 "cases of ammunition," and "4,200 cases of cartridges."[23] In Katalla, Alaska, a certain Zoleon Jaslin reportedly shared his view that the Germans had been "right" to sink the *Lusitania* "and that Americans had no business on her after being warned by the American government." The statement would come back to Jaslin once the United States was in the war. In late 1917, Governor Strong wanted to name him to a defense board in Katalla, but a community leader protested in writing, recounting what Jaslin had said two years before.[24] But in 1915, Jaslin's words, assuming he actually said them, were not so controversial. The American press voiced commentary that effectively if obliquely placed blame not on the Germans but on the *Lusitania*'s voyagers. (Juneau's *Dispatch* ran the story of the ship's sinking as front-page news but offered no related editorials.) And while there was, following the disaster, talk of war, most hoped such talk would pass.

A month after the sinking, concern remained, but there was "every reason to hope for a friendly understanding with Germany."[25] A few writers downplayed the significance of the event, referring to it as an "untoward incident abroad."[26] In

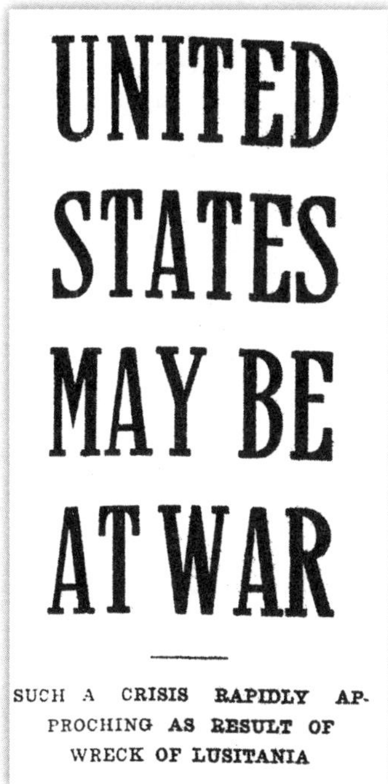
UNITED STATES MAY BE AT WAR

SUCH A CRISIS RAPIDLY APPROCHING AS RESULT OF WRECK OF LUSITANIA

*Daily Alaska Dispatch*, May 13, 1915

response to reports in March 1917 on the sinking by German submarines of the ships *Algonquin*, *Bray Head*, and *Vigilancia*, James Wickersham wrote that U.S. vessels "had been warned" by Germany, and that there is "little excitement about the matter," for such action by the Germans "seems to have been expected." As if to illustrate his point, the next line in his diary simply reports that he had spent the day "[w]orking in the office—nothing unusual."[27]

But some, with former President Theodore Roosevelt in the lead, argued for a vigorous program of military preparation. The terms "preparedness" and "armed peace" became commonly used. Juneau's *Dispatch* disagreed with Roosevelt and scorned the idea of accumulating weapons for the sake of peace. What were weapons for if not to fight? The paper editorialized that "[e]ither we must admit our distrust of mankind in general and other nations in particular and arm ourselves to the teeth, in order to show our fangs whenever any nation frowns at us from across the ocean, or else we must practice what we preach as a nation making for a world's peace."[28] There was merit in universal defensive training, the paper noted, but a "standing army for offensive purposes or aggression is obnoxious."[29]

Ruby's *Record-Citizen* suggested that Roosevelt should refamiliarize himself with the Founding Fathers' warnings to the country against foreign entanglements.

The country's unpreparedness might be taken as a good enough reason not to get involved in the war. The country was not ready for a fight, and therefore it should not fight. A writer in Seward predicted laughter in Europe's chancelleries upon an American declaration of war. "In our present state of unpreparedness, we are no match for any world state bigger than Haiti." What would Americans fight with? "Would we mobilize an army corps of housewives, armed with brooms?" As of January 1917, Alaskans had "neither the time nor the inclination for war."[30]

A month before war with Germany was declared, James Wickersham wrote that there was "much talk and fear of German war." A week after war's declaration, he still expressed doubts. "We are all talking War these days," he wrote, "and *wondering why?*"[31] Even into late August, after a state of war had been declared, Wickersham hoped for a way out. In the late summer of 1917, President Wilson received a communication from Pope Benedictus XV calling for peace. Responding for the president, Secretary of State Robert Lansing stated that everyone wanted peace, but that this depended on removing the causes of the war, among them Germany's "malign influences." Wickersham read Lansing's statement twice and called it "a very shrewd diplomatic paper." It "does *not* close down the bar to peace," he continued, "rather, it seems to me, to invite further consideration."[32]

## Peace Gesture

Most Alaskans wanted to stay clear of Europe's war, but few were pacifists. For most, life in Alaska required a degree of mental and physical toughness not well suited to the comfortable philosophies contemplated in urban armchairs. Wickersham wrote fondly of a certain Constance Reed of Nome, a "long-legged awkward girl" who "loved dogs and drove them to Arctic sleds like a man and swore at them on occasion like a trooper."[33] Almost certainly neither Constance nor the large majority of her fellow Alaskans would have thought well of an anti-war scheme, based loosely on New Testament principle, to cede Alaska's Panhandle to Canada. The purpose of the plan, put forward in the U.S. Congress by Representative Frank Smith of Maryland, was to present the troubled world with an example of international goodwill.

Smith's proposal gained some support among intellectuals with nothing to lose. In the words of a supportive seminary president, the cession of southeast

Alaska would serve as a "lesson to the nations of the world in their unjust scuffle for land." Yale University professor Irving Fisher said that the gift to Canada would be a precedent to other nations eager to find more peaceful ways to resolve disputes. Other supporters of the scheme spoke of it as the Golden Rule put into international practice. If *we* were Canadians, the argument went, we would want Alaska's Panhandle—so let us Americans do unto others as we would have them do for us! Middleton Smith of Washington, D.C., felt certain that if the decision were Christ's to make, then he would endorse Representative Smith's plan. Another said it was true that the Panhandle's cession meant the surrender of Juneau and Sitka, "but it is better to give them voluntarily now than to have them forced from us some other time by war."[34] The writer did not say which nation might take Alaska's soil violently, though the finger seemed to point toward Britain, a soon-to-be ally in war against Germany. (At the same time, it was also true that the good feelings that grew between Britain and the United States did not exist before the war. A month before Congress declared war against Germany, Ruby's *Record-Citizen* still spoke of Britain as an international pest.)

For obvious reasons, the Panhandle scheme acquired support among Canadians. Archibald McGoun of McGill University in Montreal praised Smith's "magnanimous proposal for the United States to cede to Canada the Panhandle of Alaska." The Canadian writer Stephen Leacock honored the scheme as a "splendid and statesmanlike idea."[35]

In the American Congress, on the other hand, Smith's idea was quickly, frigidly, and predictably crushed. A newspaper in Oregon summarized the scene: "The Smith resolution is being ignored by most members of Congress and will not be acted on by the committee on foreign affairs."[36] The Alaskan reaction to the goodwill plan was not surprising; it had shown the way to the "limit and pinnacle of absurdity."[37]

## War

By March 1917, it was clear that a European war more than thirty months old was pulling the United States in. The struggle had affected the lower states and Alaska from the beginning. In 1914, the United States had trade relationships with the belligerent powers equaling almost $100 million (eighty percent of it with Britain, France, and Russia). A tiny element of that trade came from furs acquired in Siberia by merchants based in Nome. In late 1914, Nome businessman C. E. Darling and his wife reported that the fur market in Nome had been "paralyzed" since the conflict had begun, partly as a result of plummeting demand in London, Leipzig, and Paris; partly as the result of the drying up of European investment in the Siberian venture; and partly as a consequence of foreign-born residents having left town "to enlist in the armies of their native countries."[38]

By the dawn of 1917, it looked certain that a war that had caused some economic and demographic dislocation in Alaska was now on the point of moving into center stage. Germany's submarine warfare remained the primary problem. In early February, the USS *Housatonic* went down in the Atlantic.

A few weeks later the British government passed the United States a captured and deciphered German telegram intended for the government of Mexico. In the case of war with the United States, the Zimmermann telegram stated, Germany offered an alliance to Mexico. Upon victory over the United States, the note continued, Mexico would "reconquer" the land lost to the Americans some seventy years before, specifically Texas, New Mexico, and Arizona.

This revelation brought two festering problems together. For reasons of proximity, the problem in the Atlantic was most threatening to the Americans living on the East Coast. The other problem was that the U.S.–Mexico border had seen American homes raided and a portion of Columbus, New Mexico, destroyed by the Mexican gangster Pancho Villa. Indeed, just one month before news of the Zimmermann note ran in American newspapers, General John Pershing had withdrawn his troops from Mexico, thus ending a twenty-month military expedition that went deep into Mexico with the goal of eliminating Villa's ability to raid American communities. And even as young men were dying in Europe, some Mexican radicals enunciated a "San Diego Plan," a key element of which was the murder of young American males living near the border.

So, even as Americans discussed German submarine activity in the Atlantic, a conflict with Mexico seemed possible—more likely, even, than war in Europe. The 1915 edition of Nome's high school annual, *The Aurora*, said nothing about Germany or England, but it provided a different prophecy for the near future: "The U.S. finally decided to invade Mexico."[39] The next year, Anchorage's *Weekly Alaskan* considered the news from the southern border and declared: "everything looks like WAR."[40] At the beginning of 1917, the *Forty-Ninth Star* wondered sarcastically if Pancho Villa might attack Anchorage.[41]

But in 1917 Mexico's government had no real command over its own territory. While Americans living near the border were threatened and, at times, victimized, Mexico did not pose a danger to the United States as a whole. The

General Pershing. Stroud Collection

threat from Mexico was real but limited. Germany's offer of the American Southwest to Mexico was a mark of desperation. In September 1918, Roy Fraisure of Cordova wrote from Iowa that he expected to be sent not to France but to the U.S.–Mexico border.[42] But the real trouble was across the Atlantic.

By March 1917, the anti-war *Record-Citizen* of Ruby had lost hope that there was a peaceful way to resolve the country's differences with Germany. "If we must kill our youth in the end," the paper announced resignedly, "we would like to feel that at least every other means had been exhausted before that tragic one was reverted to."[43]

President Woodrow Wilson had wanted to avoid war. He won reelection to the White House in 1916 under the slogan "He kept us out of the war." He had taken biting criticism from former President Roosevelt, who thought the country needed to do more to prepare for conflict. On April 2, Wilson addressed

*Seward Gateway,* March 24, 1917

Congress. He spoke of Germany's "reckless lack of compassion or of principle." He said that Germany's submarine warfare against commerce was really a "war against mankind." The United States had not wanted war, Wilson said, but neither could it "choose the path of submission and [allow] the most sacred rights of our nation and our people to be ignored or violated." The president focused on Germany's use of submarines, though he also mentioned the Zimmermann note and the German spies at work in the United States.

Rehearsing a theme that went back to colonial days, Wilson spoke of America's mission as a beacon of light and civilization to the world. It was a thesis also rehearsed in reflections on Alaska, often discussed in light of mystic ideals associated with the country's early history. "In the history of the United States the outposts of civilization have been planted, beginning with the Virginia and Massachusetts colonies and following the star of empire until they reached the Pacific Ocean," wrote one popular historian in 1905. "Up here in Northwestern Alaska is the extreme outpost of civilization in the United States. Civilization has marched westward to the Pacific, and at a single bound has gone northward beyond the Arctic Circle."[44] Now, the president said, this march of civilization would be taken back across the Atlantic. The war's basic goal was the defeat of Germany and her allies. The greater goal was to bring "peace and safety to all the nations and make the world itself at last free."[45]

In the chilly Alaska Interior, J. J. Filbin sat down to write a column for the *Record-Citizen*. A man of pointed words, Filbin had long said that if war came he would stand with his country. He had hoped that war would not come. Now it had, and it was difficult for him to accept the fact.

J. J. Filbin and the home of the *Record-Citizen*. Alaska State Library, ASL-P277-004-116

Filbin was not impressed with Wilson's "high-sounding language." If saving American lives had been the point, why had the United States not gone to war two years before, when the *Lusitania* had been sunk? "If lives are in question, how about the lives of Americans living peaceably on our own side of the Mexican border, where they have a right to protection and consideration? Have we declared war on Mexico?" How to account for the United States now being "caught in the whirlpool of madness that is spinning this senseless stream of blood down the rivers of time"? Could it be, Filbin asked, that Woodrow Wilson had been cornered and won over by the "siren of Wall Street"—the commercial interests that stood to gain so much from so huge a war?[46]

Delegate Wickersham had also wanted to avoid the struggle. But now that his country was at war, he put that sentiment aside. In the late summer of 1917, he entered a few lines in his diary about Howard Rolston of Fairbanks, whom he had recommended to West Point and who was soon to be on his way to France to join the conflict. "Bully for Howard," Wickersham wrote.[47] In July of the next year, he wrote of being "delighted with the war spirit observed at every place."[48]

As for Governor Strong, a few days after the war declaration, he sent a message to President Wilson. "From every town and hamlet in this far northern country," he wrote, "come pledges of loyalty to you and to the nation in the conflict which the country at present faces in the name of humanity, democracy and national honor."[49]

## LETTER FROM FRANCE (II)

*The following letter was written by Raymond C. Schott, who served with the Thirty-First Engineers' Regiment commanded by Frederick Mears, the Alaska Engineering Commission official who did so much to establish Anchorage and the railroad that connects it to Seward and Fairbanks. Dated July 3, 1918, the letter was printed in the* Alaska Railroad Record *on August 27. It is obvious that as of the writing of this letter, Schott had not yet visited a war zone.*

We are now situated in what is known as the garden spot of France. The country is beautiful. En route here from the seacoast, we passed fertile fields and vineyards, and ruins of chateaus. The fields are much different from those in the United States. They are cut into small tracts, the French being great on diversified farming.

The fertility of the country is evidenced by the fact that although there has been no rain here for two months, the crops are in good condition. Everything is luxuriant. The soil is sub-irrigated. Water can be obtained at any place by digging to a depth of six feet.

All the houses are of stone. The stone is a soft limestone, not affected by climatic conditions. Lumber is very high in price, costing the government, I understand, about $140 per thousand feet.

The scarcity of young men is noticeable. What young men there are here are crippled. Most of the work is done by old men and old women.

We have a great camp and the boys are well satisfied. Our quarters are brand new. Every company has four barracks, one being used as a mess hall and the others for sleeping quarters and offices. We have wooden bunks and straw on which to sleep. The food is plentiful.

We can get light wine and beer between the hours of 6 and 9 o'clock p.m. Champagne is forbidden us. Champagne is sold for ten francs—$1.80—a quart. The beer is very poor. It tastes like stale beer and is sweet. The French think it is quite a joke when we put salt into it, as they put sugar into it, if anything. None of us drink enough to hurt.

The French are of the opinion that the soldiers are all millionaires. Prices fluctuate here worse than on Wall Street, being governed by the supply and demand.

I visited a nearby town Sunday. The place is very old-fashioned. The streets run in all directions and are intersected with little, narrow alleys. On a hill there is an old chateau that was Napoleon's headquarters. It was built in 890. There is a fine Young Men's Christian Association in the town. The Association occupies the home of a rich man who turned it over to the Association for the duration of the war.

The boys recently were given a little railroading work, going out with picks and shovels to tamp ties. It sure went against the grain for some of them. We are attending school now to learn the French railroad signals. They are much different from ours—seem to be just the opposite. I think we shall start to railroading in earnest soon.

We are going to have a thirty-six piece regimental band. The instruments are ordered. It will be jolly to have some music to break the monotony. All the Alaska boys are well. We want to stay over here until the finish, but we look forward with pleasant anticipation to the time when we shall be back home again.

CHAPTER THREE

# Over Here—Words

## Strange Days

Among the clichés of American history is that once the United States entered the war against Germany, the country was swept by "hysteria." As one historian writes, the United States experienced a new "cultural atmosphere in which the flames of hysteria were kindled."[1] Another scholar speaks of a "great majority of Americans" being "caught up in fear, hysteria, and zealotry."[2] Some liked to describe American public opinion as being stoked to "frenzy."[3]

Putting aside the vast improbability of 106 million Americans falling into collective lunacy, one need only patrol the pages of U.S. newspapers from the period to see that while the war era marked an unusual and grim time, the country did not lose its basic rationality. It does seem correct to say, as one writer has, that Americans lost their sense of humor with the coming of the conflict. The Fairbanks *Alaska Citizen* acknowledged that the war era comprised "abnormal days."[4] James Wickersham wrote in his diary about a war "excitement" that burned at "fever heat," adding that a conscription bill had passed Congress with "much feeling."[5] Yet comments on the war comprise a tiny part of Wickersham's journal.

While we take claims of "hysteria" with caution, it remains true that the public culture of the United States and Alaska underwent a significant transformation in a very short time. Promoting the sale of Liberty Bonds to finance the war, D. B. Lewkesbury of the Alaska Engineering Commission noted that he and his compatriots were living in "feverish times," and in 1918, a Treasury Department official in Petersburg needed to assure Governor Riggs that he would "not let the people of this town take any radical steps in mob rule" against people perceived as less than enthusiastic for the war cause.[6] What accounts for this transformation is difficult to understand in a post–civil rights age when cynicism toward government is normal and the sense of community that existed before the advent of electronic media and the Internet is almost impossible to recapture.

Perhaps the greatest cultural alteration came in the form of opinion—what could and could not be expressed publicly. In early 1915, Juneau's *Daily Alaska Dispatch* noted that every one of the belligerent nations "can justly be proud of its soldiers," for they were "all brave."[7] This included German soldiers. And before the United States had entered the war, a headline in an Alaska newspaper declared "German Cities Provide Model for Americans."[8] By mid-April 1917, however, few would speak openly of German bravery. After Congress's war declaration, Germany was spoken of publicly only as a model of barbarism and depravity.

Before the war, debate had a significant place in public life. A few weeks before Congress declared war, the *Seward Gateway* editorialized against "forced patriotism" in public schools. Requiring children to sing patriotic songs against their will did not strengthen the nation, the paper argued, and the writer went on to suggest that there were "sections of some cities in this land of the free where there is mighty little cause for patriotism."[9] The paper's tune would change.

Before the war, criticism of government counted as constitutionally protected free speech. Fairbanks's *Alaska Citizen* published letters from readers who "condemned" the country's moves in the direction of war. Printing such letters had been perfectly proper. Once war was sure, however, the *Citizen* noted that it would "decline any communications that tend to question the propriety of the administration's actions."[10] As of April 1917, criticism of the country's cause was the stuff of treason.[11] As the *Wrangell Sentinel* put it, if someone who benefited from American liberties before the war now wanted to indulge in "pro-Kaiser talk" or to "make the slightest slur at the American flag," then such a person "should be instantly dealt with drastically."[12]

The quick turn away from free speech is on display in the pages of J. J. Filbin's *Record-Citizen*. The day after the United States formally entered the war, that paper had offered skepticism about President Wilson's motives. The president said he had been concerned for American lives, which was hard for Filbin to square with the passage of two years since the sinking of the *Lusitania*, and also with the ineffectual government response to the chaos along the border with Mexico. Filbin suggested that Wilson's turn to war might have more to do with keeping the president's Wall Street friends and arms dealers happy than it did with avenging the lives of strangers killed at sea.

The response to Filbin's editorial was quick and fierce, and the feisty wordsmith found himself digging a defensive trench. He felt obligated to say that it was not true he was "pro-German," though it was true that he had refused to award a "halo" to Britain, America's new ally. More than anything, Filbin insisted on his freedom to speak his mind. He and those with opinions like his were not "aliens," he wrote. "We are Americans and as citizens, not a subject people on bended knees before a crowned head, we have a right to voice our honest opinion." If the United States was in the war, then the United States had to fight to win, he added. But doing so did not necessitate the destruction of democracy, which the president himself supposedly wanted to promote abroad. "We want freedom of speech, not censored sheets."[13]

But censored sheets is what Filbin would get, and it is almost painful to watch an intelligent and strong editorial voice give way to the era's form of political correctness. By late July, full censorship of all messages arriving via Atlantic cables was in place.[14] The *Record-Citizen*'s editorial stance on the war became indistinguishable from any other.

The advocates of greater war preparedness had been right: the country was now committed to a war it was ill prepared to fight. In very short order, a nation twenty-five hundred miles in breadth, plus Alaska and other U.S. possessions, had to unite behind the war effort. This was a practical reason for the formation of the Committee on Public Information (CPI), which from the beginning was tasked with "selling" the war. It did so via pamphlets, posters, films, and lectures.

The work of the CPI was helped in June 1917 by the passage of the Espionage Act, which called for stiff penalties for "false statements with the intent to interfere with the operation or success of the military or naval forces." The act empowered the postmaster general to stop mail that advocated "treason, insurrection, or forcible resistance to any law of the United States."[15] In March of the next year, amendments to the Espionage Act (often called the Sedition Act) prohibited "any disloyal, profane, scurrilous, or abusive language about the form of government of the United States, or the Constitution of the United States, or the flag of the United States, or the uniform of the Army or Navy," or any words that might bring these things "into contempt, scorn, contumely, or disrepute."[16]

These laws, broad in scope, sometimes became broader in spirit when interpreted at the local level. Readers of Skagway's *Daily Alaskan* learned that in Vincennes, Indiana, authorities had arrested William Van Knalle for "libeling" Abraham Lincoln, declaring that the former president had been "part negro."[17] In the Nebraska town named after the revered Civil War president, a German farmer was arrested for cursing Woodrow Wilson.[18] In the same city of Lincoln, the University of Nebraska's board of regents demanded the sacking of three professors who had shown a "lack of aggressive Americanism in their attitude toward the war."[19]

## Socialists

In early-twentieth-century Alaska, socialism had its greatest appeal and its best chance of succeeding. The war and the speech laws Congress passed help to account for socialism's sharp demise as a viable political alternative in Alaska—or anywhere else in the United States. When the war began, the editor of Nome's socialist *Industrial Worker* was Martin Kennelly, an Irishman who mixed anti-British feeling with political radicalism. It was difficult for Kennelly to see why the United States should bail England out of its crisis, and he said so. This along with his alleged highlighting of German war triumphs in the *Worker*'s pages spurred talk and resentment. A grand jury in Nome indicted Kennelly for sedition, though juries in two separate trials failed to find him guilty. His colleague at the *Worker*, the even more radical Bruce Rogers, also went to trial and was convicted of sedition. Among other inflammatory statements, Rogers had scorned Americans who defined patriotism as a willingness to die "in defense of the trade supremacy of the British Empire and her subjugation of India and Ireland."[20]

Socialism had also made some progress in Anchorage. In the election of 1916, the socialist Lena Morrow Lewis campaigned to be elected Alaska's delegate to Congress. She gained 218 of Anchorage's votes, to Republican James Wickersham's 432 and Democrat Charles Sulzer's 336.[21] Twenty-two percent of the vote was respectable, and it marked socialism's high point in the Cook Inlet region.

Socialists faced difficulties elsewhere. In Ruby a certain Dr. Good, who reportedly had his office door plastered with International Workers of the World stickers, ran as a socialist for the Alaska legislature. The town paper sarcastically called Good a "humanitarian and world fixer" with a liking for anarchy and a "rabid pro-German." According to local lore, the doctor had refused to allow his wife to make a pumpkin pie for a Red Cross benefit. "His humanitarianism did not extend to the price of a couple of cans of pumpkin and a little pie dough." Alaska was an easy-going place, the *Record-Citizen* said, but Dr. Good was a traitor and a liar whose words and deeds reached "pretty near the limit even for Alaska where almost anything can get by."[22] To vote for Good, even in a primary election, was to "spit on the American flag."[23] Needless to say, Dr. Good never took a seat in the legislature at Juneau.

In the territory's capital city, William Waddleton was arrested for distributing an article published in the *International Socialist Review*. The fervent piece, titled "Our Action against Conscription," pointed among other things to revolutionary Russia as a good model for social action. A jury eventually found Waddleton guilty, though eight of twelve jurors had initially voted for acquittal. Only when the jurors learned that Waddleton's punishment could be limited to a nominal fine or stern rebuke did they find him guilty.[24] (This, along with the Nome jury's refusal to convict Martin Kennelly of treason, suggests why claims of wartime "hysteria" need to be reeled in.)

Meantime, Ruby's Loyal League declared itself committed to combating the pro-German sentiment that socialists in the area were trying to stoke. Alaska's gates had been open to all who came to build the territory; Alaskans had been happy to embrace those who came as fugitives from other countries to escape oppression. What could not be tolerated now, in a time of war, were residents who wanted to "take complete charge of our country and turn it over to a foreign invader."[25] Given the Bolshevik Revolution then under way in Russia and Russian Siberia's proximity to Alaska, there were some grounds for concern about threats from Alaska's own "American Bolshiviki." But the purported link between the revolution in Russia and the alleged pro-Germanism of Interior Alaska's socialists was, at best, very weak.

The nation's anti-sedition laws, the nonradical political temper of most Americans, and what Governor John Strong called the "fires of patriotism" that warmed most Alaskans' hearts were not the only things to end socialism as a viable political alternative in the territory. Certainly they did hasten that ending. By war's end, socialism was not, and would not again be, a significant political factor in Alaska.

## A Different Era

The federal laws designed to shape and contain speech help to explain the waves of conformism that washed over the United States and its territories in 1917 and the following year. The tremendous challenge that came with suddenly mobilizing a nation so expansive for a war so big helps to explain why most Americans did not resent the laws or the constriction of public thought the measures brought into being. Given the novel situation the country was in, many Alaskans concluded that the complications that came with open speech were an unaffordable luxury.

It is worthwhile to reflect on the meaning of the word *propaganda*. By the early twenty-first century the word had acquired completely negative connotations. In this later view, propaganda was what dictators fed populations to keep them duped and docile. In the early twentieth century, however, *propaganda* was usually synonymous with *official information*. There was nothing sinister in 1917 about being a propagandist.[26] Indeed, it was the postwar reaction to government propaganda that helped turn the word negative.

While criticism of government was normal before the war, and would be again afterwards, in 1917 the easy cynicism about government that became standard in the United States after Vietnam and Watergate did not exist. In an era of crisis, it was culturally praiseworthy to stand by one's country. As one Alaskan wrote, now that war had come, it was the citizen's part "only to accept and obey the orders and wishes of the captain in the fight."[27] The *Record-Citizen*, now edited by Gus Lynell (J. J. Filbin had died soon after the United States entered the war), was on board. "Every citizen should think twice," he wrote, "before criticizing any man in public office."[28]

This conformity, mostly voluntary, was assisted by the fact that early-twentieth-century Americans lived in well-defined communities with names like Seward, Skagway, Nome, Wrangell, Juneau, Ketchikan, McCarthy, Ruby, Anchorage, and Fairbanks. There was no television to seclude people in their homes; movie theaters were a new thing that brought people together. Obviously, there was no computerized "social media" to isolate citizens while providing them with the comforting belief that they were in truth well connected. Civic organizations such as men's groups, women's groups, children's groups, and church groups prospered and multiplied. People had conversations, were not afraid of quiet, and read newspapers, which referred to towns' entire populations coming together for communal observances, such as when they gathered to see local young men off to war. In November 1918, for example, the *Nenana Daily News* claimed that "almost everybody" in town came together to celebrate the war's end, despite the fact that the news arrived after "[m]any of the citizens of this town had already retired to rest for the night."[29] This sense of community spirit and obligation, substantially lost by the late twentieth century, partly explains the near disappearance of individual voices during the war.

## Hearts of Darkness

Alaskans did not become hysterical, but they did become alert, susceptible to rumor, and liable to overreaction. In this they were like other Americans who, at various times during the war, entertained rumors of Germans bombarding New York and of German provocateurs aiming to incite an uprising among African Americans living in the South. An explosion at the Eddystone munitions plant in Pennsylvania, which killed more than one hundred workers, was supposedly the work of employees sympathetic to Germany. A naval yard explosion at Mare Island, near San Francisco, led to questions about German spy networks. What appeared to be a mass poisoning of sheep in California was "believed to be the work of [enemy] aliens."[30]

Rumors, and the fear stoked by them, came closer to home. The wrecks of the *Spokane* and *Mariposa* off Alaska's coast drew suspicious eyes toward Austrian sailors, who some assumed had tampered with the ships' steering gears.[31] Some in the small settlement of Chichagof worried about a man named Adolph—"his surname being unknown"—who had supposedly escaped from "an interned German ship in the Argentine Republic."[32] Armchair strategists worried about Germans invading Canada and, from there, launching attacks on Alaska and the lower states. Americans "could be attacked from any one of a hundred points on our northern border."[33] The Alaska Railroad and the territory's mines now looked like sweet targets for a clever foe. "The German secret system is too widely known for it to be laughed at."[34]

The case of Edward Krause shows how rumor, fabricated and dispersed, could have bleak consequences. Krause, who was of German origin, was imprisoned in Juneau awaiting execution for murder. He escaped, and locals quickly connected nonexistent dots. According to a hastily arranged and frightful fantasy, Krause had been aided in his jailbreak by German sympathizers, and he would "meet a German U boat, reported to be in the waters of the North Pacific, thus making his way back to Germany."[35] Within three days of his escape in early April 1917, a famished Krause was discovered, shot, and killed on Admiralty Island. No German sympathizers or submarines were in sight.

Then there is the case of William Britt, a businessman, president of the Territorial Board of Pharmacy (1913–1917), member of Alaska's legislature (1915–1917), and a political supporter of Thomas Riggs, soon-to-be Alaska governor. In the war era, Britt was a vice consul for Norway. His opposition to Alaska's prohibition law had earned him political enemies.[36]

Captain John Hunt, an official in Juneau, penned a lengthy memo to authorities in Washington, D.C., about the scorn being heaped on Governor Strong in the editorial pages of the *Alaska Daily Empire*. Hunt suggested that the criticism was bringing government agents into contempt and thus hampering the draft. The paper had also published a letter by Britt that, "beyond question, was an insidious attack upon the officials charged with the administration of the Selective Service Law."[37]

Governor Strong knew Britt, and he knew that Britt had informed foreign-born men that if they ended their plans to become U.S. citizens, they could avoid military service. Upon questioning about this, a report produced in the governor's office noted Britt "appeared to become somewhat heated," saying "the United States would not win the war anyway" since the Germans were too well organized and because "it was impossible for this country to transport sufficient troops to Europe to combat the German troops." Britt also allegedly claimed that the Soviet Bolsheviks would win the war, not against Germany but, ultimately, against the United States, and they would accomplish this on American soil. Hunt claimed that Britt was widely known as a socialist.

Hunt worried that Britt's influence might diffuse throughout southeastern Alaska. He was concerned about the potential spreading of disloyalty among the territory's Scandinavians. A report from Juneau said the country "is overrun by spies" and asked for the authority to shutter newspapers with editorial stances unfriendly to the government.[38] Britt was charged with violating the Espionage Act.[39]

Britt's own words, the few available to us, do not reveal sedition. In a letter Britt wrote to the *Alaska Daily Mail*, he describes his work as a Norwegian vice consul, which included answering the questions of immigrants from neutral countries that did not want to serve in the U.S. Army. He recounted his loyalty to the United States and said nothing critical about the authorities. "Every word and every action of my life," he wrote, "is an open book and ready for the [closest] investigation as to my devotion to the United States."[40] The characterization of Britt's published letter as "insidious" is fictional and understandable only in light of wartime worry.

The accusations against Britt, and his own admission that he had advised Norwegians who did not want to serve in the military to leave the country, created a sense that Alaska's Scandinavian immigrants were especially keen on avoiding the draft.[41] Before the war, Scandinavians were considered particularly desirable newcomers since life in their homelands had prepared them for the rigors of Alaska. After the conflict, Norwegians, Swedes, and Finns would again be spoken of as the kinds of settlers who were "most likely to succeed" in the territory.[42] But now, during this brief, strange moment, the "Swedish element" needed special attention, for it appeared "to delight in treating the authority of the local [draft] boards with contempt."[43] The governor's office sent an appeal to authorities in Washington, D.C., asking for investigators fluent in Norwegian, Swedish, and Finnish to come to Alaska. All the better, the memo noted, if the investigators could also "at least understand" German and "Austrian."[44]

Soon another request for an investigation went from the governor's office to the national capital. It involved Oscar Anderson, a deserter arrested in Ketchikan who claimed to have been influenced by Britt.[45] Within a few days of his arrest, his body was found dashed on a shoreline near Juneau. An official wrote from the governor's office that the body's condition indicated foul play. Coincidentally, a few days after Anderson's death, an article appeared in the *Alaska Daily Mail* that essentially called for a lynch law against dissenters. Whipping, tarring, and feathering hardly seemed sufficient, the article claimed. "A stone wall and a firing squad should be the answer to the activity of the [German] spies and those guilty of treasonable acts of expression."[46]

A post mortem assessment of Anderson's body suggested "accidental drowning," but given the circumstances, this did not seem convincing.[47] In his request for investigators from Outside, Hunt wrote that it was "unsafe" to rely on civil officers in Alaska to conduct a proper examination—presumably less for their own security than for the integrity of the investigation itself. So far as the present researcher could tell, no further investigation into Anderson's death was launched. As for Britt, he was cleared of any wrongdoing and would again serve in Alaska's legislature in the years 1919–1923. He remained in Alaska until 1932, the year he died in a car accident in Juneau.

The on-the-spot shooting of a prison-escaped murderer like Edward Krause would have rankled few in the early twentieth century. And if William Britt helped men, even as the representative of a foreign country, to avoid military service, then many would have said that he deserved denunciation. It was a rough and violent time in which few cared for the rights or sensibilities of criminals, perceived troublemakers, or radicals, such as members of the far-left Industrial Workers of the World ("Wobblies"). Some headlines published in Alaska newspapers make the point:

I.W.W. Leader Hanged by Mob

Southern Mob Lynches Negro for Assault

Race War Breaks Out in Chester, Pennsylvania

Alleged Pro-German Hanged By Citizens

These are the kinds of appalling events that have led historians to write of an era of hysteria, but we bear in mind that such depredations were the work of a few.

## Germans

As far as German Americans were concerned, not all threats were imaginary. In January 1917 a German consul general, Franz Bopp, was sentenced to two years in prison for conspiring to disrupt a shipment of munitions in the United States. And Germans were arrested in New York for possession of explosives apparently intended for Wall Street. After the United States got into the war, anti-German stories made their way into speeches, newspapers, sermons, and movies. Anxiety levels rose.

Before the war, Germany was universally recognized as a land of high learning. Alaska students learned the German language, the tongue of Beethoven and Bach. The American research university had been created in the German image, and numerous American academics had taken degrees in Germany. Now, in wartime, Germany was reconstituted in the American mind into an essentially medieval entity, inhabited by brutes who, like their thuggish ancestors, "sallied forth with bludgeons and battleaxes, riding roughshod over the lands of their friends, raiding and robbing their neighbors, holding captives for ransom, stealing food, money, and virgins."[48]

Alaskans read bogus or hyped stories about German prisoner-of-war camps in which boys maliciously shot prisoners with nail-tipped arrows and of dogs trained to pick out and bite British prisoners. There were false and overblown stories about the German execution of children and of their intentional bombardment of hospitals. One headline screamed, "Fifty-Four Girls Killed in Hun Raid on Hospital." Untrue tales circulated about German troopers hoping to gain Iron Crosses not only for acts of bravery but also for the skillful looting and destruction of French property. Allied liberators were quoted as claiming to have seen the defiled bodies of women and babies in the wake of retreating Germans: "They were terribly disfigured by bayonet jabs."[49] A well-meaning but misinformed speaker at a patriotic gathering in Nome told the audience about a German passion for gouging out eyes, torturing prisoners, and crucifying Canadian prisoners.

Such tales helped to make a case for the de-Germanization of American society. The few open calls for the execution of American Germans insufficiently critical of their mother country found sustenance in fictional or overwrought horror stories from Europe. The *Nenana Daily News* published the fervent musings of George Griffith, an Episcopal priest and army chaplain, who spoke of German "hell fiends" assaulting nuns and destroying convents as a matter of policy. Mostly referring to Germans as the Boche (also called the Hun or Fritz), Griffith wrote that to "talk of [peace] terms until the Boche is exterminated is to league with Satan for a corner in hell."[50] Such talk from a person with such a job title made levelheadedness all the more difficult to maintain. The *Anchorage Weekly Times* offered its own "demand" for Germany's extermination if the enemy were too slow to agree to unconditional surrender.[51]

In this context it made sense that the names of German ships confiscated in American ports when the war began would be changed: the *Vaterland* became the *Leviathan*, the *Hamburg* the *Powhatan*, the *Rhein* the *Susquehanna*, and the *Barbarossa* the *Mercury*. Some towns with German names also converted. Berlin, Michigan, for example, became the town of Marne—adopting the appellation of a French river and battle site. In the summer of 1918, the use of German was banned from all Elks Club lodges.

Some German immigrants showed their loyalty by joining the anti-German chorus. Jacob Cratts argued that foreign-language newspapers should be abolished. If immigrants could not read English, Cratts said, "let them learn, and keep all foreign languages out of the schools."[52] Once the United States joined the war, Anchorage's *Alaska Labor News* stopped publishing articles in Greek, Italian, and Serbian.

Everyone knew that millions of people of German birth or ancestry lived in the United States. Large German populations had concentrated in the American Midwest. Many Germans and Austrians had come to Alaska. In 1910, thirty-four of Skagway's residents reported that they had been born in Germany or Austria.

Given the large number of people living in the United States who were from a nation the U.S. was now at war with, what should Americans do?

Theodore Kremmer, a Philippine War veteran living in Dawson who had recently passed through St. Louis and other areas in the Midwest with large German populations, said he did not think there was much to worry about. Others were less sure. In an open letter to President Wilson, a concerned mother contemplated the "millions" of Germans living in the United States "who quietly sometimes, and openly at other times, are doing their utmost to bring about the downfall of this country." The government should see to it, the writer continued, that disloyal Germans were dealt with convincingly or a "mob spirit" would rise up to "wreak vengeance" on the Teutonic allies of hell.[53] This view was obviously extreme.

On the whole, Alaska walked a more moderate path. So far as the research for this study found, no one of German birth living in Alaska was mobbed simply on account of his ethnicity. Indeed, at the outset of hostilities, Ruby's *Record-Citizen* preemptively denounced "prejudiced race hatred" directed against Germans. The *Alaska Citizen* reminded readers that there were "numerous German-born in and around Fairbanks who are well known and well respected, and who have formed numerous friendships here."[54] Wrangell's *Sentinel* had the same idea: "it is certain that the great majority of naturalized Germans have developed too much love for American freedom not to be loyal to the flag that has protected them."[55] And Juneau's *Alaska Daily Empire* defended William Britt (discussed above) as a "patriotic American citizen" who had been maligned by small, ambitious men.[56]

But there is no doubt that Germans in Alaska were watched, and that whatever culture of easy trust that existed in Alaska's communities came under pressure. In January 1918 Governor Strong noted that "a spirit of distrust [and] suspicion" could be seen in Alaska's communities.[57] Governor Riggs also looked into allegations made by "well-meaning but mistaken" residents in Bethel who claimed that a "state of sedition existed at Good News Bay."[58]

The *Alaska Citizen* recognized the difficult position German immigrants were in, but also said that Germans needed to prove themselves worthy of the "square deal" the United States had given them. Most German immigrants understood this, though they probably also winced at some of what they heard and saw. In Haines, even before Congress had declared war, John Schmidt went to trial for posting an American flag upside down at half-mast. In his own defense, he said that he had lifted the flag that way as a sign of mourning upon learning about his cousin's death on a European battlefield. The court dismissed the case, but not before ordering Schmidt to kiss and salute the U.S. emblem, which he willingly did. Not much later, a German flag was hoisted with other national symbols in Fairbanks as a customary part of a Seward Day celebration. A government official ordered the flag down. Also in Fairbanks, G. Hinton Henry was found guilty of emitting "pro-German utterances" and sentenced to a year in jail.[59]

Bernard Hettel was arrested for saying that "what the United States needed was German discipline and the sooner it came the better."[60] Had he not fled apprehension, he might have been given the same punishment meted to Dick Windmueller, who was found guilty of breaching the Espionage Act, sentenced to a year in the federal prison at Valdez, and fined $250. He allegedly claimed that America had abandoned its isolationist principles "by sending soldiers to Europe and that...all American soldiers who had gone to France should be killed and that Germany would clean them all."[61] In Fairbanks, a jury found Charles Pyne guilty of sedition, though it recommended leniency in sentencing. Pyne had called military conscription a joke and a "slur" on the United States. He said that the war was being fought by the poor for the benefit of the rich. He said that, to him, "it makes no difference if the allies or the Germans win the war."[62]

During this period, German heritage could be a political liability. Alaska's congressional delegate James Wickersham successfully cast political darkness on his chief opponent, Charles Sulzer, by reminding Alaskans that Sulzer's father had been a German soldier. The seed of doubt successfully planted, Wickersham was then careful to say that he did not mean to suggest that Sulzer himself was pro-German, even if he did intend to say that Sulzer was a "slacker." Otherwise, the older Wickersham noted, the thirty-nine-year-old Sulzer would be in uniform. "My brother is forty-three years of age," Wickersham wrote, "and he is a soldier in France."[63] Sulzer, a veteran of the Spanish-American War, had reason to be offended. But Wickersham felt no regret. Summarizing the episode in his diary, he recalled the audience's cheers and added that Sulzer's secretary "retired very badly beaten and crestfallen." He had "denounced both [the assistant] and Sulzer as 'slackers'," he wrote, and "the house applauded."[64]

As was the case throughout the United States, in early 1918 residents of German citizenship fourteen years and older were required to register at Alaska's post offices and supply four photographs of themselves.[65] The registration of the thirty-five Germans living in Anchorage passed without trouble. By late September, Alaskans of German origin were prohibited from traveling from port to port—say, from Anchorage to Nome—without a permit.

Germans were prohibited from all fishing on boats. Austrians could fish, but only if the master of the vessel they worked on was a native-born citizen of unquestioned loyalty. Fishing permits given to Austrians had to be carried at all times and "exhibited to any Citizen of the United States upon demand."[66] As of late 1917, Germans could leave Alaska only with a permit signed by a U.S. attorney.[67]

These rules were set by the federal government. Probably many non-German Alaskans agreed with them. But, on the whole, it is also true that Alaskans made distinctions. Germans *over there*, across the Atlantic, were a problem—a big and definite problem. At one point, Anchorage's *Weekly Times* suggested the German nation's "extermination" as a justifiable war measure.[68] As for the Germans in Alaska, they were watched, but if they caused no problems and demonstrated loyalty to their adopted nation, they carried on with their lives. Thus, while a certain Miss H. W. L. Albrecht needed a letter from Governor Strong to cross from Alaska into the Yukon, he felt no hesitation in supporting her. The young woman was a person "of excellent character," Strong wrote. And while he could not be completely certain of her political views, he had "no reason to doubt that she is just what she represents herself to be," a person who adopted the customs and habits of democracy.[69] Residents of German birth and heritage needed to be careful about what they said and how they said it, but the same was true for everyone.

The war brought new tensions to Alaska, but there was no reason why all loyal, law-abiding residents in the territory could not work to contribute to its development. Alaskans needed to exercise "sound judgment and forbearance," Governor J. F. A. Strong wrote in his proclamation of April 1917. Alaskans should do nothing that might "incite racial feeling or create prejudice against those who have come to the territory for the purpose of bettering their condition and enjoying the inalienable right to life, liberty, and [the] pursuit of happiness guaranteed by that Constitution of the United States." As "strangers in a strange land," Strong said, Alaska's immigrants were "entitled to the utmost consideration, always provided that they comport themselves in accordance with our laws and with due respect for our institutions." The governor did not name German immigrants specifically, though he obviously had them in mind.

All Alaskans, the governor also noted, had been warmed by the "fires of patriotism." They were "ready to respond whenever duty calls." Their response, varied and demanding, is the theme of the next chapter.

# LETTER FROM FRANCE (III)

*In September 1918, L. C. Keely of Cordova received the following letter from B. D. McMasters, his uncle, who served with the U.S. Army in France. It appears that McMasters was serving with the Thirty-first Railroad Engineers, organized and commanded by Frederick Mears, formerly of the Alaska Engineering Commission and instrumental in the early formation of Anchorage. The letter was reproduced in the* Cordova Daily Herald *on September 24, 1918.*

You will observe that my address changes quite often and will no doubt change again in a day or two—but there is one satisfaction in changing—one has an excellent opportunity to see France and I have already seen quite a lot of it.

I left [my recent address] Sunday to report here and am now awaiting orders for another move. Have had a fine rest the last two days and feel quite equal to any occasion now. But boy, I was tired when I reached town. It was later at night and while we were trying to locate billets we ran into several guards; and when I finally got a place to unsling a pack and spread my blankets, I was ready for [sleep]. We had ridden all day on a French train, quite crowded, and I had not eaten anything but a piece of bread and drank some water.

Well, I arose about 7:15 a.m. and set me up a "barber shop" and after shaving took my mess kit and proceeded to the mess hall and filled up.... As you know I am...a part of the railroad transport corps....

Sorry you are not with the engineers. They are some organization to be with all right and one sees many interesting sights daily. However, we have all learned the use of a pick and shovel.

You would...be much amused at the French girls. Many of them are not "nice," but when you do happen to find a real nice educated French Miss, one can have a very nice time and be royally entertained—which has occurred to myself on two occasions of late. They are learning English faster than we are French. However, I can get along very nicely by signs. They are also very affectionate and polite.

The French soldiers term us comrades and often stop and shake hands. I got my French badly mixed recently at a restaurant. I asked for butter in French and got a nice bottle of beer, La Bierre. Butter is pronounced "burr" and beer La Bierre. I forgot to put "La" before the word. However, I did not send it back. Think I will look around and secure a French tutor and study French if I can get settled in a town where I will be permanently located for a while. But by the way boys are moving Fritz just now, it may be necessary to learn the German language. Guess Fritz has learned something about the Sammies [the Americans] that he won't forget soon. What do you think?

I suppose you have become very adept in tripping the light fantastic by now. Only you must be careful and not get tangled up with some of those Eskimo maidens or Indians. As for myself—being a decent married gentleman of mature years, there is no danger of falling from grace or becoming attached to some French widow, although I must say there are a number of perfect "stunners" over here and if I was not a staunch church member I might get led astray.

Stroud Collection

CHAPTER FOUR

# Over Here—Deeds

## Vulnerability

The United States had experience with total war. In the colonial wars, the American Revolution, and the War of 1812, communities became battle sites. During the Civil War, Southern towns and cities learned personally about the truth of the saying, coined at the time, that "war is hell." During the First World War, the military threat was distant, but some Americans worried about the possibility of a German invasion. German submarine activity off the East and Gulf Coasts was a danger.

In the war's early days, Alaskans had local worries. The army's presence in the territory—spread among widely separated forts—was skeletal. Even in 1940, when the threat to Alaska was far greater than at any time before, only about five hundred soldiers were stationed in the territory.

Following the frantic gold rush at the end of the 1800s, the army's main purpose in the territory was to stand guard and respond to emergencies, such as outbreaks of disease and potentially violent labor strikes. In 1916, forty military men went from Fort Seward to Anchorage to guard the property of the Alaska Engineering Commission. They were led by Frederick Mears, an army captain with experience building the Panama Canal and the Alaska Railroad who would soon leave for the war in Europe. In the next year, two hundred enlisted men with the Army Signal Corps, along with twenty-five foot soldiers, maintained the Washington-Alaska Military Cable and Telegraph System, better known simply as WAMCATS. These soldiers did useful work, but they hardly comprised a serious defensive force.

Most soldiers would have been grateful not to have duty in the territory. Official records of life in Alaska's forts point to workplace monotony combined with limited social opportunities, fewer in some locations than in others. Soldiers marched through town centers on the Fourth of July, and fort teams often played baseball and other sports against town clubs. John Tatum, a veteran stationed before the war at Fort Gibbon near Tanana, remembered that the locals organized a dance to mark the soldiers' arrival in their region, "for we were as much an event to the community as it was to us." Tatum writes of battling the dreariness of life in the Interior with an uninspiring "endless round" of events: dances, boxing matches, bowling tournaments, and competitive games. The oppressiveness of the winter darkness, the sleeplessness of the summer sun, and the clouds of gluttonous mosquitoes put the men in a "receptive mood for the bottle," Tatum recalled, and "we had narcotics to combat."[1] In 1907, Fort Gibbon's soldiers could not have known the future relevance of a lecture given by a visiting German titled "The Daily Life of the German Officer and Soldier."[2]

Alaskans, living in small communities, had long felt vulnerable. The presence of troops based at the eleven military posts established in gold rush days brought some comfort but not much. Few of the forts hosted more than a hundred soldiers, and all of the installations' men combined could not stand up to an organized invasion. Fort Seward's strength of nearly 350 officers and men in 1912 was impressive by Alaska standards, but such a band could not be expected to throw back a committed invader.

By 1914, Japan had been on the rise as an imperial and military power for over a decade, as its colonization of Korea and its defeat of Russia in a war of 1904–1905 showed. In 1907 the *Nome Nugget* suggested that the "Japanese have always looked with a covetous eye on this region," and that in the event of an American war against the Asian nation "a Japanese cruiser might easily sail into Nome harbor someday . . . hold up the shipping, land a strong body of troops, and under cover of quick-firing guns sail away with the whole result of the winter's clean-up." Presumably the 130 or so soldiers at nearby Fort Davis would respond, though the writer suggested that they would be not much more than "helpless" in the case of an organized Japanese incursion.[3]

A year before the United States entered the Great War, Governor Strong sought unsuccessfully to persuade the federal government to form a militia in Alaska. In the event of war with Japan, the governor wrote,

> Alaska would be among the first points of attack, and I regret to say that, without an organized militia and with no harbor defenses of any kind, the Territory would be at the mercy of a hostile country, and the towns of coastal Alaska and the rich gold and copper mines could, and no doubt would, be laid under tribute.[4]

Another indication of concern about potential military problems for Alaska in the Pacific is the presence among archival papers from the Alaska Engineering Commission of a manuscript on naval defenses that called for the building of a naval base somewhere on the Aleutian chain.[5]

As for the instability of Russia, that too was a security concern. The *Skagway Alaskan* editorialized in 1912 that in the case of a war between Russia and the United States, Russia's former colony would "be the first target for Russian occupation, and with no troops, no forts, and a hostile nation but a few miles across the Bering Strait, our citizens would be taken in a fortnight."[6] At the end of his reflections on army life in Alaska, Tatum considered the territory's place on the "flank of the world," and wondered if Alaska would someday need a greater military presence.[7] And as war raged in Europe, congressional delegate James Wickersham spoke at a Kiwanis Club meeting in Washington, D.C., calling for the development of Alaska defenses in order to protect the territory "against a possible future Asiatic enemy in the Pacific, or the permanent occupation of Russia by Germany."[8]

Such worries were justified. A generation later, the United States would fight a ferocious war with Japan that did briefly reach Alaska soil; and for more than forty years following the Second World War, the United States and Russia faced off in a global cold war. But in the struggle that began in 1914 and drew in the United States three years later, Japan and Russia would be America's nominal allies. The isolation Alaskans felt and the sense of urgency this isolation spurred was not much appreciated Outside. In 1912 Secretary of War Henry Stimson was looking to send soldiers to defend the Panama Canal, which would open two years later. It seemed to him that soldiers served little good purpose standing "police duty" in Alaska when they could be meeting more pressing needs elsewhere.

With the coming of the Great War, Alaska's undefended position raised questions. What if Germany captured Alaska and then used it as a base of operations against the American West Coast? What if Germany had access to safe ports in Mexico or Central America from which to harass and attack American shipping in the Pacific?

These concerns soon dissipated. Less than a month after Congress declared war, informed observers could see that whatever trouble Germany caused in the Pacific would be directed against Japan. And even if Germany was able to connect with anti-American insurgent forces in Latin America, that would hardly amount to a threat against Alaska. In any case, Latin American nations aligned themselves with the United States. Alaska newspapers carried stories about pro-American demonstrations in Brazil, and they learned that Guatemala, Panama, and Cuba had broken diplomatic ties with Germany soon after the American declaration of war.

Then again, some wondered if the very unlikelihood of an attack on Alaska was reason enough to bolster Alaska defenses. The Germans might strike Alaska, some thought, precisely because so few would anticipate it. Certainly, the vulnerable territory provided Germany with an alluring stockpile of natural resources. A "hostile cruiser could land marines without opposition at any town on Alaska's coast and destroy [the] commerce between Alaska and the states," valued at more than one hundred million dollars.[9] Most of all, Germany would covet the coal of the Matanuska region, the value of which the U.S. Navy was investigating when war was declared. According to this view, the federal government needed "to protect Alaskan harbors so that this supply of coal may not be endangered by enemy attackers."[10] (Alaska's coal was soon found not to be of sufficient quality to fuel naval ships.)

Alaskans had to be vigilant, even if their distance from centers of influence served as a buffer from the world's chaos. From one point of view, Alaska's isolation was a blessing. "In these troublous times," Fairbanks's *Alaska Citizen* observed, "when the world is in turmoil and in the travail of a new order of things, it is good to live in Alaska."[11]

## Service

Most Alaskans wanted to play their part in seeing the country to victory. As one newspaper put it, "Let us show the world that Anchorage, the newest city in Uncle Sam's greatest territory, is with the president in this fight for freedom."[12] Once war was declared, Alaskan civilians focused on security. Under the auspices of service organizations—the Arctic Brotherhood, Elks Club, and Eagles Club—men too old or otherwise ineligible to join the battle overseas drilled and stood watch in Nenana, Juneau, Fairbanks, Wrangell, Sitka, Anchorage, McCarthy, and probably every other Alaska town. They guarded important sites saboteurs might want to strike, such as train depots and radio and telegraph stations. Nome's home guard, one of many in Alaska, drilled for an hour on Monday, Wednesday, and Friday mornings.[13]

Initially, Alaska Natives were not required to register for military service, but they contributed to the cause from the beginning.[14] The week following the war declaration, Wrangell's *Sentinel* reported that within the town's boundaries lived "people from every country of Europe, and we have a good percentage of people who are of Indian or mixed blood."[15]

For Alaskans the Great War was a total war in the sense that it touched every aspect of public life: shopping, school, work, play, conversation, and church services. Some worshipers agreed with the popular Midwest preacher Billy Sunday, who shadowboxed with imaginary Germans, shouted "to hell with the Kaiser," and declared that "the great guns of the United States" would end the problem of German militarism.[16] (Alaska's delegate to Congress, James Wickersham, was impressed by Sunday, less for his theological reflections than for his "cunning, shrewd and skillful... use of slang.")[17] Alaska ministers could be fierce, too. In early 1918, the Reverend Paul Kern of the Church of the Holy Name in Ketchikan learned that his name had been placed on a list of anti-Americans. Kern wrote (and not quite in the spirit of the Sermon on the Mount) that putting his name on that list amounted to "the insane act of a diseased brain, inspired by ill-advised, over-zealous, ignorant, or pinheaded bigotry."[18]

Some Alaskans sought secret knowledge in biblical prophecy. Richard Collier, whose lengthy and complicated musings found space in the territory's newspapers, linked the antichrist of the Book of Revelation to the German kaiser and predicted the war's end in January 1918, eleven months shy of the actual finish line. Alaska's Christian Science churches published long, if not always easily comprehended, philosophical essays. With the advent of war, these essays promoted loyalty to country in spiritual terms. St. Philip's Episcopal Church in Wrangell also linked good Christian conduct to good citizenship. As in previous and later wars, public figures connected Christ's work on the cross to the work of battle: "as he died to make us holy, let us die to make men free."[19]

Most Alaskans readily came to terms with the demands the nation's involvement in the war presented. After months had passed, those demands would come to feel more burdensome. And while a majority faced the war's requirements with equanimity, everyone felt some pressure. Alaskans reminded themselves that what they were enduring was nothing compared with what the boys faced in France.

Indeed, the front-line soldier's responsibility was the standard by which every act of service was judged. When the military registration process began, the lawyers designated to manage it learned that they would not be paid.[20] After some protest, Governor Strong offered modest economic compensation to those who needed it, but not without reminding the attorneys of the soldiers who "in many cases have been delighted to sacrifice large incomes in order to work and fight for their country twenty-four hours a day for thirty dollars a month."[21] Perhaps it was unfair to browbeat professionals with the soldiers' example, since army responsibilities were repaid in currency, room, and board. But the lawyer's potential sacrifice, as compared to the warrior's, seemed trivial. Acting on this ideal, Carl Lomen, the leading draft registration official at Nome, spent three hundred dollars of his own money to meet inductees' basic needs.[22]

In the early months, when energy levels were high, calls to give to the war effort were broad and positive in tone. Alaskans heard that they were free to help the war effort, or not, as they wished: "It is up to you."[23] Alaskans were encouraged not to assume that everyone should contribute to the war in the same way. "Because our fellow citizen does not take the same method of showing his love for his country that we do should not be the cause of any unpleasant feelings."[24]

Participation brought benefits—the good feeling that comes with lending a hand, supporting a worthy cause, and being alongside a neighbor whose son had just shipped off. But there were also costs. And as fatigue set in and the pace or value of work flagged, appeals became sharper and more demanding. In Alaska's small communities, where everyone knew what everyone else was or was not doing—where everyone, officials said, comprised the "police force of the Food Administration"—the pressure to pitch in was great.[25] In late 1917, a few Skagway residents declined to sign a self-denying "food pledge," part of a national effort to make more food available for the men at war. The local paper assumed the refusal had been due to a misunderstanding. Until "we know that everyone understands [the food laws] completely, we will refuse to believe that anyone will deliberately not conform to the pledge."[26] It did not seem possible, the paper suggested, that someone could understand the purpose of a war measure and still

*Seward Gateway*, April 4, 1917

decide not to participate. The *Seward Gateway* was more emphatic. It editorialized that if you had a chance to assist the war effort and did not do so, then "you are just to that extent a traitor and an ally of the Kaiser."[27] Such words offered on behalf of volunteerism approached coercion. Yet it remained true that most Alaskans did not need extra prompting. The country was at war, and everyone had a part to play.

What could Alaskans do? The list of possibilities was long.

Some "ardent little Patriots" of a Sunday-school program in Ruby sewed blankets for soldiers recovering in France.[28] Anchorage's Woman Patriotic League hosted events to raise $100 of the $600 cost of an "Alaska bed" in the hospital for wounded soldiers at Neuilly, France. The league's members also vowed to wear the U.S. flag's colors until the war was over.[29]

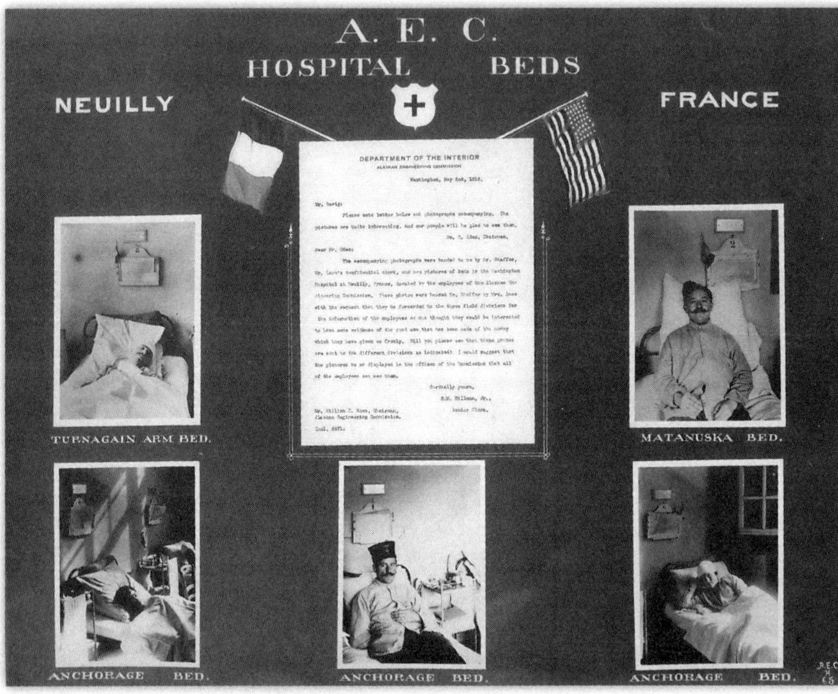


Alaska Engineering Commission Hospital Beds. Anchorage Museum, AMRC-aec-h65

Anchorage's Fatherless Children of France Fund gave Alaska's "hard-handed miners" a chance to show their sensitive side as they gazed on the photographs of sponsored children that had come "all the way from sunny France to the frozen north."

> In actual distance it may be a far cry from France to Alaska, but in the question of saving the lives of precious children, humanity materially lessens the distance, and the generous arm of Alaskans easily spans the breach.[30]

The Emergency Italian Refugees Committee, based in Anchorage, had its own focus, and Juneau's Treasure and Trinket Fund collected items useful to airmen and their families. The people at McCarthy hosted a Starving Armenians Fund. "Once more," an editorial explained, "we are asked to contribute towards the relief of a nation that has suffered untold horrors and humiliations from the Turks," Germany's allies in the war.[31] For the same reason, an official with the Alaska Engineering Commission received the task of organizing an Armenian and Syrian Relief Fund.[32] No one in Anchorage could know at the time that the depredations the Turks had launched against the Armenians would be counted as the twentieth century's first genocide.

It is not clear why Native women in Teller donated their hair to the military cause. Perhaps they had heard stories about hair being used for machine belts in German factories. But the deed's actual lack of usefulness mattered less than the motivation behind it. Women in Pennsylvania also had learned that their hair's sacrifice was not necessary, though their gesture was said to show the "height of devotion."[33] Some ideas did not come to fruition. In response to an article published in *McClure's Magazine*, C. G. Wilford of the Alaska Engineering Commission wrote that he would be glad to found branches of the My America League in Alaska's towns. There is no evidence that the league ever took hold in Alaska, perhaps because plenty of service opportunities existed already.[34]

## Liberty Bonds and the Red Cross

As for financing the war, the U.S. government offered interest-bearing Liberty Bonds. In the language of the day, Americans could "subscribe" to the Liberty Loan project and help the country while also saving money and investing for the future.

The response was enthusiastic. James Wickersham, passing through Boston, witnessed a "gala day" that involved thousands of people parading in support of a Liberty Bond drive. "The whole city is covered with flags and filled with enthusiasm."[35] Wickersham himself purchased at least $1,350 in bonds (equal to about $21,000 in 2013 dollars).[36] In May 1918, the people of Nome bought bonds worth nearly $42,000.

In all of Alaska's towns, contributors' names appeared in print. Thus we learn that Harry Pigeon purchased bonds valued at fifteen hundred dollars, A. N. Kittilsen at three thousand dollars, and that Al Gawne paid five thousand dollars. Most purchases were in the fifty- to one-hundred-dollar range, still heavy sums at a time when miners on the Seward Peninsula were content with a daily compensation (wages plus board) of seven dollars. Officials in San Francisco paid tribute to Nome's financial contribution to the war with an "honor flag."[37]

As for the residents of nearby Candle, they raised an average of almost ninety-six dollars for every adult in the town, and they were eager to see their effort distinguished from Nome's. "We do not wish to discredit Nome in any way,"

# HAVE YOU BOUGHT A LIBERTY BOND?

By special arrangement with one one of Skagway's patriotic citizens a new plan for smaller payments and longer time is allowed. You can now buy a $50.00 Bond for $5.00 down and $5.00 a month or a $100.00 Bond for $5.00 down and $10.00 a month. You CAN AFFORD this. Come in and see about it.

You can help win the war by buying a Bond for $50 or $100 payable in installments

## LIBERTY BONDS

Protect you, your family, your home, your business and your country. By buying your share you will be doing your part to encourage our officials, strengthen our allies, and show our enemies that our resources, an irresistible force, are backing our fighting men on land and sea.

## *DON'T BE A SLACKER*

Campaign Closes Noon, October 27th, 1917

**Do Your Bit And Do It Now**

Applications received and Further Information cheerfully given

# BANK OF ALASKA

*Daily Alaskan* (Skagway), October 25, 1917

wrote the town's Council of National Defense, but Candle was a distinct town and "it would . . . please the general public of this community if they knew that our efforts . . . received some recognition beyond Nome."[38]

So each town sought distinction. The *Daily Alaskan* said that Skagway's Liberty Bond "honor roll" would be the pride of every "true Alaskan." Included on the roll were Phil Abrahams, Jennie Bender, Frank Fowler, Helen Lynch, Joe Toyozumi, and Frank Wurzbacher. Opposite these, the newspaper argued, were the "poor Americans" who withheld support from the bond program and, in so doing, held back support from soldiers and sailors "fronting death on battlefields and oceans."[39] Among these potentially fake Americans of Alaska residence were one hundred town dwellers who had not subscribed to a bond issue. They were easily identifiable by their names' absence from the published roll. Some of these—Evelyn Curtis, Karl Larson, and G. C. Siprella—acted and must have been relieved to see their names added to the next day's list.

We have seen that, when the war was new, Alaska editors had called for a generous view of war participation. The quotas linked to Liberty Bond sales made this line harder to toe. As of April 1918, Ketchikan, Cordova, and Anchorage had won recognition Outside for their high bond subscriptions. The news about Anchorage appeared in newspapers from Idaho to South Carolina. Fairbanks, on the other hand, needed to improve its game for "the sake of the Flag."[40]

The government gave towns financial goals related to their population. Anchorage's quota for the third of four Liberty Loan campaigns came in at $59,000. In the event, Anchorageites subscribed $113,000. In the popular phrases of the time, Anchorage had gone "over the top" and "done its bit" in helping to meet the war's costs. To use another word that pervaded wartime speech, the people of Anchorage had shown their "loyalty." Anchorage's *Weekly Times* noted that the town's Japanese had "been ultra-loyal in purchasing liberty bonds," even though, as a result of federal law, citizenship was legally beyond their reach.[41] And after the war, Native purchases of Liberty Bonds and donations to the Red Cross were added to legal arguments for the recognition of Alaska Natives as U.S. citizens.[42]

The government understood that bond purchasers' self-interest needed to be considered. Interest rates for Liberty Bonds ranged from over three to four and a half percent. Similarly, local merchants found ways to do well for themselves while also doing good for the nation. Nome's Arctic Bakery and Candy Store enticed patrons with a lottery offering a one-hundred-dollar bond in exchange for a twenty-five-cent meal. Albert Reinert, a merchant in Skagway, promised to donate ten percent of his profits to the Red Cross. The battle overseas even found its way into want ads:

> FOR SALE—At a great war sacrifice, 43-Mile Roadhouse, fully equipped. Apply at Fowler and Morris.[43]

Since its founding in the United States in 1881, the Red Cross has been an indispensable institution. During the First World War, more than any other time, the Red Cross's work was constantly before the American people. Following the war declaration, Alaska chapters formed throughout the territory. In Fairbanks, the organization's inaugural meeting convened at the George Thomas Memorial Library.

Some Alaska women joined the Red Cross and went overseas. Among these was Molly Smith of Valdez who wrote home about the hardship of nurse life near the battlefront. In Alaska, the organization's chapters appealed for financial help to assist "the boys who are now fighting OUR battles in Europe."[44] This meant darning socks, packing bandages, and collecting and shipping books to help keep the men in Europe usefully occupied. The Red Cross of Skagway placed "com-

Red Cross workers in Anchorage. Anchorage Museum, AMRC-aec-g872

*Daily Alaskan* (Skagway), December 7, 1917

fort bags" in shops for the collection of pencils, writing paper, handkerchiefs, tobacco, cigarettes, and "other things [for] the soldier boys at the front."[45] Meantime, laborers with the Alaska Engineering Commission sent baseball equipment, and members of the Eska War Relief Club committed to donating a dollar each month to the Interior Department's War Work Association.[46]

Like other newspapers, McCarthy's *Weekly News* printed names. The Red Cross was happy to have Al Anderson's dollar, though Mrs. Boutin's $5.99 was better, and Tom and Mrs. Cloninger's combined $50 was best. Donations came

Red Cross volunteers in Nome. University of Alaska Fairbanks, UAF-2010-50-27

in from Long Creek (George Pike—$2), Poorman Creek (Billy Morton—$20), Nulato (Mr. and Mrs. Ostrander—$25), Kaltag (John Somers—$25), and Koyukuk (A.W. Aston—$10).[47] In Wrangell, Natives contributed more than $100. "The Native people," the town's *Sentinel* said, were "surely banner Red Cross workers."[48]

In another community, Natives donated money to the war cause that had originally been saved for a new sawmill. As the money had been earned selling furs and trinkets to occasional visitors to their village, it would "take them years to make the money back."[49]

## Doing More

Alaskans could—*should*—subscribe to Liberty Bonds. They could—*should*—donate to the Red Cross. They always could—always should—*do more*. Responding to a call from Secretary of the Navy Franklin Roosevelt, for instance, they could send their binoculars and "spyglasses" to Washington, D.C. They could forgo gas-guzzling outings, since "[t]oo many picnics mean gasoline waste in auto or boat."[50] Alaskans could also join organizations that sponsored war-related projects—the Alaska Women's Patriotic League, Alaska Council of Defense, and the Alaska Loyal League, among others.

*Daily Alaskan*, October 19, 1918

Throughout the territory, appeals went out for old shoes that could be sent to needy French and Belgian civilians. One Skagwayan was seen purchasing five pairs of shoes at the Kennedy and Company store, only immediately to deposit them in a box destined for Europe. The Women's Christian Temperance Union at Skagway contributed $36.50 for the aid of a French child who had lost his parents. The youth of Ruby did the same. The Alaska Committee for the Fatherless Children of France noted that French soldiers would be stouter warriors if they knew their fallen comrades' young ones were cared for.

Civic leaders constantly promoted the idea that one's actions directly affected the men overseas. An extra helping of beef for you, they said, translated into one helping less for the soldier in the trench. And where in times past an "insignificant spot" like the town of McCarthy would have had no role in war, this conflict had become "our own personal affair," an occasion on which "we all can put our shoulders to the wheel just as efficaciously as the soldier in the trenches and sailor on the sea."[51]

The question forced itself: did anyone honestly want to compare sacrifice at home to what the boys overseas were facing?

> When you are out on a shell-swept hill and the shells are going by like bats out of hell, as the soldiers say, and it's dark as the grave, and every man…stands strong and true camouflaging all his own feelings for your sake and for the sake of what he has back home, meatless days and wheatless days, and Liberty Bond campaigns seem cheap as your support of him in such an hour.[52]

So Alaskans showed their mettle. "In the great outside world," wrote one traveler, "one would not imagine that these far-away towns were doing more than 'their bit.'"[53] According to one contemporary, the residents of Nenana, whose number stood at about 630 in 1920, had given almost $23,000 to various war-related causes.[54]

In all this, Alaskans, like Americans generally, submitted to an unprecedented government reach into their daily lives. Most saltwater fishermen now needed to acquire government licenses while German noncitizens without written permits from a U.S. attorney or the Department of Justice were prohibited from ocean fishing altogether. As of April 1918, workers needing access to docks, like Stephen Adelman of Seward, had to have a pass with the pass holder's photograph and a deputy U.S. marshal's signature.[55] James Wickersham noted in his diary that the federal government had taken control of the country's railroads as a war measure, adding that it was "a remarkable event in history."[56]

## Conservation

Government action touched Alaskans' lives most directly in their kitchens, restaurants, and food stores. This effort was spurred nationally by books with titles like *War Vegetable Gardening and the Home Storage of Vegetables*, *Recipes for*

*War Bread, Food and the War: A Textbook for College Classes, Food Saving and Sharing, War Cook Book for American Women: Suggestions for Patriotic Service in the Home,* and *War Economy in Food* (all published in 1918). Housewives gained a new title: "soldiers of the kitchen."[57] In the interests of allowing more professionally farmed food to be sent overseas, they planted "Liberty Gardens" that produced spinach, cabbage, cauliflower, and potatoes. In Nome, they planted radishes, turnips, and lettuce.[58] The mayor of Skagway promised to enforce the town's livestock laws to ensure that such gardens would be safe from the appetites of horses and chickens.[59] The *Alaska Citizen* admitted that Alaska's vegetable contribution would not amount to much in the overall war effort, but it was better to do something than to have it said after the war that "Alaska or Alaskans stood back and let others fight America's battles."[60]

So Alaskans altered their diets in conservation's name. On Tuesdays and Fridays, most of the people of Anchorage went without meat. On Saturdays, they declined pork; on Wednesdays they refused wheat. "I have come to the end of a wheatless day," a lighthearted Anchorage poet wrote,

*I have eaten no cookies or pie;*
*I have had no bread that was made with wheat,*
*It was made out of corn or rye.*
*And I liked it so well that when war is past,*
*And glorious victory won*
*I'll keep observing "wheatless days"*
*And I'll eat "corn pone" for fun!*[61]

Bakeries sold "Victory Bread," and a recipe for "war cake" went around:

> ½ cup fat, 1 cup sugar, yolks of 2 eggs, ½ cup milk, 1¾ cup flour, equal parts white and rye, 3 teaspoons, baking powder, 1 teaspoon cinnamon, whites of two eggs.[62]

As was true of other efforts on the war's behalf, food conservation was initially taken with some enthusiasm. But as months passed, restrictions felt more onerous, bureaucratic, and intrusive. Soon local committees had the power, under the authority of the U.S. Food Administration, to determine food prices and, therefore, merchants' profits. (As of late October 1918, a retailer in Cordova could expect to receive twenty-six cents for a pound of pot roast, with a profit of nine cents upon sale.) Anchorage was divided into ten districts for the purposes of organizing food conservation. A captain was assigned to each district, and these would "personally visit every home and secure pledge cards and once every week will collect personal reports from the pledgers showing the saving effected during the period."[63]

As of early June 1918, Anchorage's bakers had to inventory their stocks and submit reports on food conservation to the local federal food administrator. Alaska's bakers soon faced a loss of their business licenses unless they substituted at least twenty-five percent of wheat in their "victory bread." All establishments that used "three barrels or more of wheat flour per month were required to obtain licenses from the United States Food Administration."[64] Fats, too, had to be conserved, since "[g]lycerin, which comes from fat, is one of the chief things for making modern explosives."[65]

Then there was the steady stream of editorials, speeches, and personal exhortations. "The armies of today are fighting three thousand miles ahead of their food bases," asserted the *Alaska Railroad Record*, and there was "a food base in every kitchen." Alaskans should "help keep up the supply of foodstuffs by production and conservation, and thus be of material assistance to our country in achieving victory in the war."[66] William Gerig, Alaska's Federal Food Administrator, make the point more starkly. If Alaskans, like other Americans, failed to conserve food, then the United States would not be able to win the war, "and the nameless horrors and suffering of the women and children in Flanders, northern France, Italy, Poland, and Serbia will be repeated in America." It may be true that Alaska's women had already volunteered with the Red Cross, bought Liberty Bonds, and seen a husband or brother go to battle—all "splendid in themselves." But, another official said, "you haven't done enough yet." Where America's great-grandmothers had sacrificed for the sake of the nation, this generation of ladies was called on to sacrifice for the good of the whole world: "Don't help the Hun at meal time."[67]

In this charged context, small wastefulness could be spoken of in absolute terms: "He who wastes a crust of bread prolongs the war" and puts himself at odds with the "moral forces of the universe." To waste food was a "sin" because "food has become sacred." To have leftover "sugar at the bottom of your [coffee] cup is pro-German." To be careless with food in this time of crisis was "nothing short of criminal."[68]

Citizens had the responsibility to see that others were living up to the demands of the nation's need. As a government document reprinted in the *Alaska Railroad Record* put it:

> If the restaurant and hotel in your town don't follow the [government's] food conservation program it is your fault—your fault! Because if you insist upon their doing it, and take an interest in their doing it, they will follow it, if you explain it to them.[69]

Not even the elderly could catch a break. If children would do with less sugar, Governor Strong wrote to the director of the Pioneer Home in Sitka, then the elderly could do with less meat and wheat. Obviously, the governor added, food regulations would not apply to invalids; and

> the Lord knows it is not my desire to exercise such food economy as would result in any individual . . . not receiving sufficient subsistence. But it is up to us, as American citizens, with our country facing such tremendous responsibilities, to give our best efforts for the ultimate success of the cause and the principles for which we are fighting.

Besides, the governor added, a little dieting would do the residents' health some good.[70]

Food became a topic of discussion in other ways. Sauerkraut, sounding German, fell into unpopularity until people learned that the dish was really of Dutch origin. Sauerkraut was a "valuable food," an official reported in the *Record*, "and its use should not be curtailed as a result of over-zealous and ill-advised patriotism."[71] This was good news for Alaska's cabbage farmers.

The war presented Alaska's farmers with some opportunities. A few thought, incorrectly, that wartime conservation of beef might open a market Outside for Alaska reindeer. More successful was D. M. Lynch of Anchorage, who developed syrup made from birch sap—the beginning of a small industry that survived in Alaska into the twenty-first century.[72] Consuming the Matanuska Valley's potatoes had been a matter of local convenience, but it was now raised to the level of patriotic duty since Alaskans buying Alaskan products meant more food produced Outside being sent to the troops. Thus, the Alaska Engineering Commission's Land and Industrial Department pledged to purchase only Alaska-grown potatoes, cabbage, carrots, and lettuce. E. L. Wagner, a cook with the AEC, devised a recipe for thirty-six pounds of bread using twenty-five pounds of dry mashed potatoes as a primary ingredient. Alaska's potato farmers were now "potatriots"—a "fighting corps" in their own right who would help to "spud" the Kaiser. As for the potato itself, it was a "good soldier" and was best eaten "uniform and all."[73] However, while this homegrown demand gave Alaska agriculture business, it was insufficient to prevent farmers from "becoming discouraged," as a memo to Governor Strong from officials in Anchorage put it. Even after accounting for the AEC's requirements, there remained a potato surplus of about one hundred tons.[74]

The use of Alaska coal was also a patriotic act. As with food, the more local coal Alaskans used, the less they would have to import from Outside and the more there would be for other necessities. By the latter half of 1918, the conservation focus turned to paper. William Gerig wrote a memo to AEC employees reminding them that not wasting paper was "as necessary to the winning of the war as the purchase of Liberty Bonds."[75] Even personal orderliness had war implications, since a disorganized desk in the workplace indicated a lack of attention to tasks at hand, and "it helps the Kaiser to have matters lie over night without attention."[76] Every ounce of human energy, every cent, and "every life if need be" had to be devoted to Germany's defeat.[77]

The constant admonitions and appeals inevitably taxed energy levels and pocketbooks. And as the war's toll on Alaska's economy became heavier, war work on the home front became more burdensome. McCarthy's *Weekly News* noted that giving to the Belgian Relief Fund and the Red Cross, along with purchasing Liberty Bonds, had been "somewhat of a tax on people's finances."[78] And where the Alaska Loyal League in Anchorage had sixty-five members as of early February 1918, for two weeks running only thirty-two had come out for drill. "These figures need no comment," the league's secretary wrote with disapproval, adding that drill perfection was hard to attain in the face of such high absenteeism.[79]

Tiredness and shifting attention spans made home-front ardor more difficult to maintain, but this was countered by the concern that slacking could lead to charges of being soft on the enemy. The AEC itself was forced to counter accusations of pro-Germanism leveled by a disgruntled employee with tallies of commission workers' contributions to the Red Cross, the hospital at Neuilly, and other projects.

## History

Alaskans did their bit. They went over the top. They responded to President Wilson's call to promote American democracy versus German savagery. Like other Americans, Alaskans knew that the vast conflict in which they were participating would go into the history books. Some looked to the past for insight into the present. As with other things in that time of heightened anxiety, these historical reflections met current needs and avoided complication.

At the outset of the war, the only veterans organization existing in Seward was composed of the "boys who fought for our flag" in the Spanish-American War.[80] The nasty conflict that spun off from that war against insurgents in the Philippines had been controversial. (Mark Twain was one of the struggle's prominent critics.) The war with Spain had made the United States an empire, which conflicted, in some Americans' minds, with republican ideals. But now, references to these wars were few, brief, and sanitized. The popular reflections on America's previous military episodes offered in the wartime press had less to do with past struggles than with hopes about the present one. Thus, the War of 1812 ended when Britain recognized the "soundness of the principles for which the Americans fought," and the Mexican War of the 1840s had occurred because "the Mexicans had not been very careful of American rights."[81] Neither of these claims could withstand stand significant argument.

Some aged veterans of the Civil War lived in Alaska's towns. One of them, E. H. Flynn, of St. Michael, offered his services in 1918.[82] All such warriors, Yankee or Confederate, now seemed the stuff of pure principle. Old disputes were put away. Every ancient fighter, regardless of what had really been said or fought for at the time, was interpreted as having stood for the defense of basic democratic principles, "just as they are fighting today."[83]

During the First World War, most public historical references were to the American Revolution and the Civil War. In the words of the *Daily Alaskan*, the present war rose "to a plane of standards as ennobling" as those previous conflicts. The Alaska women who volunteered to work with the Red Cross were demonstrating the "same spirit of patriotism that made heroines of American women in '76 and '61."[84] The names Washington and Lincoln, already revered, now seemed sacred. Martha Washington was morphed into a kind of model Red Cross worker.

Articles for children, serialized in Alaska's newspapers, posed weighty questions. At school and church the young learned that fighting was bad, so how to make sense of the millions of adults hurling themselves into a deathly maelstrom? How to make sense of the glorification of military enlistment? Up came the specter of adults doing what they told children not to. But, queried the popular writer George Ade, is it always wrong to fight? Did Americans want to criticize George Washington for fighting the British to secure America's liberty? In 1917 children learned that Americans were fighting for the freedom to sail the seas, not to mention the liberation of the conquered and suppressed French and Belgians.[85]

Reflection on the American Revolution also sparked a romanticized mutual regard between Americans and the French. In that olden conflict, the French had come to the aid of the Americans. Now, America was returning the favor. "Compared to the French, we do not know what sacrifice means," said someone in Ruby.[86]

Eleven months into the American effort, the French ambassador to the United States, Jean Jusserand, spoke of how the France of yore had gone into mourning upon learning of George Washington's death. Now, the diplomat continued, Washington's memory fortified both the French and the Americans in their common struggle against German autocracy. In their daily newspapers, Alaskans read that the French and American republics had always been of the same democratic spirit—the world's equal cradles of liberty. "France stands erect today unconquered and unconquerable. America stands beside her."[87]

Anchorageites celebrated Bastille Day (July 14) with a picnic at Lake Spenard.

## LETTER FROM FRANCE (IV)

*The following rather lengthy letter provides a wealth of information about the life of a young American nurse in France. It was written by Molly Smith of Valdez. Her sister, a Mrs. W. H. Caswell, lived in Cordova. In the summer of 1918, Molly had gone to France with the Red Cross. As her letter indicates, she worked long hours among French refugees and wounded soldiers, many of whom died in spite of her care. At times she was close to the battlefront. Her letter, dated September 3, first appeared in the* Valdez Miner *and was then reproduced in the* Cordova Daily Herald *on November 6, 1918, five days before the war ended.*

I wonder if you and the other Red Cross workers have any idea of the great need for the dressings which you all are so willingly giving your time to make. They are greatly needed and also greatly appreciated. Rarely are the dispensaries fortunate enough to get sterile dressing, as such dressings are greatly needed by the hospitals. This military hospital, [which is] French, has received Red Cross supplies from California; also adhesive plaster. There is no adhesive plaster in France, consequently all the French military hospitals have to depend upon the generosity of America for them.

The French military hospital here at Corbeil was formerly a girl's seminary.[88] It is a large, one-story building with a court in the center, and consequently most inconvenient. It is used mostly for convalescing patients.

I am again at Corbeil. Now I am training three French nurse's aids. These girls have had four months' training in a hospital under the auspices of the Red Cross. Now I have to train them to do visiting in the homes and dressings in the dispensary. One speaks English, another understands it, and they interpret it to the third one. It is much more difficult than training the pupils in the hospitals at home. I would much rather nurse soldiers and hope after I get these trained I [will be able to] go back to the front. Of course, everyone wants to go to the front; then when one gets in to the front line hospital, she is not satisfied until she gets into the dressing station or first aid station.[89] In fact, I do not think the American over here will ever be satisfied until they can march into Berlin.

The eagerness of the American soldier is beyond the comprehension of the allies. However, it is one of the traits which make them so much loved by the French. I heard that some of the Illinois soldiers were in the front line trenches and they kept bobbing up over the top so much without orders that they were retired into the back trenches.

In one of the recent boats all the nurses were gassed [by the Germans]. It was a slow-working gas, as they were not taken seriously ill until they reached Paris, then three were taken to hospitals and the remaining eight went to a hotel. These eight recovered in five or six days but the others were in a hospital for two weeks and one has not been able to go to work yet.

On July 21, I and some other nurses and aids went to the front to care for American soldiers. As you recall, a big attack was launched on July 18th and 19th, consequently a great need for extra nurses. We left Paris in the morning. We rode in a large French camion, which is an automobile truck with two boards running along the side. On the way, amidst clouds of dust, we lunched on bread and cheese, but we did not mind, as all were so happy to be going to the front.

About 2:30 p.m. we reached...a wrecked town. After finding the hospital we learned that the Americans had evacuated the night before. After receiving as definite instructions as possible, we started to find where the Americans had removed to. [The town] was being bombed every night, consequently was not safe, and the bombing is terrible on the nervous system of sick men. In about an hour we located the new American hospital of 3,000 beds. The hospital was in a field almost entirely surrounded by woods. Here we were greeted with shouts of joy, as all the workers were worn out. Having just gotten my cap on I walked up to the operating tent, where I was asked to assist, when one of the aids and myself were selected to go to a French hospital. A messenger had just come asking for four American nurses to take care of American soldiers in this French hospital. This time we rode in an ambulance of American make, one of those put out by Henry Ford. I understand the ambulance...costs the American government but $90.

About dusk we reached the French hospital called Ambulance 5–11. Madame Trancenf [*sic*] turned her large estate over to the military department at the beginning of the war. The chateau contained an operating room, dressing rooms, a kitchen, and five wards. Besides these were five tents, capacity in all about 250 beds.

We had all our patients in the chateau, or rather, they moved all of the American soldiers into one ward. Miss Margaret Lee, my aid, spoke French, but of course, was unfamiliar with the hospital terms, as she has just come over.... Then after many questions we were told that they did not expect any of these American patients to live, which, to say the least, was discouraging. Then after many questions, we learned the few orders which were necessary for our night's work. Four delirious men, all the rest terribly ill. Someone was always getting out of bed, or raving for water. The few who slept had nightmares, and talked incessantly about going over the top.

Patients with wounds in the stomach or intestines can have only a few drops of water, consequently you can imagine their thirst. Only about half of these patients live.

During the first night two of our men died; one married and one single. We felt very sorry but knew everything had been done which could be. Both of these men had been injured in the stomach.

Life was very strenuous for both of us for a few days, but as some of the soldiers were gaining it was possible for us to arrange to be off duty, each one taking a few hours off.

Later [another of] the soldiers died. He was injured in the spine but as he had lived several days we had hoped that he would recover. As soon as the soldiers were well enough they were evacuated to the next line of hospitals. Consequently our boys began leaving one by one. They go from the hospital in an ambulance to the train, which is a train for carrying the wounded.

Do not infer that the soldiers were well, as in peace time it is supposed that anyone with arms or legs off could not be moved; in war times it is different. From one hospital to the next the patients are evacuated until they reach the coast and then back to America.

As our American soldiers began to leave, the beds were filled with English, Scotch, Italians, and French. Our ward was called the Salle of Aliens. The French were very polite. They never were too sick to say "thank you," and were exceedingly grateful for our care.

One French soldier from our ward was moved down stairs. After being down there a short time he demanded that his physician have him moved back so that he could be taken care of by the Americans. His reason for this was that we gave all our men baths, and also that every man in our room has a washcloth, towel, and toothbrush.

For this they had to thank the Red Cross, for they sent us towels, soap, and washcloths. Not only the Americans were grateful, but all patients; and most of all, Miss Lee and myself. For until these supplies arrived, we had but one towel and one washcloth for the whole ward. We had plenty of sheets, night shirts, etc., but very few towels. However, no baths were ever given except what we gave. First, a front line hospital is a very busy place, and second, the French male nurses do not give baths, probably not thinking it necessary, as they do not love water.

Miss Lee and I were the only women in the hospital; also the village.... Also a few inhabitants of the village had moved back. It is wonderful how quickly the people move back to their homes.

The French surgeons are wonderful, not only skillful, but will take time to understand each patient, and speak so beautifully to them. Miss Lee said that anyone seeing these surgeons could not help but believe in a God for only a God could have made them. I think the same was true about the ward orders and everybody attached to the ambulance or hospital. For the help had been all formerly wounded but now able to work in a hospital, and how these nurses could be so kind to the patients day after day and month after month is nothing less than marvelous.

All the stretcher bearers were old men, and sometimes I was afraid that they would not be able to climb the stairs. If they had a few minutes to sit down, they were so weary they fell right to sleep.

None of these people had any diversion, for if they had an evening there was nowhere to go. They might walk through the woods, as this estate was very large and very beautiful. But walking is no pleasure when one is so physically weary.

I feel sure that the American surgeons, ward, orderlies, and ambulance drivers also deserve a great deal of credit. For all of these people must work night and day following a big attack.

We could hear the cannon night and day and were soon able to distinguish the difference between a German and an American barrage. Also airplanes visited us frequently. Occasionally they appeared in the daytime. Germans seem to enjoy hitting hospitals but we escaped the bombs.[90]

I forgot to mention that the only light allowed at night is a lantern. All shutters must be closed. If any airplanes appear even the lantern must be put out. The first few nights were rather uncanny, but later I became used to doing many things in the dark.

Only two meals were served, one at 11 a.m. and the other at 5 p.m. At 7 a.m. coffee and milk were served. The... two meals were good and those who could eat had enormous appetites. Nothing was served during the night for any of us who worked. I suppose it was customary but we would have gotten very hungry except for the chocolate we took with us. Chocolate is very scarce in France and very expensive.

We were at the hospital nearly five weeks and as our last American was evacuated, we had orders to return to Paris. The chief surgeon wished us to remain and the last night I assisted him in the operating room, and Miss Lee cleaned instruments. We were sorry to leave, for while the work was strenuous it was all so interesting.

Thirty ambulance drivers who had been loaned to the French army lived in a tomb about a mile from this hospital. After they heard American nurses had arrived they would drop in at the ward to see the sick men. After we were there about 10 days these ambulance drivers invited us over one evening. They were very eager to talk as they had not had the pleasure of visiting with an American woman for some time. One of the crowd mentioned that they were having such a good time that something would surely happen. And it did, as the next order came for them to go to another sector. We missed them as they would get newspapers, cigarettes [and other items] for the men when driving through a town where these could be obtained. They also helped to keep the ill men cheered up.

One day when Miss Lee was walking in the village she met two ambulance drivers, Americans, who had walked 8 kilometers, or 5 miles, to see us. She brought them up to the ward and as they seemed to have no intention of going home, I was able to give them dinner. As one of our French nurses offered to look after our patients for a couple hours, we went for a walk that evening. These men were so eager to talk that both talked at the same time. After leaving us, they had to walk 5 miles back to their camp. These two men came three times to see us, and the last time they brought us German caps and coat buttons. You can realize how these men miss American women when they are ready to walk 10 miles just to be able to see and speak a few words to one. Both of these men were about 21 years old but they looked much older.

One day I was looking out of the window and saw an American ambulance drive in. I spoke to the driver. He gazed all around and exclaimed, "My God, do I hear an American woman's voice?" I said, "Yes, I am coming down to talk to you for a few minutes." The man was so stunned that he could not speak for a few minutes. He stayed and chatted as long as he could and told us that it was the happiest day he had had in months. He has been over here 18 months and most of the time has been driving for the French, consequently never sees any American women.

I fear the American nurses near the front may become spoiled by the admiration bestowed upon them by the American soldiers. But hardly, for these little things are what make life endurable, for no one can [describe] the tragedy or strenuousness of a front line hospital. And I am sure, at least, most of the nurses would be glad to change places with the soldiers and have the opportunity of going over the top.

Today on my way to visit a family in Essones I stopped to see the American coffee roasting plant which belongs to the army and now supplies coffee to a half million men. They expect in time to be able to supply coffee to one million men. I did not have time to go through the plant. As far as I could learn it is in charge of a lieutenant and sergeant and the rest of the help are French.

We have many people in need of clothing. Everything is so very high and food is so dear that it takes all the wages a man makes to provide for the family table. Eggs are now $1.20 a dozen; butter $1.19 a pound; and meat even more expensive.

I cut a girl's hair today and then dressed her in American clothes, which we were able to get since she was a refugee. I bobbed her hair and she looked like an American child. She was very proud and is now envied by all her friends. I forgot to say that first I gave her a bath and it was the first time she was ever in a tub. I could not get her clean; it will take several washings to do that. The most cosmopolitan and wholly American restaurant is at the Y.M.C.A or Petrograd Hotel. Luncheon is 80 cents and dinner $1.00. When there you can see privates, officers, Y.M.C.A workers, canteen workers, physicians, nurses, etc. It is a very popular restaurant. The hotel is very large. However, I have no idea how many guests it can accommodate.

Today is Tuesday and it has been a hard day. This afternoon we took care of nearly 100 at the clinic.

This has passed so rapidly, I can hardly realize that four months have passed since I left home. Everyone here hopes that the war may end soon as the greatest majority miss America very much.

Yours sincerely,<br>
Mollie B. Smith

CHAPTER FIVE

# Organizing

In early April 1918, Governor John Strong wrote to Thomas Riggs congratulating him on his appointment to Alaska's governorship.[1] Strong had recently described himself as "very, very tired and worn out."[2] This had something to do with scandal. The Canadian-born Strong was not a U.S. citizen, had no right to serve as a U.S. territorial governor, and accordingly had been dismissed by President Wilson. But his fatigue was also tied to the relentless demands on his energies. In a short period of time, the governor helped the Anchorage Rifle Company secure five dollars in goods from an arsenal in California; requested arms and ammunition from the secretary of war for the Anchorage Home Guards; and assured Fairbanks's mayor, Henry Ray, that in due course the city's contribution to the Rocky Mountain Club–Hoover Fund for Relief in Belgium would be formally acknowledged. He advised an official in Sitka that, while an Orthodox church did not have an absolute right to fly a Russian flag, he would have no objections to such a display so long as an American flag was posted above it. He responded to a letter from Selma Katzenstein of the Dallas Conservatory, saying that he would promote her patriotic song "All Hail America" (though there is no evidence that he did so). He sent a letter to the founder of the Anti-Saloon League, Howard H. Russell, describing himself as "a total abstainer [from alcohol] for a considerable number of years"; he responded to the query of a U.S. marshal at Valdez saying that he knew of no institution "that takes care of imbecile children"; and he published notices that the relatives of a Swede named Albert Johnson, from whom they had not heard in eleven years, wanted to know what had become of him. Meanwhile, Cedric Davis, who wanted to serve in the navy, Robert de Journal, who wanted to join the army's intelligence corps, and Burnett Ashley, who was aiming for an officer's commission in the army, asked the governor to write letters of recommendation.[3] He met these requests, and many others. One petition Strong could not meet came from the editor of the *Farm Journal*, based in Philadelphia, asking the governor to officially proclaim a Bird Day. The "subject of the protection of birds," Strong responded, "has as yet received but little attention in Alaska."[4]

Indeed, the opposite would be true. With the thought of stopping birds from eating the eggs of fish that would otherwise grow to be captured and eaten by Americans and their battle allies, the governor's office briefly considered seeking permission from Washington, D.C., to kill the legally protected creatures. "The sea fowls and many sea animals are not only useless to humanity," an unsigned memo declared, but they were "weeds," "miscreants," and "voracious swarms" (as great a menace to humanity as German U-boats) that needed to be wiped out in the interests of humanity.[5] Fortunately for Alaska's ecology, no plan of extermination went into effect.

The governor was also confronted with the fact that the war presented a multitude of possible economic advantages. Entrepreneurs wrote to Alaska's nonexistent "adjutant general" offering a booklet titled "Memoranda Court-Martial Procedure," acetylene hand lamps "suitable for camp purposes," and field saddles.[6] Edgar Banks from New York asked the Alaska Historical Museum if it would like to buy "genuine ancient Babylonia tablets . . . dating from 2400 to 500 BC," his claim being that he would then use the money to buy war stamps.[7] William Pallister, a doctor in Juneau, sought unsuccessfully to work for the Russian government with the aim of establishing an American Eye and Ear Hospital in Petrograd.[8] Given the high number of schemes—some noble, some less so—devised to capitalize on the war's circumstances, Governor Strong felt compelled to note in a letter of recommendation that James Hogan, a man offering his services to the government, was "not actuated by any other motive than a desire to serve his country."[9]

More than any other concern, military registration consumed the governor's managerial capacities. In all, almost sixteen thousand men in Alaska registered for military service. The labor involved in organizing the paperwork associated with that number taxed nerves and spurred bureaucracy. Strong distributed memoranda to doctors informing them of "regulations, systematic methods, disqualifications, and physical examinations," which should be "conducted by experts in the most exhaustive manner possible."[10] Incompetent officials were few, but these added to difficulties. Strong wrote to Ernest Blue, director of the draft board in Ketchikan, relieving him of his responsibilities, for he had "failed lamentably in becoming familiar with [government] regulations."[11]

Alaska's vastness, some settlers' remoteness, and slow mail services made keeping accurate military registration lists very difficult.[12] In some cases, unreliable mail delivery gave cover to men who wanted to shirk army service while also making the lives of the well intended more complicated. One man claimed to have requested a registration questionnaire three times and he never received one.[13] Another swore in writing that he had registered but was nevertheless arrested and jailed.[14] Others, like Soichi Hayakawa, left the United States altogether. Authorities were left to uncover such facts for themselves.[15]

Transient workers, more interested in earning a living than in waiting for official notices, traversed the territory. A report from Juneau observed that registrants were "scattered all over Alaska, in canneries, and almost impossible to reach at short notice."[16] Arthur Shea left Nenana for work in Whitehorse, Canada, and, as a report concluded, it was well known that communication between the two towns was effectively closed for half the year. "It is apparent," the official wrote, that Shea's failure to send in his paperwork was "not a case of willful delinquency."[17] On the other hand, William Falk, who registered at Skagway, appeared to use labor at sea as a cover for evading the draft. His case was turned over to a special investigator.[18] Other men, unable to read English, needed interpreters to guide them through the registration process. It was not always easy to peer into motivations and, in the absence of significant evidence to the contrary, delinquents usually received the benefit of the doubt.

A few men preempted the army's process by signing up with the navy or by joining the military of an allied nation. A few Alaskans, eager to get into the fight, crossed the international border and comprised a small part of the thirty-five thousand Americans who served with Canadian forces. Among them were H. L. Faulkner of Juneau, John McEwan and Walker George of Nenana, and Richard Green of Cordova.[19] After the United States had entered the war, Leander James, an attorney from Seward, tried to enlist with American forces but was rejected on account of a football injury. To no avail, he appealed to Governor Riggs for help.[20] Then he turned to the Canadians who, having already been at war for three years and needing men, received him.

So much transience within the territory had practical consequences. The *Alaska Railroad Record* reported in the summer of 1918 that where military registration questionnaires had been sent to 1,740 men living in the Anchorage region, 350 of them (or twenty percent) were not returned.[21] Later, when Anchorage's quota of 184 draftees was called to muster, forty of them did not show up. (Anchorage's quota was the largest of Alaska's towns. By comparison, Juneau's requirement was eighty-five, Fairbanks's forty-seven, Cordova's forty-four, and Nenana's twenty-two.)[22]

It was grueling work, sorting out where men were and where they stood in relation to the military. Over two thousand names came to be entered into Alaska's enlistment files for delinquents and deserters. At one time, close to five hundred names appeared on Anchorage's list alone. Inquiring government agents in San Francisco needed to be told that Louis Martinez had registered at Nushagak, Alaska, and messages from Juneau informed authorities in Portland that Hisao Yazawa had registered in Alaska. Governor Strong's office wrote to the president of the University of Washington to ensure that student C. Denham Greer registered, since he had not done so at home in Alaska.[23] Meantime, unusual surnames appeared differently on different forms, such as when Wekan became Vekan.[24]

Then there were questions about who was and was not eligible to serve. William Martin had a short right leg and a paralyzed right arm, and so would not put on a uniform. Rangwald Overaa, owner of a "rapid irregular heart," was ineligible.[25] Nenana's Alek Kalissoff did not have to serve "by reason of fast operative hernia" that followed, so says the report, an "offendectormy [*sic*]."[26] Charles Thomas was "morally unfit" for military service.[27] Henry Schafer was excused on account of schizophrenia.[28]

Others gained exemptions for economic reasons. Some miners and fishermen, doing work deemed essential to Alaska's economy and the overall war effort, kept their civilian employment. The Alaska Pacific Herring Company pled to keep Magnus Halvorsen on the job, "as he is the only one who understands Norwegian method of smoking herring."[29] Not all such requests could be approved. The Quandra Cannery petitioned to keep five workers. Governor Strong's office responded that at least four of these could be replaced by Natives or men exempt from military service.[30]

In the late summer of 1918, the registration board in Anchorage received a list of nearly forty names, including Christ Treatafelopealos, whose once-reported delinquency needed to be corrected. This single list represented myriad hours of investigation and telegram writing devoted to finding out where men were and what they were doing. Nine additional names were listed as *perhaps* liable to being excused from the delinquent list. Whether they would be excused was left to the local board's discretion, which, of course, meant more investigation and paperwork.[31]

Inevitably, some paper went missing. Grachino Del Piero was counted as delinquent until his misplaced document was found mixed with another file. An official admitted, "[I]t was simply by accident that we ran across it."[32]

## Dogs

The first Alaska battle contingent to form did so two years before the United States declared war. French officers had gone to Nome to recruit the famous dog driver Scotty Allan, who would gather four hundred sled dogs for transportation work in the Vosges Mountains of France. Of these, 106 were rounded up in the Nome area, along with sleds, harnesses, and two tons of dried salmon. "I knew all the Eskimos," Allan recalled, "and they liked to talk dog." The rest of the canines he acquired in Quebec, from where they and he left for France. He had promised his wife not to see the animals all the way to Europe, but only to "keep peace in the family." [33] At eastern Canada's safe distance, he scrapped his promise and made the trip.

Allan and his French handlers wanted to keep the mission secret, but this would be hard to do in Nome, where the "entire population…applauded" as dogs and men boarded the S.S. *Senator.*[34] News spread through Alaska and then to newspapers Outside. Minnesota's *Duluth News-Tribune* and Mississippi's *Daily Herald*, among many others, reported on the Alaska dogs and their road to war.[35] "These animals are the chief means of freight transportation by the icy regions of Alaska, where camps are many miles distant," one report noted, suggesting that the dogs were ready for what was to come.[36] By 1917, the story found its way into a children's book that mixed the romance of Nome's sled dogs with the dash and pluck of battle. The four-legged "immortals of the trail" could now be called the "War Dogs of the North."[37]

Allan stayed for a while in France and helped to ensure the dogs' success in their work of transporting war materiel "up the steep, snow-covered side of the Vosges Mountains."[38] By the end of 1916, he was back in Alaska and again in the news, this time for having sledded from Nome to Valdez in a record-setting ten days.[39] The dogs that survived the war remained in Europe.

## Canada

Canadians and Alaskans had long mingled. Sometimes this led to disputes. Early in the century, a Canadian agent in Skagway had hoisted his country's customs revenue flag—not easily distinguished from the Union Jack—over the office building of the White Pass and Yukon Railway in 1901. An offended Yankee tore the emblem down to the acclaim of locals. This incident briefly gained the attention of the U.S. secretary of state, and Alaska's governor, John Brady, wrote that it was indicative of the high anti-Canadian feeling that existed in Skagway. In the background lay a simmering border dispute between Canada and the United States that was decided in the Americans' favor with British concurrence.

Also in the background was the persistent sense among Canadians, and perhaps especially British Columbians, that the United States was set on annexing Canada, in whole or part. Arguments in favor of the Alaska Purchase had noted that the territory's acquisition would mean caging "the British lion on the Pacific Coast" and the quick "consolidation of the North Pacific Coast line as an American possession."[40] Such occasions show that the close relationship between Britain and the United States that took shape later in the twentieth century did not exist in 1914. As recently as 1895, there had been talk of war between the two nations, the result of a border dispute between Venezuela and Britain's colony of Guiana.

The First World War pulled the countries together. Once the United States entered the conflict, American and Canadian pennants flew together on both sides of the border. Alaskans crossed into Whitehorse in the Yukon to celebrate Empire Day; Canadians crossed into Alaska to observe the Fourth of July. "This is the new spirit, born of relations now existing between the United States and Great Britain." Before the war, relations between the North Americans had been simply civil; now Canadians and Yankees met as "family."[41]

Most American forces would not arrive in Europe until 1918. In the meantime, Americans seeking information about the conflict learned from Canadians in the war zone. H.B. Eastman of Atlin, British Columbia, wrote of snipers and trench warfare's ebb and flow. "One day you chase Fritz [the Germans]," he wrote, the "next day he comes back at you." Eastman said he looked forward to the Americans' arrival in France and to their joining him on his hoped-for march to Berlin.[42] Another Canadian passing through Skagway shared war stories and explained his early return from war in terms of the thirty-four shrapnel wounds he claimed to have sustained in France. Canadian letters printed in Alaska newspapers offered thanks for socks, tobacco, and other items sent to them from Americans.

Before the war, it had never been much in the American mind to look to Canada for models. This changed during the brief period between the U.S. war declaration and the arrival of American forces overseas. Now Canadians were seen as having shown the way in service and sacrifice. There was Mrs. L.G. Bennett of

Dawson, who had sold her home and gone to Britain as a nurse. There was E. G. Lester, formerly a fire department chief in the Yukon, who lost his life in battle: a reminder to rookie Alaskans that war is real. But the Canadian experience also showed Alaska mothers that most of them could expect their sons to come home alive. A report published in Skagway's *Daily Alaskan* claimed that of the thirty-three thousand Canadians who had gone to Europe in the war's first year, about thirty thousand remained alive three years later. (In the end, about sixty-seven thousand Canadians would die in the war. The United States would lose about 117,000.)

## Joining

Canadians had gone to war, and some Alaskans had gone with them. Now, it was time for the rest of Alaska's men to face the possibility of battle. An army officer from Fort Gibbon had written that the men from Canada's Yukon Territory had "made a splendid showing in Europe" and that, if called on to do so, Alaskans would do the same.[43] From Whitehorse, an American miner wrote in early April 1917 that the Americans in the Yukon were eager for a "stampede" against Germany and were ready to be made into "cogs in an Alaskan fighting machine."[44] Now the time had come. At the end of June 1917, President Wilson declared that between July 2 and September 2 all men between the ages of twenty-one and thirty were required to register for the draft. Alaska's minimum draft quota on this occasion was 696. In the event, the military inducted more than twenty-two hundred Alaska men during this first of three registration drives. About fifteen hundred more men left Alaska to enlist Outside.

Enthusiasm for military service varied. Within a few weeks of war's declaration, Raymond Johnson of Juneau went to the Naval Academy, and brothers R. J. and Fred Sheppard of Haines left for army officer training. Daniel B. Pullen of Skagway was Alaska's first West Point cadet. J. W. Pigg of Wrangell quit his physician's practice to enter military service. W. H. Grigg, a Spanish War veteran, traded his position as mayor of Nenana for a return to the military. Colonel Frederick Mears left his leading position with the Alaska Engineering Company to serve in France with the Thirty-first Railway Engineers. Lieutenant Colonel M. A. Saville, commander at Fort William Seward in Haines, received some three hundred applications for twenty officer training slots. Sixty-one-year-old Harry Lott's offer of army service was gratefully declined, so he turned his energies to a three-acre liberty garden.

*Seward Gateway*, March 26, 1917

Motivations differed. Some Alaskans were attracted to the supposed romance of battle; others joined for lack of something more interesting to do. Some were motivated by a sense of patriotism; others faced their duty with grim determination. Gene Zoraeff, an immigrant from Russia, had lost several family members in the war against Germany. He went to war to exact revenge. In Anchorage, a Serbian flag flew in honor of fifteen Serbs and Russians who left the city for the war. "My prayer and prediction," their spokesman said, "is that the flag raised by you in Anchorage . . . will never be lowered or surrendered but will rise to the eminent height where it will lead a free and united people."[45] Early in 1918 Governor Strong received a letter from the Serbian National Defense Committee assuring

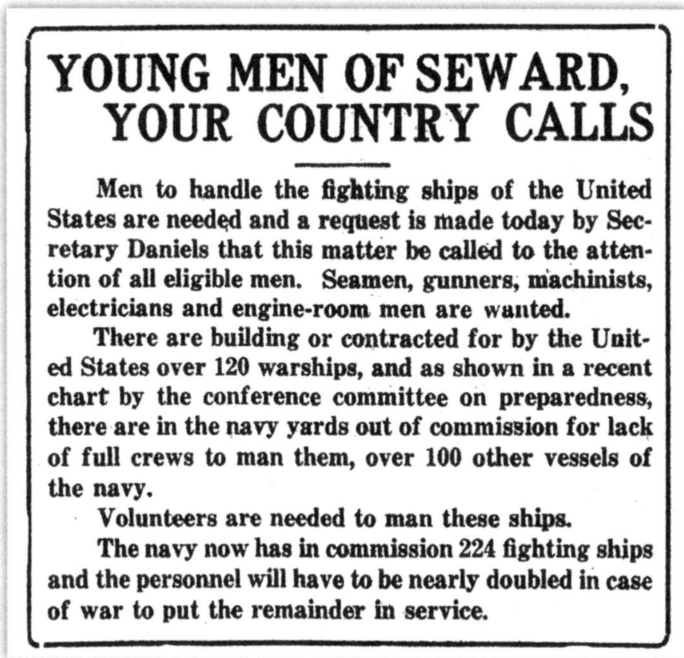

# YOUNG MEN OF SEWARD, YOUR COUNTRY CALLS

**Men to handle the fighting ships of the United States are needed and a request is made today by Secretary Daniels that this matter be called to the attention of all eligible men. Seamen, gunners, machinists, electricians and engine-room men are wanted.**

**There are building or contracted for by the United States over 120 warships, and as shown in a recent chart by the conference committee on preparedness, there are in the navy yards out of commission for lack of full crews to man them, over 100 other vessels of the navy.**

**Volunteers are needed to man these ships.**

**The navy now has in commission 224 fighting ships and the personnel will have to be nearly doubled in case of war to put the remainder in service.**

*Seward Gateway*, March 24, 1917

him of "our loyalty to this, our adopted country, and we pledge our utmost in support of the prosecution of this war."[46]

Every soldier who left home, family, and friends for military service had a personal story. In his usually reserved and terse diary that focused primarily on political struggles, James Wickersham added an unusual passage about an unnamed "matronly lady about 50 (or more years of age)." Living in Anvik, the woman was eager to have a letter she had written taken to her husband, who had been drafted and was stationed at Fort Gibbon. "I knew that only men from 20 to 30 years were drafted," Wickersham wrote, "and thinking she had made a mistake I corrected her by a question—saying that her husband could not be among the drafted." But the woman's husband was only twenty-one.

> She was the matron in charge of the Episcopal Mission schools and had married a boy [who had studied] to begin Christian work among the heathen! I could just imagine her disappointment to have him drafted! She is certainly not less than 50—but rotund, full breasted—with possibly strong old age passion for a youthful lover! Too bad to lose him![47]

As for Native participation in formal military work, there was complication and confusion throughout the war period. Early on, the army registration of Alaskans of "mixed Indian blood" was allowed. Then, for reasons that are not clear, in early 1918 this registration was suspended. Governor Strong wrote to one such Alaskan, telling him that his registration card, "in which you are described... as being part Indian," had been annulled.[48] In Haines, a draft agent who did not know which Natives to count as citizens learned that citizen status went to "a half-breed who is leading a civilized life separate from and apart from Indian tribes."[49] The registration chairman in Petersburg was told to fill out the correct paperwork for "half-breeds."[50] But then word came down that "no person having Indian, Aleut or Eskimo blood in his veins is to be registered."[51] So what about "half breeds who have Indian blood in them but who live in a white community and exercise the rights of citizens, and who do not live as Indians"?[52]

Adding to the lack of clarity, Alaska Natives residing Outside *were* subject to service. Governor Strong wrote that a certain Paul Albert Kinninook needed to register in Oregon since the rules in place in Alaska did not apply Outside. Thus, Alaska Natives living at the Salem Indian School in Oregon were registered, among them Charles Milne of Metlakatla, Nick Hatch of Unalaska, and Paul Moody of Ketchikan.[53] "I think an erroneous impression exists with reference to the status of the Alaskan Indian," the governor wrote. "He is not absolutely exempt from registration, but the requirement for his registration was suspended during the registration period."[54] This was a clarification that did not clarify.

In Alaska's vastness, where information traveled slowly and imperfectly, government distinctions did not much help. In the fall, an official on St. George Island learned that while Aleuts were subject to military registration, the impending winter made it impossible to get the proper paperwork to him.[55]

Noting that Natives would be included in the military registration drive that began in October 1918, Native school superintendent Charles Hawkesworth wrote that military service would "put the native where he belongs—beside the rest of us, in the world-wide cause of democracy." Alaska's Natives, the *Wrangell Sentinel* said, were "buying spades to dig the graves of the Huns."[56] Some Natives did put on the military uniform, among them Newton Kaska and Louis Paul, who, with his brother William, would later found the Alaska Native Brotherhood.

In early 1918, the *Anchorage Weekly Times* spoke of the "most loyal and intense patriotism in helping the government" that had been demonstrated by Natives from the far Southeast to Barrow. The "American patriot is of no particular

# FIRST ALASKAN TO VOLUNTEER IS FROM KODIAK

## Peter Dobrovolsky, Former Carlisle Man, Seeks Place in the Navy

Peter Dobrovolsky, native Alaskan, was the first to present himself at the office of the Gateway today as a volunteer in answer to Secretary Daniels' call for recruits for the United States navy.

Dobrovolsky was born at Kodiak and is 28 years of age. He is a Carlisle man, having studied at that university five years.

Others have indicated that they may offer their services but are await ing word from Washington as to how volunteers from this part of Alaska are to be received. At present it is necessary to go to Seattle for examination and it is possible that a recruiting office may be established in the territory.

In the meantime the names of those who volunteer will be reecived at the Gateway office and forwarded to the proper officer.

*Seward Gateway*, March 27, 1917

race or color," the paper said, and it called for a "splendid organization of fighting men" to be recruited from among willing Natives.

Where Native volunteers were praised, a special contempt was reserved for immigrants who had planned to become citizens but now renounced that intention to avoid the war. Locals in Ruby and Long denounced Fred Neilson, Theodore Svindlund, Olgat Anderson, and Albert Bylund as blots on the community. Ruby's Loyal League resolved to "use its best efforts to lawfully force . . . Neilson and Svindlund from the community and cause them to lose all rights to exploit the natural resources of the public domain."[57] It is not clear if this sentiment led to concrete action.

As the Alaskans selected for military service gathered for transport to the States, communities bid them goodbye. To Fairbanks's *Alaska Citizen* this send-off seemed to lack the "romantic glamour of the days of our forefathers." The paper surmised that perhaps war had become "strictly a matter of business."[58] But this was not the general perception. Alaskans spoke of soldiers in reverent tones and praised them as the best men Alaska had to offer. At a reception for the men at the Loyal League Armory in Fairbanks, the Reverend H. H. Lumpkin "made a stirring address" in the inductees' honor that "kept his listeners applauding continually."[59] In Cordova, soon-to-be soldiers received a going-away party with "plenty of smokes," nonalcoholic beer, and a boxing match between sailors from the U.S.S. *Saturn*.[60] The town's *Daily Herald* sent encouragement to Fred Brotherson, Carl Edmund, Carlos Spinoza, and twenty others. "You are offering your all, your life if necessary, and the people of Cordova who know you so well, love you for your sacrifice."[61] Fairbanks's *Citizen* said that the departing men were leaving a gap in the community's life that would not be filled until they returned.

> But we are proud of them—every one of them. They are a credit to Fairbanks and we have no fears for their future. We know that wherever they go they will be a credit to Fairbanks and Alaska and in that knowledge we pledge ourselves to give them the support they deserve.[62]

Some Alaskans held romantic ideas about battle. A few old-timers remembered the Civil War's carnage. Well-informed residents knew that modern weaponry was deadlier than ever. Watching their men leave town for the war's sake,

Fairbanks inductees, 1918. University of Alaska Fairbanks, UAF-1989-166-195-Print

Parade for Anchorage's recruits. Anchorage Museum, AMRC0b77-5-5

Soldiers march in Nome. University of Alaska Fairbanks, UAF-1980-68-257

they prepared themselves for the "unspeakable horrors which we must of necessity be party to."[63] It was not surprising if there was a spirit of seriousness among the new troops. A few years before, they had been "happy and carefree" in the Alaska "land of gold." Now, they seemed "grim and determined."[64]

On their way to the war, men from different parts of Alaska stopped first at Fort Liscum (Valdez), Fort William H. Seward (Haines), Fort Davis (Nome), and the fort at St. Michael. En route to Nome on the *Victoria*, James Wickersham met soldiers heading to Fort Davis. Another time, passing down the Yukon River from Nulato to Ruby on the mail boat *Jefferson C. Davis*, Wickersham found himself among "250 draftees—bound for Outside and the war."[65]

## Letters

Before long, letters began arriving from friends and family members in the army. Wickersham first received a letter from France in January 1918. Alfred H. Brooks, who had served as the chief geologist for the Alaska Geological Survey, sent him a French book about the territory—probably *Mon séjour en Alaska*—and described himself as "hungry for word from Alaska."[66]

# NENANAITE TELLS OF ARMY LIFE NEAR THE FRONT

**Late Employee of the A. E. C. Is Helping to Build Roads In France Now.**

Lyman Longfellow, who was for some time instrumentman in the employ of the Alaskan Engineering commission, is now a sergeant in the 318th Regiment of Engineers in France.

His regiment arrived 'Over There' last May, and are now preparing to go to the front, where the actual fighting take place, soon. Lyman has been permitted to mention in his letter to a friend in Nenana, the name of the town in which his regiment is stationed temporarily, which he says is called Gievres, and is somewhere near Paris.

They are engaged at present in construction work on the railroads of France, and Lyman is doing transitman's work, but ever so much more of it than he was ever called upon to do here.

He speaks of having visited a nearby town, provided with a pass from his commanding officer, where he had a pretty good time. France, he says, is not a dry country by a long way.

From all accounts the former Nenanaite is getting along well and says he likes his work and that he expects soon to be given an opportunity to take part in actual battle.

*Nenana Daily News*, August 28, 1918

From the time the men came under military supervision, their letters were censored. The notes they sent home were usually upbeat and spoke in generalities. Soldiers from Fairbanks wrote to thank the YMCA for sending them games, books, stationery, and other items that lessened the possibility of soldiers falling for "amusements of a less elevating character."[67] Nenana's J. H. Flower penned a letter from Camp Fremont in California saying that he was "tickled to death to be in the army"; he called his comrades a "big bunch of school boys."[68] C. F. Ingersoll, also from Nenana, sent a note from Fort Lawton in Seattle to say that he was looking forward to getting to Europe to "take a crack at the Hun."[69]

Missives from or near the field of battle were less cheerful, though they betrayed little of the hardship of war. The Alaskans' relatively brief participation in the war helped to ensure that they, like Americans generally, experienced less trauma than the Germans, British, French, Canadians, and others who had joined the war many months before. Whatever mental turmoil they did experience was kept from the mail partly by censorship and partly by the requirements of a culture that did not honor male expressions of anguish.

Ralph Keys from Fairbanks sent news of meeting other Alaskans in France. Ralph's brother, George, wrote that the Yankees were on the job and that the Germans were "catching H—l right now, and I hope it keeps up," adding that the Americans and their allies "will soon have the Kaiser where they want him."[70] H. B. Eastman wrote from "somewhere in France" about the sense of brotherhood life in a war zone created.[71] Former Alaska Engineering Commission accountant H. M. Rydholm, a sergeant in Company D of the Thirty-first Engineers' Regiment, wrote down his expectation that the "Alaska boys" would try "hardest of all to set the pace" in France.[72] Frederick Mears sent a letter from his camp near Saumur, France, to say that, with all the "Anchorage boys" around, the rear echelons of the war zone seemed like home. Sigurd Gilbertson mailed a German helmet to Andrew Christensen of the AEC, either as a present or for safekeeping. T. J. Case, from Wrangell, sent home a "souvenir" in the form of a German psychological warfare pamphlet, written in American English and calling into question President Wilson's "'high falutin' words about 'liberty,' 'humanity,' and 'making the world safe for democracy.'" Why, the pamphlet asked, put one's life at risk for such foggy themes? The American soldier "might as well [surrender and] be a free boarder in Germany till the war is over."[73] Case found the German message more amusing than tempting.

Reading reports about what would come to be called the Second Battle of the Somme, a two-week bloodbath that led to 416,000 casualties on all sides, James Wickersham wrote of his concern that things were not going well. "Disaster may result to the Allies," he noted, adding two days later that there was a "big battle raging in France with the advantage somewhat against us."[74] His brother, Frank, was in France with army engineers, but whether or not he was in the battle zone, Wickersham did not know. He was reminded of war's harm when a veteran who had lost an arm in France offered a "patriotic speech" at a Kiwanis Club meeting.[75]

Near the end of the war John Strong, formerly of the AEC (not the former governor), wrote home about surrendering "German soldiers coming in by the trainload." The "boys on the front lines were 'mopping up' the Germans," he continued. "The American has proved himself the greatest soldier in the world. They go to the front yelling and singing and they don't stop when they collide with the German line. I certainly am proud to be an American."[76]

Censored news did not allow for detailed, current reports from the war front, but the outlines of the general story got through. By the fall of 1918, headlines suggested steady progress:

Patrols Are Very Active on the Western Front,
With the Americans Taking a Big Part

Yanks Make Fierce Attack on the Boches

Americans Again Push Back Germans and Clean Up Some Strategic
Points—German Raiders Are Repulsed

Yankees Shell Metz and the Nearby Forts

In Hour of Desperation the Hun Press Grows Hysterical

Contempt for the enemy survived the censors. Lieutenant-commander L. F. French sent a letter to Juneau's *Empire* rehearsing accounts of German atrocities. "The Hun is an unspeakable beast," he wrote. The "best thing would be to have every one of them wiped out."[77]

## Africans and African Americans

Much has been made of what American boys saw "over there" during the First World War. As a popular song of the day asked, how could returned American soldiers be content to live on a quiet farm again after they had visited Paris? A memo to Governor Strong about the "country-wide movement to combat venereal disease" suggested that the sudden uprooting of young men by the tens of thousands had stirred challenges to given morals.[78]

Certainly Alaskans saw the difference of civilian life in France. A soldier from Douglas said that French village people were very pleasant, though he was struck by the villagers' wooden shoes and surprised to find the French "so husky." He could not help but notice that some of them lived under the same roof with their livestock.[79] But Alaskans' outlooks were probably less altered by the experience overseas than were other small-town Americans'.

In the first chapter, we saw that Alaska's public culture, hosting a multitude of accents and national backgrounds, was generally easygoing and pluralistic. Alaska's human diversity was illustrated by the fact that just forty-four percent of draft registrants in the fall of 1918 were native-born U.S. citizens. The territory's military registration lists illustrate this ethnic mix. From Skagway there was a Reynoldson, Rogers, and Rapuzzi; from Fairbanks an Otsuba, Rose, Bucci, Hall, Rozenstain, and Sabanoff; from Ruby a Mead and a Chung, along with Sam Moe and Bozo Luko Vukovich. Registrants from Anchorage accounted for all English vowels: Agbaba, Elliott, Ifantis, Olson, Urnnmoff, and Yip.

Given the cultural variety Alaskans were familiar with, French difference would not strike them as great. More noticeable were African American and French colonial troops from Tunisia, Algeria, Madagascar, and Senegal. Given legal segregation in the American South and parts of the Midwest and the de facto segregation that existed in most of the rest of the country, Americans were surprised by the 163,000 African colonial troops that fought for France in Europe. One American soldier wrote from France about how "strange" it was "to see how the colored troops are received over in France. There seems to be absolutely no race question, such as exists in America."[80] Newspapers in the United States reported on the "dashing" and "heroic" exploits of the colonial forces, such as when they captured an important point near the French village of Craonne. Along with Canadians, France's colonials were among the first to suffer as a result of German poison gas attacks.

**Drafted From Wrangell**

COLLIS EVERETT GREEN
LOUIS ARTHUR SCRIBNER
ANDREW BERGER JOHNSON
JOSEPH ARTHUR REINHART
EINO JUSSILA
BERNHARDT ALBERT DUBKE
CHARLES BRYAN MOORE
CHARLES ERNEST DEINING
OLIVER NICHOLS
ARTHUR OLIVER MOA
[Mr. Moa will entrain at Ketchikan]

CHARLES E. WHEATON
[Mr. Wheaton is a Ketchikan registrant who will entrain at Wrangell.]

*Wrangell Sentinel*, May 16, 1918

LIST OF THOSE DRAFTED

FOR SERVICE JUNE 13th.

From McCarthy and Kennecott

| | |
|---|---|
| Eric Intze, | Kennecott. |
| Demet S. Glasos, | Bonanza. |
| Tom Olson, | Cordova. |
| W. B. Noel, | Cordova. |
| M. A. Range, | McCarthy. |
| OlausFrederickson, | Cordova. |
| John Erickson, | Mile 158. |
| Ed. O'Neill, | Latouche, |
| Steven Duffy, | Cordova. |
| John Wald, | Kennecott. |
| Henry Boyden, | McCarthy. |
| Driss Soskief, | Bonanza. |
| Roy Snyder, | McCarthy, |
| V. Popoff, | Cordova. |
| N. Rasovich, | Valdez |
| Herman Maki, | Kennecott. |
| Yovan Rasovich, | Ellamar. |
| Rich. Gustafsen, | Cordova. |
| Arvit Hill. | Cordova. |
| Donald. C. Gilbert, | |
| H. Allison | |
| O. W. Nyberg | |
| F. V. Olman | |
| J. J. Candow | |
| Jas. Hay | |
| Rad Layovich | |
| Joseph C. Morgan. | |

*McCarthy Weekly News*, June 1, 1918

Americans fought alongside France's colonial forces at Chateau-Thierry, and Africans made an important contribution to the defense of Rheims. The sight of Africans in Europe fighting alongside French, Canadians, Britons, and Americans drove home the global reality of a war fought between empires. As a South Dakota newspaper put it, the "fact that the European conflict is indeed a world war is emphasized by the spectacle of negroes from the French African possessions fighting with the allied armies against Germany."[81]

Inevitably, the experience of France's colonial troops figured into American thinking about African American soldiers. Americans learned that France's colonial troops had given a good account of themselves in battle in the early stages of the war. This called to mind the American experience in the Civil War and the Spanish-American War, in which black troops fought well. "The African colored citizen as a soldier can fight well when well led."[82] Some saw that France's use of colonial troops on European soil and its bestowal of military decorations on black American soldiers made that country a counterexample to Germany, a "hotbed

French African colonial soldiers. Stroud Collection

of racial prejudice."[83] Indeed, just after the United States entered the war, some black leaders exhorted African Americans to embrace the war cause, for good service in the war would "secure recognition to the negro race in the councils of the nations." One speechmaker said in May 1915, "there are... African troops on the battlefields of Europe, battling for civilization and democracy, who have won immortal fame in the military annals of this great war by their intrepid valor and courage."[84]

The work of soldiers of African heritage was not an Alaska preoccupation, for few went to the war from the territory. In 1918, "negroes" comprised a tiny fraction of Alaska's military registrants. The Nenana authorities counted two in their district. In the fall of 1918, Alaska was required to provide 574 whites for military service and just five "negroes."[85] An official report of early September listed 844 "whites" and five "colored" men as physically fit for army life. As for territory-wide draft delinquents, ten were "colored" as opposed to 827 "whites."[86]

Among the African Americans living in Alaska who did serve were Abe Wimpe and Charles Beasley, both from Ketchikan.[87] We know Beasley went to New Mexico to be inducted into a "colored regiment." Writing to friends in Alaska, he reported that he was lonely and would like some books, cigarettes, and candy sent to him.[88] In 1921 he expressed admiration for the black nationalist Marcus Garvey, writing that Garvey had done "more than any Negro of [the] day to put a lime light on the colored race." But Beasley apparently felt at ease in Ketchikan, for he returned there after the war.[89]

Most likely, no one in Anchorage was scandalized by news of American Red Cross nurses tending to wounded forces from Senegal at the hospital in Neuilly where Alaskans sponsored beds for American casualties. As for Americans of African descent, an Anchorage newspaper article titled "Colored Boys, Members of Pershing's Army, Are Heroes in Most Daring Feat of War" might have made for more difficult reading in other regions of the United States.[90]

## Women

Alaskans writing home admired the work of American women overseas, primarily as volunteers and nurses with the YMCA and Red Cross. Since few single women lived in Alaska, only a small number went overseas. Among those who went was Mary Patton, a nurse in the territory since 1906.[91]

The efforts of Alaska's women added to a monumental national effort. Nurses served in field hospitals close to the front, on hospital ships, and in established medical facilities. American women also served as clerks, ambulance drivers, cooks, and telephone operators, or "Hello Girls." In the course of its membership drive during the 1917 Christmas season, some twenty-two million Americans signed up to assist the Red Cross in its work. A few months later, the army called for five thousand new Red Cross nurses to be added to the seven thousand already serving. "A great responsibility rests upon the nurses of the country," an official said.

> They are the only group of women recognized as part of the military establishment. While thousands of nurses will be needed, the number is relatively small compared with the number of women in America who should stand back of them and make possible the service for which they are so greatly needed at this time.[92]

The *Wrangell Sentinel* spoke of Red Cross work in grim, if admiring, terms. No organization's work was nobler, the journal said. The Red Cross went forth

> into the blood splashed arena of carnage, picking up from among the dead the living fragments of a shattered humanity—doing everything that human agencies could do to relieve poor unfortunate creatures writhing in the agonies of death by an unholy and cruel fate.[93]

In terms of body count, the bloodletting of the First World War was unprecedented. Nurses and other Red Cross workers confronted new kinds of casualties, such as bodies riddled with machine gun bullets and the suffering inflicted by poison gas. Sometimes artillery, the cause of the majority of battle wounds in the war, sent dirt flying with such velocity that it caused injuries. The fact that much of the fighting on the Western Front took place on well-fertilized farm or pastureland made infection a serious problem.

As American casualties in France mounted, staffing in the war hospitals became difficult to maintain, and at times, nurses' assistants with little experience found themselves supervising hospital wards while nurses helped doctors in operating rooms. "The need for American Nurses, especially in the operating rooms, is desperate," a journalist wrote in 1918, "and those already in France are working beyond their strength. . . . They cannot go on forever, and it is obvious that unless nurses are supplied to take their places, and give them a chance to get back their strength, they will go to pieces."[94]

Nurses' letters give us insight into the war's hardship. Alaskans learned about the medical workers' long and grueling hours and about the dangers they con-

SAVE OUR MEN FROM GERMAN POISON GAS

To make carbon to protect our men from German Poison Gas, the Government needs

Peach Stones Plum Pits
Apricot Pits Olive Pits
Prune Pits Date Seeds
Cherry Pits
Brazil-Nut Shells
Walnut Shells
(English or Native)
Hickory-Nut Shells
Butter-Nut Shells

Collect all you can of all or any of these and turn them in to the nearest Red Cross Chapter, which will ship them to the proper authorities. You will help to save a soldier's life.

*Wrangell Sentinel*, October 17, 1918

fronted. By the end of the war, about two hundred American nurses had been decorated by the British, French, and American governments for bravery under fire. As a result of accidents and the influenza epidemic of 1918, four hundred American nurses died.

As difficult as life for the nurses was, they could see that frontline troops had it worse. This was most obvious in battle's aftermath. They brought coffee, cookies, and kind words to the wounded and shell-shocked; they scraped dirt from the bodies of soldiers who were covered with vermin after being in trenches for days or weeks. "I have just come back from the canteen," wrote one nurse whose letter was reproduced in the *Anchorage Weekly Times*.

> Such an afternoon. A great train of seriously wounded, which is tiring, as one has to climb in all the carriages. The men adore cocoa. We get into the sanitary trains and begin with the men who are well enough to sit up and

AN RED CROSS
EATION HUT

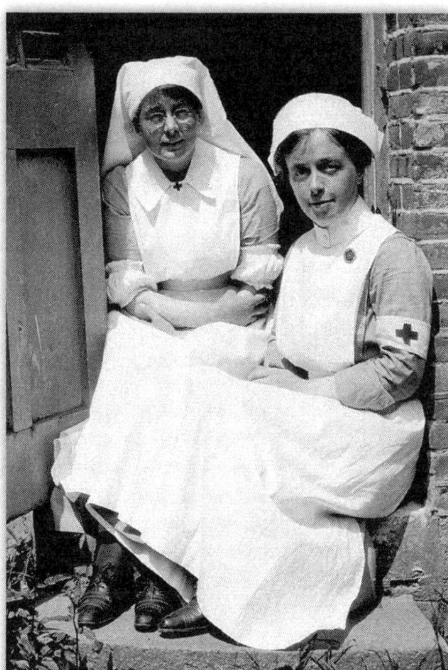

Nurses and the Red Cross in France. Stroud Collection

> handle tin cups, and afterwards those who are too ill to lift their heads or use their hands. Those, of course, we have to lift and feed ourselves; as there are usually two and three hundred men in a train, you can see one has to work quickly to get through.[95]

Exhaustion set in; the feeling that one might break under continual strain threatened. "Together," said one tired nurse, "the Matron and I stood there for some minutes surveying the rows of beds, with those mechanical contrivances that mean war."[96]

The Great War marked the first time that a significant number of women moved into positions formerly held by men in military service. American newspapers reported on English "conductorettes" now driving public buses, and an American soldier commented on the ways French women were bearing the brunt of war. "You will find women cleaning the streets; women working in the powder factories; women driving delivery wagons and operating street cars. However, they don't seem to mind in the least and they seem very glad to see Uncle Sam's boys here in France."[97]

The employable ranks in Anchorage became thin enough by mid-1918 to justify hiring women to wait tables in the AEC and YMCA lunchrooms. The executive board of the Council of National Defense at Juneau advocated moving more Alaska women into the workforce, noting that this had already happened in the fishing industry. "By making labor, for the good of the nation, a patriotic duty, ... no social barriers will be raised against honest women workers," the memo noted. "And a greater, more liberal spirit of democracy will thus prevail."[98]

## Casualties

While details of combat were scarce, the news wires conveyed some of the war's costs.

> The casualty list in yesterday's fighting at the front names forty-one including four killed and twenty wounded.... American army casualties in yesterday's fighting on the western front were seventeen killed in action and seventeen wounded. The Marine Corps casualties were one hundred fourteen, including twenty-one killed and seventy wounded.... General Pershing reported today to the state department that during the fighting yesterday forty-three casualties occurred among the American soldiers.

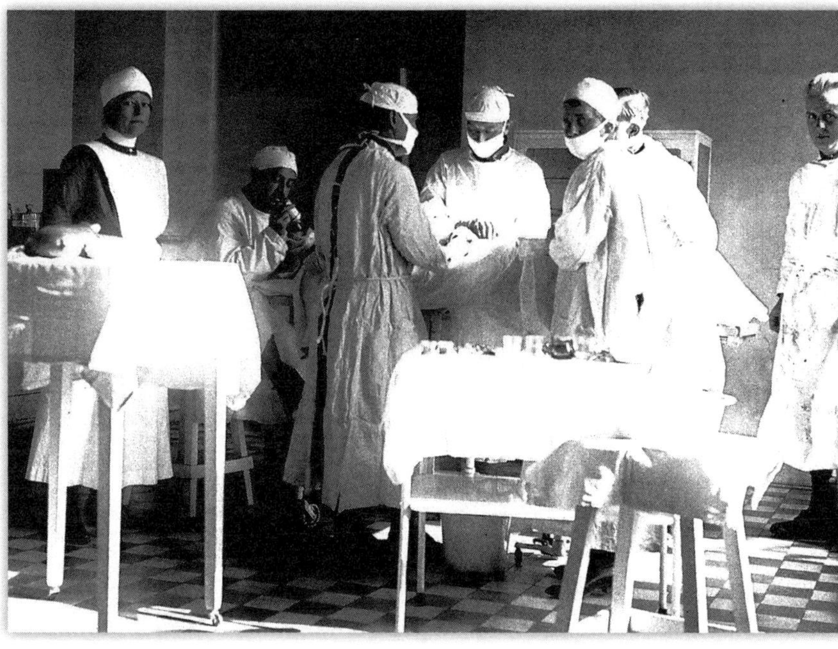

Stroud Collection

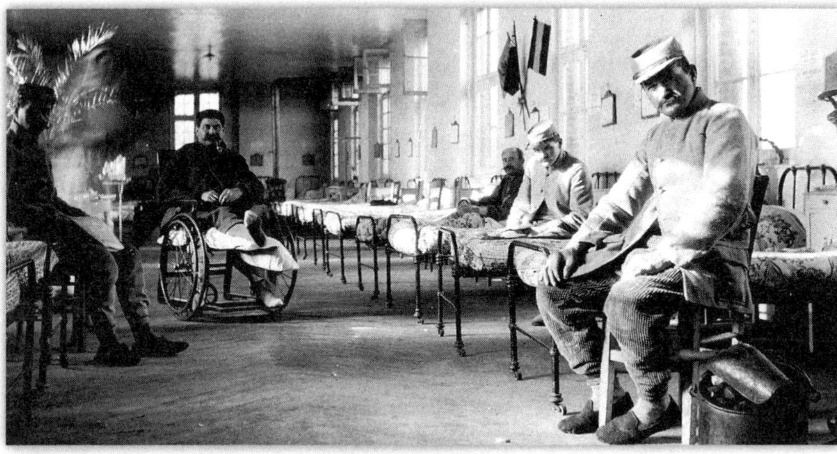

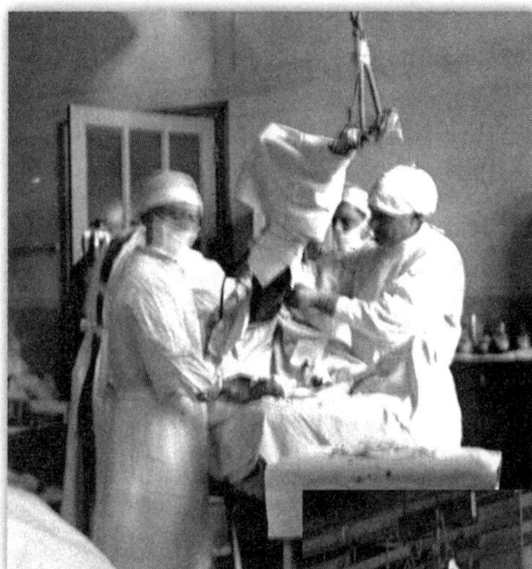

Stroud Collection

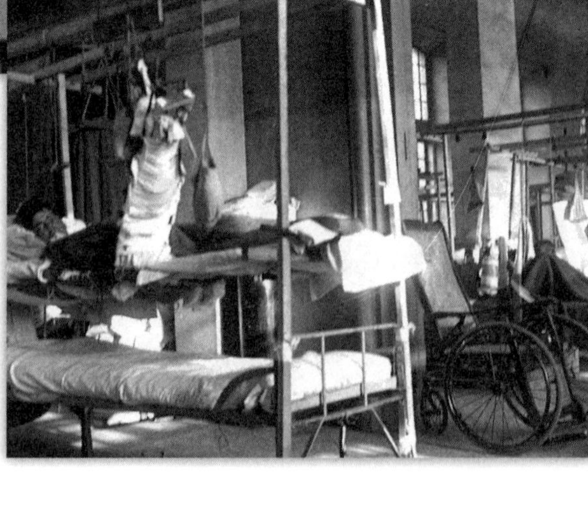

Stroud Collection

An official roster of Alaskans who served in the war is useful but not completely reliable. Of the more than two thousand Alaskans who saw military service, eighty-one are listed as having died in uniform, the majority from influenza. Just two are listed as having died of battle wounds.[99] Local reports provide additional information. In the late summer of 1918, the Alaska Council of National Defense sent a letter of condolence to the parents of Clem Summers, "the first Alaska boy to be reported killed in defense of his country."[100] Carter Koon was the first Nenanaite to die in battle. Robert Blee, Jack Henry, and James Meechan, all of Anchorage, were reported to have died from battle wounds. Merlin Palmer, a marine from Wrangell, was killed in combat. A motorcycle crash in France killed Robert Blee and injured A. G. Balls, both former employees of the AEC in France serving Frederick Mears's railroad engineers. Mears himself reported that an unnamed young man from Cordova had been killed by an accident on a train.

In their early postwar letters, some soldiers talked of returning to Alaska. The *Nenana Daily News* reported, "All of the boys heard from, without exception, express themselves as being well-pleased with the army life and are also agreed

Stroud Collection

that civilian life in Alaska is a whole lot better than in the States."[101] James Wickersham was also hopeful. He said that the "rugged, manly, self-reliant life of the great North" would offer an irresistible appeal to the war veterans. A month before the war's end, he claimed that Alaska would begin to prosper. "The boys who have made the world safe, democracy will find the most hospitable people on earth in America's newest frontier."[102]

But many of those who left Alaska for the war did not return. Some would not come back because battle or illness had taken them. Many simply chose not to. Before the war, Grady Sumerlin had been a fireman with the AEC. In late 1918 he wrote to friends of his plans to resettle in Oregon. Kenneth Case, another worker with the AEC before the war, said that he planned a move to South America.

Such messages challenged Alaskans' hopes for good economic times once war was done.

# LETTER FROM FRANCE (V)

*George Fawcett of Chitina wrote to his town newspaper before the war ended on November 11, 1918. "Fritz," a term used in the letter, was one of several names Americans used for the Germans. Fawcett describes himself as wearing a kilt. Perhaps he was an immigrant from Canada and had returned to fight with British forces. Fawcett gives his address as the Forty-third Battalion, a Canadian unit also called the Cameron Highlanders, which served with the British Expeditionary Force. Perhaps he was an American volunteer with the Canadians. (In October the Minnesota* Duluth News-Tribune *had announced the death of Nick Marion, an American serving in the same battalion.) Whatever the case, Fawcett's letter indicates an obvious Alaska attachment. It appeared in the* Chitina Leader *on November 23, 1918.*

I am on a Lewis gun... [and] so far, I have been lucky, and hope it continues, for I would sooner make a Fritzie die for his country than I would for mine. I want to eat cake and candy with real sugar in it again before I say "Good morning [to St.] Peter"... I can duck into a shell hole so fast when Fritz is putting [artillery shells] over [and] I can get every part of my body under my tin lid, except my feet, when the shells are flying, and unless he tilts the lid I'll see you all again someday and tell you all about it.

I guess the news suits you better these days, and know it does me, too, for the better it is the quicker it will be that I can dress like a white man again. A pair of pants is what I crave. They have me camouflaged like a woman. But one thing about it, we have Fritzie frightened when he sees the kilts coming over the top. He calls the Kilties "the Ladies of Hell," or the "Devil's wives." There is nothing to these kilts, especially from the knees down.

I would like to see the Fritzies run to Berlin and then run out of breath and die. They are bad actors, believe me, but they started things and we will finish them and beat them at their own game.

I am enjoying good health all along and the experience is great, even if it does frighten one a bit... it has its funny side, too. Even when [things are] hot one has to laugh at some of the funny things he sees. I know one thing—it has done wonders for me physically. Have the boys all write once in a while. Letters help win the war. They make a fellow feel better. Write to the boys from Alaska that are in France. They will all appreciate it, believe me. I have seen many a lad miss a meal to get a letter quicker. My address is "B Co., 43rd Batt., B. E. F., France."

It is hard work here, but the boys go to it like a bunch of kids to a picnic. Of course, there's lots of kicking, too, but it's forgotten in a minute, as they don't take it half as seriously as one would imagine. Well, the last post has blown "lights out," and so I will close with best wishes to all my friends.

George W. Fawcett.

# CHAPTER SIX

# Aftermath

## Promise

In the fall of 1918, C. J. Porter sent home to Juneau a quote from General Pershing: "We will be in Heaven, Hell or Hoboken by Xmas."[1] The prediction was basically right; Germany agreed to an armistice on November 11. Wagoner Nussbaumer from Wrangell described a victory celebration in France. The whole country "was lighted up for the first time in four years," he wrote.

> [P]atriotic parades were formed by civilians who were joined by soldiers from all colors; bands of all kinds played; church bells were sounded, whistles and sirens were blown, big guns were fired; everyone simply was overjoyed. Kisses and wine were cheap; nothing is too good for *les americains.*[2]

They celebrated in Alaska, too. Nenana's "big peace celebration" began around two in the morning. News of the armistice had been "flashed over the telephone from Fairbanks." A crowd gathered at the town's grandly named Coliseum. Several latecomers found "not even standing room" available. Mrs. Leon Kellum sang "God Save the King," Luella Shaffer offered the "Marseillaise," and Lucille Diven inspired the crowd with "America." Sergeant Thomas Galvin shared his own lyrical creation.

*Now, friends the war is over, if we's got the news alright;*
*And everybody in this house should celebrate tonight;*
*And sing and dance and give three cheers, and pray to God they're free,*
*and glad that they are living in the land of liberty.*
*And our friends so far away should hear from us today;*
*we should send a postal or a greeting right away,*
*and show that we are praying for their safe return once more,*
*and waiting with our arms outstretched outside our cabin door.*[3]

The war was over. Alaskans hoped the same could be said of the economic depression the war had brought.

Before the United States entered the conflict, Alaska's future glimmered. As one writer put it, Alaska was "the only bit of Uncle Sam's territory where it is still possible for a man to get in on the ground floor."[4] The book title, *Alaska: An Empire in the Making* (1913), directed readers to the lofty vision some people had for the territory. According to this outlook, Alaska was a promise composed of land to settle, natural resources to tap, and opportunities to create.

Outside commentators had written of Alaska in familiar phrases: the "nation's treasure house"; an "Arctic Empire"; a "frontier wonderland"; a "land of vast resources"; a "strongbox full of treasure." Rhode Island's *Providence Journal* took note of Alaska's promising oil, coal, and copper stores. The New Orleans *Times-Picayune* commented on the territory's salmon, cod, herring, seals, and timber, as well as its farming possibilities—potatoes, oats, wheat, and barley. A few months before the United States entered the war, Seward's *Alaska Evening Post* looked forward to a new "stampede" to Alaska.[5] The *Seward Gateway* declared that the "prospects in sight for fishermen in Alaska were never brighter."[6] At the beginning of 1918 it looked certain to observers in the States that Alaska would "help us win the war."[7]

Now that the fighting was done, some Alaska soldiers were eager to return. Governor Riggs asked authorities for James Bogan's release from military service, as he had been elected as a representative from Nome in Alaska's territorial legislature.[8] But appeals even from a governor's office did not speed up the dismissal of military personnel. In memos to army officials, the governor noted that Alaska's men in uniform were badly needed in the territory's mines. Seward's only prospective pharmacist was in military service in San Francisco, the governor noted six weeks after the war had ended, but getting the Alaskans released quickly from the army seemed "impossible."[9]

*McCarthy Weekly News*, January 1, 1919

In January 1919, James Wickersham confided to his diary that about six hundred Alaskans stationed at Camp Grant in Illinois wanted release from the army. He received a telegram from Camp Dodge in Iowa asking him to use his influence "to get the Alaska boys there released & sent home."[10] Others based at Camp Lewis in Washington State complained to him that their travel stipend of 3.5 cents per mile was insufficient to pay for the trip to Alaska. The delegate intervened with the War Department, which agreed to transport the soldiers to camps in Alaska and to discharge them from there.[11] "Working in office," Wickersham wrote. "Much correspondence about discharging Alaska soldiers—many trips to War Dept. about the same.... Am being flooded with telegrams & letters from Alaska soldiers who are seeking discharge from the Army."[12] A month and a half later, in mid-February, he penned the last entry on this theme in his diary. Later in Fairbanks, he claimed that "all signs point to good times in Alaska this year." He said that "all" of Alaska's soldiers were going to return to Alaska, "and there will be immediate increase in all activities."[13] The economic darkness the war had brought would weave a different story.

## Siberia

Among several blows to Alaska's economy was turmoil in Siberia, which some had seen as a "second pioneer Alaska" before the war.[14] A book published in 1912, *Through Siberia: The Land of the Future*, tapped into this sense of promise. But the Great War had also changed conditions in eastern Russia. Trade between northeastern Siberians and Americans, many of them based in Nome, had never been well organized.[15] Before the war, merchants in the Siberia trade had hoped for the establishment of a formal customs house there, but by the fall of 1918, Russia, weakened by its war against Germany, had undergone a communist revolution followed by civil war. Economic activity in Siberia became more dangerous and less predictable. Merchants returned to Nome speaking of having to buy licenses from opposing sides in the civil war.[16] Trade slowed. Nome's mayor wrote to Governor Thomas Riggs that the "Siberian situation may without warning require military protection."[17]

Reportedly, there was some actual fighting between Alaskans and Russians on the Siberian side. In the summer of 1920, L. M. Quirk and Corbett Bland arrived in Nome with a story of a battle between Bolsheviks and Alaska miners that had led to the death of a dozen Russian aggressors.[18] The Bolsheviks had sought to shut down all trade with foreigners, and

> [a] mere handful of American miners, mostly Alaskans, fearful their supplies would be seized, rallied the people to organization, resulting in a good old time western massacre. Mikoff, the leader of the Bolsheviks, was first riddled with .30-30 bullets from the rifles of the armed Alaskans, followed by the killing of many of the Bolsheviks.[19]

Whether or not this really happened, Nomeites worried that Siberia's instability might make its way across the Bering Strait. Community leader Carl Lomen recalled in his memoirs the concern that Russians might "sail right into Nome and make off with whatever they happened to want."[20] In this context, the postwar closing of Fort Davis nearby looked less like federal government neglect and more like cold malice. Nome's residents were lacking in military protection "since the government saw fit to abandon Ft. Davis," the *Nome Nugget* observed. "Nome is fully justified in...raising a strident voice for troop protection, even though there is small hope that it will be heard in Washington."[21]

Commentators who knew nothing, or had nothing to say, about Siberia nevertheless did see the lack of Alaska development as a missed opportunity. English travel writer Charlotte Cameron had always wanted to visit Alaska, drawn as she was to Nome—"a spot on the map.... this Mecca of mine."[22] After the war, she made her way to the far northwest and was surprised by the community's access to electricity, telephones, automobiles, newspapers, and shops. She saw Alaska's tremendous natural wealth, and she took note of the territory's human wealth—"the hospitality and kind-heartedness of these Northerners know no bounds." An American government that was "so busy" it was unable to appreciate the worth of its northern treasure trove mystified her. But someday America would be able to see the territory clearly, "and Alaska will then come into its own." Alaska, Cameron observed, "is now Cinderella in the opulent family circle of Uncle Sam."[23]

## Hardship

Alaska's economy stumbled. Important mining districts went unvisited by government geologists because professionals with the Geological Survey's Alaska division had been "depleted by the entrance of most of the geologists into the Army or into various activities connected with the prosecution of the war."[24] This mirrored a dramatic fall-off in mining productivity once the United States was in the war. Excepting coal extraction, mineral production in Alaska declined by nearly forty percent in 1918 compared to two years before. In the words of a technical report, mining in the territory had experienced a "general retrenchment."[25]

The trend was evident in the Alaska Engineering Commission's workforce. The November 13, 1917, edition of the *Alaska Railroad Record* reported that the AEC had 2,798 employees on its payroll. In March of the following year, the number had fallen to 1,084. With the return of summer, the figure had risen to 1,438 (mid-July), still nearly a fifty percent reduction from the period immediately before the United States declared war. For shops and cafés, this meant a dramatic decline in economic activity along the rail line that would eventually connect Fairbanks and Seward.

Alaskans had celebrated the service of military volunteers and draftees; they had understood when laborers left the territory to take less arduous and better-paying work Outside. (The shipbuilding industry alone appealed for one thousand Alaskans to go Outside to meet wartime demand.) But the economic consequences of these departures were significant. Alaska's population declined from about sixty-four thousand in 1910 to fifty-five thousand ten years later. That drop was partly related to the end of Alaska's gold rush but was mostly a legacy of the war.

Signs of Alaska's economic hardship were easy to see. Numerous letters bearing the same message crossed Governor Riggs's desk: "I am leaving Alaska," said one, "[and] I regretfully tender my resignation [from] the Territorial Council of Defense."[26] "I am leaving Candle for a temporary stay in Nome," another letter noted, "and if not finding business in a professional way encouraging, will proceed to San Francisco."[27]

This movement had practical consequences. The George Thomas Library, where the Fairbanks chapter of the Red Cross had first met, closed its doors for lack of funds. St. James Methodist church, also in Fairbanks, ended services when its minister left the territory and no one replaced him. In the spring of 1918, Nome's famous All-Alaska Sweepstakes dogsled race had been canceled for the war's sake: the funds set aside for the race were better donated to the Red Cross, and, in any case, most of the Seward Peninsula's best dogs had gone to the war. By the end of 1918, there were too few people living in Nome to provide for a substantial winner's purse. "If things settle down," Scotty Allan said, "we can work up a big trade with our neighbors, the Siberians, and thus bring enough people and money to Nome to make it possible to stage the old races again."[28] But, as we have seen, the Siberian trade did not improve.

Few settlements were as hard hit as Ruby, built by gold rush in 1911. At its peak about three thousand people lived there. (A century later the figure stood at fewer than two hundred.) The town's descent began with the dwindling gold recoveries, but the war's effects quickened the slide. By late July 1918, the *Record-Citizen*'s editor notified his shrinking readership of the paper's likely demise. The people of the Ruby district would have "a virile newspaper only so long as they give it the support that will keep it alive enough to be a potential and progressive agent in the community."[29] The editor wrote that there were a few hopeful signs for Ruby in the form of announcements about possible new gold finds. And there were predictions of good times to come once the "best blood and brawn of the Northland" returned from military service. But Ruby's residents could not wait until then. Ruby's most prosperous days had passed and its "darkest hour is yet to come."[30] On August 3 the paper announced that, so far as it could see, the town no longer had a physician among its population of nine hundred (including three hundred Natives). It also no longer had a newspaper. "We leave Ruby in the war on the side of the Allies and America. Good night."[31]

Natives also felt the downturn. The exodus from Alaska meant fewer customers to buy fish, and a decline in tourists meant a dearth of customers for arts and crafts. "No baby in Belgium or France," an Anchorage journalist wrote, "has suffered more than these untutored sons of Uncle Sam, and none have given to the war cause more patriotically than these."[32]

During the war, grumbling and complaints had to be tempered, but workers could express their unhappiness by leaving the state. Once war came, Anchorage's "labor temple" could no longer be a place to promote agitated socialism, but it did serve as a gathering place for the disappointed. In late January 1918, some five hundred workers had come to Anchorage to express their opposition to the suspension of an eight-hour workday as a war measure. At the meeting, workers heard that patriotism did not necessitate submitting to indignities, that railroad workers' pay in Anchorage was ten percent lower than it was in Seattle, and that each person who left Anchorage accounted for nearly seven hundred dollars less spent per year in the local economy. Laborers, said the unhappy workers, could stay in Alaska and freeze or go Outside and prosper. If the government did not believe that railroad work was necessary, then "they should shut it down and let the men go out to do their patriotic duty."[33]

Government officials tried to convince workers to stay in the territory. The Alaska Engineering Commission raised wages by ten percent. Now machinists could make between $6.00 and $6.60 in an eight-hour day, and sheet metal

*Nenana Daily News*, January 4, 1918

workers could be compensated up to $7.60 per workday. This was helpful but did not really address the economic malaise. Perhaps a few found consolation in the thought that Alaska's hardship was just another wound of war, another demonstration of high loyalty. "Alaska," someone wrote, "was made up of the kind of men that would respond most quickly to the needs of the Government and it is on this account that Alaska became depopulated."[34]

Editorialists and town boosters sought to minimize the news of a war-related economic boom Outside. It was true, some said, that the cost of living had risen in Alaska, partly because fewer ships available for the Alaska trade made commodities scarcer and thus more expensive. But costs had also risen Outside, and while opportunities were always plentiful in Alaska, jobs in the States would be scarce once the soldiers returned from the war.

Alaska's Bureau of Publicity tried appeals to sentiment. Why should Alaskans bother looking for work Outside when their hankering for life in the territory would only compel them to return? "You are in Alaska now and Alaska is in your system."[35]

Others spoke of the territory's open spaces and its room for individualists. Perhaps it was true that more money could be made Outside, they said, but how high was the value of the freedom that came with life in Alaska? What about the greater chance the territory provided of being one's own boss? What about the greater sense of equality that existed in Alaska? "Things you could do here [in Alaska] without a question being asked would get you fired [Outside]."[36]

It was helpful that some who had gone Outside wrote back to Alaska with less-than-glowing reports. Walter DeLong sent a letter from Utah to advise his Anchorage friends to think again before leaving the territory. The economic situation in the States might look good from Alaska's distant perspective, he wrote, but workers living in the territory "better consider their steps before they make a move," for conditions were just as unsettled Outside as they were in Alaska.[37]

None of these campaigns worked. The U.S. Geological Survey's 1919 assessment of economic conditions in Alaska included the phrase "much worse than ever before." The news was sharpened by its proximity to another report on a growing economy Outside. "The country, as a whole...was never more prosperous."[38]

Some who stayed in Alaska looked for as-of-yet-unrealized possibilities. John Kehoe of Tanana thought about building a goat ranching industry "to which in future years the people of Interior Alaska will point with pride."[39] Seldovians hoped for a great future in fishing. Delegate Wickersham proposed legislation giving "every deserving soldier and sailor" some property in Alaska.[40] Emphasizing his "boundless faith in the future prosperity of Alaska," Franklin Lane, secretary of the interior, wondered if the territory's reindeer and muskoxen might not eventually supply the entire Pacific coast with meat.[41]

Meantime, the old anger felt before the war—the disgust that came with living in a trove of natural riches while Uncle Sam, dumb and distant, did nothing—rose again. Sometimes this manifested itself in pettiness, such as when complaints were raised about Alaska's portrayal on many American maps as greatly reduced in relative size and placed southwest of San Diego. The aggrieved said this was the work of "slander...perpetrated by cartographers."[42]

Rigid government bureaucracy stirred feelings of resentment. Delegate Wickersham wrote that Alaska "must yet break through the maze of red tape and duplication of governmental labors created by executive proclamations and orders and bureaucratic rules and regulations."[43] It seemed that Alaska was hemmed in—on the one hand by immovable government regulations and paperwork, on the other hand by indifference.

The stage was set for the reemergence and strengthening of the "Seward's Folly" myth. It appeared, among other places, in Governor Thomas Riggs's report on the year 1918. During the war, Alaskans had "responded more nobly to the call of duty than did the people of any other state or territory," he wrote. "In three [Liberty] loan drives Alaska headed the Nation in oversubscription of her quotas; and, in its support of the American Red Cross, Alaska, in proportion, completely eclipsed all competitors." And what was the result? Government "neglect and repression."[44]

Alaska's situation was grim. Wilds P. Richardson, the first president of the Alaska Board of Road Commissioners, encouraged the *Atlantic Monthly*'s readers to disregard all they had heard about the Alaska Purchase as a stellar deal. Predictions about the territory's speedy growth following the construction of the Alaska Railroad had busted, Richardson wrote. "The little state of Iowa alone produced…more than the total output of Alaska." He offered little sympathy to the "credulous and hopeful" Americans who had invested their money and energies in the government's faltering Alaskan project, including the town of Anchorage.[45] In Alaska, America's Roaring Twenties never roared.

## Another Fight

The Great War, some said, was the conflict that would end war. But in 1920, the world was as troubled as it had been six years before. As we have seen, one spin-off of the First World War was a small, ambiguous, and unsuccessful fight in Siberia and northern Russia that pitted Americans, British, Czechs, Japanese, French, and other nations against the revolutionary Soviet forces that had recently toppled Russia's government. Meantime, the British, wanting to hold on to their empire, faced resistance from nationalists in India. And news of Japanese military action in the Pacific—chiefly in Siberia and China—was worrying to Americans. After the war, General Pershing unsuccessfully advocated universal military training for every adult male living in the United States.

*Anchorage Weekly Times*, October 3, 1918

After the armistice of 1918, political dissent reemerged in the United States. The soldiers having put down their weapons, it was safe again publicly to denounce President Wilson's policies. The president's hopes for U.S. participation in the League of Nations, forerunner to the United Nations, foundered in the Senate. This was partly due to regrets about American entry into the Great War and partly related to a desire to leave the troubled world to itself. Many Americans again embraced the idea that a nation could trade globally while standing aloof from the world's conflicts. Senate Republicans felt that American entry into the League might drag the nation into other countries' fights.

While political argument within the American mainstream went public again, political radicalism fell into deeper disrepute. Through the early 1920s, anarchists, communists, and other radicals—many of them of eastern European origin—were imprisoned and deported. Some of these were genuinely dangerous; most only held to ideas perceived as dangerous. But since 1917, the country had seen too much. In the words of the Republican slogan during the presidential election of

1920, the American public wanted a "return to normalcy." The *Alaska Citizen*, which before the war had maintained a firm but even-keeled editorial voice, now offered terse advice on the question of immigration: "deport them all."[46]

As the war against Germany was closing, another international struggle—this one against deadly influenza—began. In short order, the virus killed many more people than human weapons had. Of the nearly thirty Nomeites who went into military service during the war, at least five died from influenza or pneumonia. A list of First World War soldiers from Alaska held at the state library names more than seventy men who died of influenza or pneumonia while in uniform.

Alaska towns took quarantine measures. Early on, the disease may not have seemed serious, as James Wickersham wrote in his diary about being disappointed by a quarantine placed on Juneau since that made it impossible for him to campaign there for reelection as Alaska's delegate to the U.S. Congress.[47] The diary of Nome's Carl Lomen offers a less self-interested chronicle:

> Many under some sort of spell (October 19).... The army post in quarantine. Schools closed, movies, churches (October 20).... We fear the influenza, now raging through the States (October 28).

While aboard the *Victoria* en route to Seattle, Lomen wrote, "Many of the Vic passengers seriously ill" (November 6). By November 15, several passengers had died, and Lomen's entries combined sobriety and hope: "The influenza has been malignant—many deaths, but seems [to be] dying down."[48] The following month, Wickersham wrote less hopefully, "The influenza is about to destroy the natives of Alaska."[49] Arthur Moa wrote from an army post to his godparents in Ketchikan. "None of us Alaskans like it here as it is so hot and dusty," he noted, adding that there were "many cases of Spanish Influenza in camp and several deaths have occurred from it. The camp is under quarantine now."[50]

Alaska's towns had no choice but to turn inward. One headline declared "Seward Places Quarantine Ban on Anchorage."[51] Nenana also banned nonresidents from entering the town, and "Natives and white persons who are residents of the Nenana Mission [were] prohibited from entering the grounds of the Alaska Engineering Commission."[52]

While coastal towns were hard hit, quarantine policies limited the disease's spread in the Interior. As of November 1918, McCarthy had had no cases of flu. In Nome, on the other hand, some 175 Natives and nearly one hundred non-Natives (including seventy-five soldiers at Fort Davis) were afflicted. By early

December, Seward had seen 250 cases of influenza and six deaths. Anchorage experienced about five hundred cases and twenty-five deaths. At the end of December, Governor Riggs estimated that 450 deaths in the territory were attributable to flu. Announcements appeared in local papers: "All through its course this epidemic has taken its toll of the lives of the brightest and best."[53]

The body count had risen substantially by the time Governor Riggs set down his report to the secretary of the interior on fiscal year 1918. His comments on the flu outbreak focused on Native communities in the Far North, and they make for heavy reading amidst what is, overall, a drab government document. By the time of writing, officials in the Bureau of Education had informed Riggs that fifteen hundred people, mostly Natives, had died in the Seward Peninsula and adjacent areas. Nearly five hundred more Native children, whose parents had perished, would have lost their lives without the territorial government's intervention.

> Particularly in Nome and on the Seward Peninsula was the epidemic most severe. Whole villages of Eskimos lost their entire adult population. Many infants were frozen in their dead mothers' arms. To make matters more gruesome, the half-starved dogs mangled and mutilated the dead and dying. . . . Medical relief was given where possible, destitution was relieved and the orphan children gathered up and placed in institutions until appropriations should become available for their permanent care.

Even as he assembled his report, messages arrived "of several villages having been entirely wiped out and the bodies eaten by dogs."

The governor went on to describe the spread of flu to Kodiak and Bristol Bay, where, he added bitterly, the "Indian question" had been "solved." "Two hundred and thirty-eight orphans, so far reported, are practically all that are left of the Aleut and half-breed population of between 800 and 1,000." Riggs wrote with admiration of naval personnel and doctors who had done what they could to help, some of them contracting sickness and dying: the sailors, "with Navy spirit, cooked, nursed, laundered, and sewed garments for the sick."[54]

Riggs brought his narrative to an end with the observation that Alaska's financial resources were too small to face another flu outbreak. The difficulty the territorial authorities had in dealing with the epidemic was yet more evidence of a federal government that was glad to take Alaska's natural wealth while doing little to ensure that Alaska had the infrastructure and development it needed to prosper. Like all Alaskans, Riggs looked to the day when, in the words of another writer, the "territory shall have increased in happiness and well-being," offering benefits not only to Alaskans but to all Americans, particularly those who were "land hungry" and looking for a new place to begin. Alaska had the stuff to be counted among the greatest of the "sisterhood of states."[55]

On January 26, 1920, Alaskans learned that, except for those who would tend to the graves of American dead, the last of the U.S. troops in Europe were coming home. Like all Americans, Alaskans knew that they had passed through a strange era and that their country had changed. Never before had Americans sent their own sons across the Atlantic to slay offending Europeans. Never before had the country come together so quickly to act on so significant a matter. The price the country paid for having done so was a degree of conformity that would later lead to some regret. The word *propaganda* acquired negative connotations. Works published in the decade after the war with titles like *Propaganda Technique in World War I* (1927) and *Falsehood in War-Time* (1928) point to this transition.

For all its carnage, within a little more than two decades, the Great War would almost seem small. In July 1917, Ruby's *Record-Citizen* had denounced Germany's air raids on London as "terrorism" and as a sign that the world had lost its "sense of balance."[56] The writer could not know of the obliteration of the next world war to be hurled down on cities like Coventry, Dresden, and Hiroshima.

It is often noticed that the Second World War sprang from the failed peace of its grim predecessor. Even before the Great War ended, observers in far-away Ruby, Alaska, could see that if the conflict closed with the losing side feeling only smoldering hatred, then that country—Germany—would possess only a "vindictive intent to begin afresh."[57] The causes of the Second World War were many, but the writer had a point: the public rage of a First World War veteran, Adolf Hitler, would resonate with a dispirited German population.

Governor Strong also thought that if a postconflict peace were not set on a firm foundation, then "the war that has been waged . . . shall have been waged in vain and [German] militarism will overshadow the world."[58] Come 1939–1944, the governor's words would seem prophetic. Sometime after the First World War, Governor Riggs wrote a memoir that was disorganized and never edited for publication. In it, the governor reflected on the "battered, crazy old world" that, he hoped, would one day right itself.[59]

Alaska had been battered, too. But as Alaskans had done since the latter 1880s, they looked to better times, knowing the wealth their territory had to offer, and knowing that someday the nation as a whole would see Alaska for the prize it was. Travel writers like Frank Carpenter still passed through and wrote of America's "Polar Wonderland"—a "land of surprises" inhabited by "the most patriotic Americans . . . who can see straight and shoot straight." Carpenter saw a bright future for Alaska and predicted a steady population of three million or more.[60] One hundred years later, Alaska's population stood at less than one million, but perhaps Carpenter's figure will eventually be reached.

Through the 1920s and 1930s, economic prosperity was something Alaskans would only hope for. As always, life in the territory required a special kind of toughness, endurance, and perseverance. "The people of Alaska," James Wickersham wrote in 1923, "will courageously carry on, discouraging though the contest is." They would keep looking to the bright time when Alaska would emerge from "territorial darkness" and take its place among the greatest of the American states.[61]

APPENDIX I

# Primary Sources

## Chapter 1: The Alaskans

### ALASKA'S NEW ERA

*Alaska Citizen* (Fairbanks), October 12, 1914

All history shows that human progress is ever traveling westward. Ancient civilization, such as it was, started in Asia. Then it went westward throughout Europe. Then crossed the Atlantic and took root in New England. For more than 100 years, the settlement and development of North America has been slowly working westward, and now the only remaining frontier is Alaska.

This westward movement of civilized humanity which follows the course of the sun is always promoted by men and women of more than ordinary energy and enterprise. It is their superabundant vitality that urges them restlessly to search for greater opportunity in underdeveloped countries such as Alaska.

Until now, the opportunities offered by Alaska to people in the thickly settled sections have been limited practically to a few placer mines of a richness that would make their development possible under adverse conditions. But the new government railroad is the magic wand that is promising to change it all and make of this neglected land a country of almost unlimited opportunities.

One worthy thing promotes another and the new government railroad is certain to be the cause of other important public enterprises. It can be expected that the coal mines that the government will control will be utilized in a hundred different ways to make more available the rich resources of Alaska. There will be power plants from which will radiate feed wires to a thousand industrial undertakings. There will be further railroad extension as population and industry grows. There will be factories that will convert the raw products of the Territory into articles of commerce, and there will be farms and homes and cities where there are now only trees and underbrush and wasted vegetation.

The men who come to Alaska now and take part in its initial development will be the men of local importance a few years hence. Thus the young men of energy will find in Alaska opportunities that, if taken advantage of now, will mean riches and good social standing in time to come.

What we need to do now is to let the world know what Alaska has to offer to the proper kind of people. We want to keep out of Alaska the men who are habitual faultfinders and encourage boosters to come.

Much of Alaska's present population is made up of men who are doing everything in their power to promote the Territory's best interests. It is to be expected that they will attract many others of their kind.

## STATEHOOD FOR ALASKA

*Daily Alaska Dispatch* (Juneau), April 1, 1915

Alaska has reached the point where it can throw off its swaddling clothes.... Alaska is over-ripe for statehood. The time has come when its affairs should be handled by its own people and when the people and their interests should no longer be made the political chopping block for hordes of administrative officials, either Democratic, Republican or any other federal party in power.

## SKAGWAY

*Daily Alaskan* (Skagway), December 31, 1917, and January 1, 1918

Skagway is a home city where children may be reared free from the smoke and the danger of larger cities, and where they may have the great out-of-doors in which to grow. Skagway is a city of flower gardens, green lawns, and is the gateway to many pleasant hikes and tramps in the mountains and through the valley.

Today, Skagway has a permanent population of about one thousand, with practically no illiterates, even among the small native element. Its people are substantial, home-loving citizens, loyal to their city and confident of its future. No city of its size can boast more efficient public service and utilities.

Crime and disorder are of such rare occurrence that the twenty-four hour police service is purely precautionary. The organized fire department…has time and again demonstrated its ability to safeguard the city from any fire menace.

## NATIVES OF THE NORTHLAND

*Anchorage Weekly Times*, April 11, 1918

The Alaskan Indian is capable of a high state of civilization if the government but recognized the racial difference between them and the plains Indians of the Fenimore Cooper type, and placed them in a position to learn the ways of the white man. They are sturdy and independent, with a high degree of patience in whatever they undertake. An Alaskan Indian with no tools but those used by his ancestors generations back, will labor patiently for months to produce an article a white man with civilized implements could make in five minutes. They are wonderful mimics, and possess a rudimentary faculty for drawing and sketching articles that is marvelous.

Many an Aleut can sit down and draw a portrait of a white man or a white man's boat or dog or weapon that is a marvel of accuracy. They have an inordinate craving for sweets, and a family will consume a case of Condensed milk of the Gail Borden brand at a sitting. Candy is consumed by the pound and sugar by the sack at these family potlatches, and as long as their money lasts they stuff to repletion on the white man's dainties.

Their instinct is as keen as an animal's. Within twenty-four hours after the arrival of a cannery steamer from the south with the crews and supplies a swarm of [boats] will be seen approaching. The manner on which these frail crafts are handled in a heavy sea is remarkable.…

The Headmen are generally intelligent and competent to look after the welfare of their people, and distribute justice with a fairness and an effectiveness that might well be copied by the white race.

These villages are necessarily on salt water, as their inhabitants depend largely upon the annual supply of fish for their food. Nearly all the Indians own good gas boats and are experts in taking care of their motors. They are natural mechanics and can do work with primitive tools which cannot be surpassed by a white joiner or metal worker. Most of the natives of southeastern Alaska dress and live like the whites, and many of them accumulate considerable money by their fishing for the canneries.

Many cases have been known where natives have cleared from two to five thousand dollars fishing, and they are cheerful spenders.

They are anxious and willing to learn and rapidly adopt white ways upon contact with Caucasians. Many villages the past year have thrown off old tribal customs and are electing councils and mayors, and running their civic affairs in a model way. Naturally temperate, the natives until taught the use of whiskey, used no intoxicants. With the arrival of the white man and the accompanying intoxicants, the natives quickly acquired a craving for liquor and would go to any ends to get it.

The government in late years has appointed an earnest, conscientious body of men to see that the use and sale of intoxicants to natives is suppressed, and much good has been done.

## NENANA

*Nenana Daily News*, August 28, 1918

Nenana is probably the best town in the Interior of Alaska at the present time. If it were not it would behoove us to think so for our own good; but the fact remains that it is.... The ... plan is to get together and keep together and make this the one town in Alaska that is known all over the coast and throughout the Interior as being in good, prosperous condition. Boost all the time. If you can't say a good word for the town, keep still. Remember that "as a man thinketh so is he" applies also to cities.

## ALASKA, LAND OF OPPORTUNITY

Agnes Rush Burr, *Alaska—Our Beautiful Northland of Opportunity* (1919)

Alaska is a land of beautiful scenery and of almost inexhaustible resources.... It is also a land of many opportunities. In size about one-fifth of the whole United States, in resources almost equal in variety to those of the entire country, Alaska as yet has but comparatively a small population and few industries. New business enterprises in almost countless number await the seeing eye and earnest hand of the shrewd business man and woman.... In the larger towns of Alaska life is much the same as in any city. These towns have their telephones, their electric lights, their telegraphic news from the outside, their newspapers, theatres, churches, libraries, and schools. They all have many fraternal organizations and usually a progressive women's club.

## FAIRBANKS, METROPOLIS OF ALASKA

Charlotte Cameron, *A Cheechako in Alaska and Yukon* (1920)

At Gordon's, the emporium for women's clothes [in Fairbanks], we found beautiful furs, model dresses—in fact, a very good selection of fashionable goods. In the old days, when money was plentiful, the proprietor imported gowns straight from Paris. The ladies of Fairbanks, it should be added, are noted for stylishness and the elegance of their dress.... Fairbanks enjoys a fine public-school system, which would reflect credit on any city.... The full four years' course of the high school... meets all the requirements of the Pacific Coast universities.

## Chapter 2: The War before the War

### THAT MILITARY SPIRIT

*Daily Alaska Dispatch* (Juneau), August 28, 1915

There is something stirring about the clank of the sabre and the call of the bugle and the glint and sparkle of the war's accoutrements. Generals and warriors wise in human nature have their troops march along the streets of crowded cities and as the "brave boys" go swinging past, and the trumpets blare and the horses prance, the waiting crowds are carried off their feet. The poet, the artist and writer are all inspired with the scene and play up the highlights in the most dazzling manner. It helps to get recruits.

However, there is no one to picture the misery and heartache of the grief-stricken women at home, no one to express the bursting heart of the soldier-parent when he kisses his little ones before leaving for the front. The artist and the poet and the writer are not permitted by the generals and the press censor to dwell later upon mangled limbs, torn bodies, ditches running red with blood, bodies rotting on the field and the terrible nightmare strain which drives men insane and brutalizes them. Such horrible details might interfere with the work of recruiting. Rather must the writers dwell upon the "comforts" of trench life and the glory and splendor of the strategic movements conducted by generals in the field. Men are simply the pawns of the great game and do not count. The state gives their widows and orphans a mere pittance and considers it a duty done. That is the military spirit.

And yet that is the spirit which many are trying to inflame in the United States. If the munitions dealers and the writers and others so keen on war would be the first to volunteer and could be sent to the front, instead of the great body of workingmen who have no quarrel with their fellow men, there might be some small excuse. But those who clamor the most loudly for war are always the last to want to enlist. If these long-distance fighters with pen and voice tried half as hard to secure the goodwill of the people of other nations, as they do in inciting suspicion and fear and hatred, all cause for war would be removed.

## NEW CRISIS

*Record-Citizen* (Ruby), February 10, 1917

Amid these exciting, troublous times, America is fortunate in having, at her helm, a man of the coolness and balance of Woodrow Wilson. It is so easy for the excitable to lose their heads and to be carried along on the swift current of popular clamor into channels that are uncharted and strewn with rocks.

All of America that is sane and normal is now awaiting expectantly the next move. War is the last thing that we desire—the last thing President Wilson would draw upon his country. Yet, if war [comes] let there be no doubt but that Wilson would prove a dangerous antagonist. Those who are slowest to engage in a fray are almost universally desperate fighters. Once rouse them and the opponent is amazed at the ferocity of the encounter.

It is a desperate move that Germany is making when she antagonizes a neutral world, especially a neutral of the importance of the United States. It may be that her diplomats misread President Wilson's noble endorsement of their peace overtures into a stronger sentiment than was intended. Her official circles may have come to the erroneous conclusion that America would go to any length to bring about immediate peace.

The preparations being made in this country in the event of a conflict are ominous. No problem as terrific as this has knocked at our doors since [the Civil War in] 1861. It would seem as though all the world were going blood crazy and was bound to drag with it to destruction every atom, large and small.

If, at this particular crisis, we had at our head a firebrand who used no forethought, no caution, our plight would be bad, indeed. And war, if war should come, could never be laid at Wilson's door. He has done all that superhuman efforts could do to keep us from being embroiled.

## AMERICA JOINS THE WAR

*Record-Citizen* (Ruby), April 7, 1917

Well, at last we too have been caught in the whirlpool of madness that is spinning this senseless stream of blood down the rivers of time and now stand upon the brink of war.

President Wilson states that America accepts Germany's gauntlet of defiance and that she will now vindicate her honor. His high sounding language to the effect that American lives are being destroyed each and every day with wanton brutality, and that Germany is cutting into the very roots of civilization, somehow fails to convince.

If it is true that the preservation of lives and not property is the motive for our grandstand play at this particular crisis, it seems, in our humble opinion, that that same issue faced us two years ago in the sinking of the Lusitania. Germany, intent upon destroying Allied munitions supplies, has, over and over, endangered American lives and often destroyed them when the pressure of her need was upon her.

Why did we not go to war then? Are the recent lives lost at sea more precious than the earlier ones? Has Germany done anything lately that she has not done before?

Yes. She has begun the destruction of American property in the shape of shipping. She is jeopardizing, by her ferocious fighting, the return of the big moneyed loans of capital which, at the outset of the war, was positive of a reasonably early victory by the Allies.

If lives are in question, how about the lives of Americans living peaceably on our own side of the Mexican border, where they have a right to protection and consideration? Have we declared war on Mexico? Is it that the American capital in Mexico is less influential or less in value than the billions invested in Allied bonds?

The slow enlistment complained of at Washington shows how the people regard war. If we have a just cause for war now in the destruction of life, why were we so tardy in the recognition of it? Why did we not go to war two years ago? Can it be that Woodrow Wilson is listening to the siren of Wall Street? How else to explain his inconsistency in making an issue of a question that is old?

We are not advocating peace at any price. We simply would like to have explained consistently and with full satisfaction to our powers of judgment this change of heart. The average layman cannot understand the difference between the tweedledum and tweedledee of statecraft. It takes a lawyer, no doubt.

## ANSWER TO THE CRITICS

*Record-Citizen* (Ruby), April 14, 1917

Our editorial of last week... has been commented upon pro and con by so many, that we find it absolutely essential to take some recognition of that fact.

The point that stands out most glaringly in that of the [anti-editorial] clique's opinion is its stigmatizing of our attitude as pro-German. This newspaper never has been, is not, never will be pro-German. It has been, is and always will be pro-American. America first, last and always. True, we have never been pro-Ally. We have absolutely refused to align ourselves with either side. We have been neutral.

There is not one single statement in our editorial of last week that in any way could be construed as approval of Germany. We simply will not be blinded by our leaning toward either to award a halo to the one or the other.

Let it not be imagined, however, that we intend embarrassing the situation any further by criticizing the government's plunge into the melee. We are in it now and useless, idle fault finding will encompass nothing. We will attempt, to the best of our abilities, to hold up the hands of leaders and will do everything that red blooded America finds need for.

However, we are not aliens. We are Americans and as citizens, not a subject people on bended knees before a crowned head, we have the right to voice our honest opinion.

## Chapter 3: Over Here—Words

### GERMAN FLAG GOES DOWN IN FAIRBANKS

*Daily Alaskan* (Skagway), April 6, 1917

In celebration of Seward day [in Fairbanks], when flags of all nations were raised with the others, up went the emblem of Germany. When the district attorney's attention was called to the flag of Germany he ordered it down, and it was removed, with no show of feeling one way or the other.

### THE AMERICAN SPIRIT

*Alaska Citizen* (Fairbanks), April 9, 1917

There are numerous German-born in and around Fairbanks who are well known and well respected, and who have formed numerous friendships here. The fact that war now exists between their mother country and their adopted country renders their position trying and doubly hard, but we know of few, if any, who will hesitate about supporting their adopted country, much as it will grieve them. To such men there will be no change in their present friendly relations, and the regard of their American associates will be only increased out of respect for the difficulty under which they are handicapped. It is hoped and believed that they will be deserving of the square deal which is being accorded them by the American government and justify it by their actions.

## A PROCLAMATION

Alaska Governor John F.A. Strong, April 1917

This is a time in the history of our country which calls for self-sacrifice and devotion to those democratic institutions and ideals that have been a beacon light to the oppressed of all nations; and now, in obedience to those principles of right and truth and justice, in the struggle now being waged between the forces of democracy and autocracy, the citizens of this great republic may be depended upon to act well their part. There should be no division of sentiment, but each and all laying aside every consideration of partisanship, should remember that they are called upon to defend those great truths upon which this republic was founded, and should uphold and strengthen the hand of the President and his administration in the international crisis that has been forced upon the country. The time for action is here, and I am sure that the people of Alaska stand ready to do their part and to do it well.

## U.S. AT WAR

*Daily Alaskan* (Skagway), April 9, 1917

The die is cast.... Our old United States is at war with a powerful foreign foe, and there is no turning back with patriotism or honor.... [T]he time for analysis and discussion has passed.... It is now the plain duty of every American to keep his own counsel, as best he may, and be ready to render such service as lies within his power for his country. It is no longer his to reason why. It is his part only to accept and obey the orders and wishes of the captain in the fight.

## WHAT ALASKA CAN'T TOLERATE

*Record-Citizen* (Ruby), July 6, 1918

Alaskans will not permit any man to state that he desires to see the President of the United States hung, or that he would not support his country in time of need, without suffering for his sentiments. Conrad Mauritz Olson Einnes tried it, according to the complaint, and is now in jail in Juneau, with a suit filed against him by the United States government to cancel his citizenship certificate. The defendant is, or was, a fisherman at Ketchikan.

## Chapter 4: Over Here—Deeds

### A PROCLAMATION

Governor John F. A. Strong, April 1917

Whereas a state of war exists between the United States and the Imperial Governments of Germany and Austria...the duty devolves upon me...to remind the people of the Territory that we have within our borders many men who are subjects of those countries with which the United States is at war. The present crisis...calls for the exercise of sound judgment and forbearance, and no word or deed on the part of American citizens should operate to incite racial feeling or create prejudice against those who have come to the Territory for the purpose of bettering their condition and enjoying the inalienable right to life, liberty and pursuit of happiness guaranteed by that Constitution of the United States. As strangers in a strange land they are entitled to the utmost consideration, always provided that they comport themselves in accordance with our laws and with due respect for our institutions....I have, therefore, to urge upon all the people of Alaska that the course they shall pursue during the continuance of this war be marked by the exercise of the best judgment they can summon to their aid in all circumstances; law and order must be preserved, and careless, seditious or treasonable speech on the part of any person or persons will be at their peril. There will be no trouble, and no serious situation is likely to be created, if each and all will remember the duty they owe their country and flag, whether they be citizens of America or sojourners owing allegiance to the countries with which a state of war now exists.

### PATRIOTIC SERVICE

*Wrangell Sentinel*, April 12, 1917

Times of National danger and great crises bring out the best in men. It is the church's business to inspire and be a leader in this. The theme therefore at St. Philip's [Episcopal] church Sunday Evening...will be "Patriotism and what it is doing for civilization." Come and help in this service of patriotism.

### ALASKA COAST UNDEFENDED

*Daily Alaskan* (Skagway), April 21, 1917

Alaska, with all its tremendous extent of coast line, is still undefended. Distance from what would seem to be the probable points of attack if Germany should send ships against the United States tends to make Alaskans free from danger, but the menace exists and should be guarded against. There is an awakening...as shown by the formation of home guards at different points, but there should be a united effort to see that the government has steps taken without delay for the defense of Alaskan waters.

### THE CALL

*Daily Alaskan* (Skagway), April 30, 1917

Deeds of those at the [battle] front may be more heroic but they are no more important than the work of those who remain at home, soberly doing their bits in shop or office or on the farm. Only by their patriotic and self-sacrificing cooperation can the army be supported and enabled to win a victory. But, those who remain at home have another duty. They must be prepared to protect themselves against any local disturbances. Though there seems to be no probability that such will arise here, still wartimes require preparedness for any emergencies that may arise.

### WAR TO END IN JANUARY 1918

*Daily Alaskan* (Skagway), August 30, 1917

The great mystery of the most occult book of the Bible is the verse in Revelation relating to the Beast and his number, 666. A comprehensive study of this verse, this number and the relation of combinations of this number to the present world war, the German Empire and the German Kaiser, would seem to establish without a doubt the identity of the Beast as the German Kaiser, and the number 666 as being prophetic of his character and acts. And furthermore, it is established from this verse that forty-two months is to be the duration of the war, which will bring to an end the power of the Beast in January [of 1918].

### DANCE GIVEN FOR A HOSPITAL BED

*Record-Citizen* (Ruby), September 15, 1917

In last Saturday's mail, Mrs. R. Graham of Ruby, received a personal letter from Mrs. J. F. A. Strong, wife of the governor, requesting her to aid in obtaining funds for a hospital bed to be put in the Washington ward of the Neuilly hospital just outside of Paris. As a first measure, a dance was given at Eagle Hall on Tuesday night and $42 was realized—$36 in receipts and voluntary donations of $6.

## WHERE THE LIBERTY LOAN MONEY GOES

*Daily Alaskan* (Skagway), October 17, 1917

The money you lend to your Government when you subscribe to the Liberty Loan will enable it to supply our boys who have been drafted or who have volunteered to give their lives to protect our liberty and property with the necessary arms with which to fight; the necessary life insurance and means to support their dependent families while they are at the front. Every family should own a liberty bond.

## HAVE YOU BOUGHT A LIBERTY BOND?

*Daily Alaskan* (Skagway), October 25, 1917

Liberty Bonds protect you, your family, your home, your business and your country. By buying your share you will be doing your part to encourage officials, strengthen our allies, and show our enemies that our resources, an irresistible force, are backing our fighting men on land and sea. DON'T BE A SLACKER. Do your bit and do it now.

## SMOKES

*Daily Alaskan* (Skagway), February 14, 1918

Other cities in Alaska have been having their "smoke" campaigns to provide tobacco for the boys fighting at the front. Skagway as yet has had no campaign as such, but a great deal of tobacco has been sent by individuals and the soldier boys. We have done our share, and more too, in the Red Cross and other lines of work, and the *Alaskan* feels that Skagway will not be lacking provision of tobacco for our boys.

## PROUD ALASKANS

Proclamation of Governor Thomas Riggs, May 11, 1918

Alaska has exceeded her quota of enlistments in the military service. Alaska has exceeded her quota of purchase of Liberty Bonds. Alaska stands among the first, if not the first, in the purchase of War Savings and Thrift Stamps.

Alaska has always responded nobly to every war call sounded. The people of Alaska are generous and true Americans, irrespective of the Nationality of their birth. We are proud to be called Alaskans.

## THE PARADE

*Record-Citizen* (Ruby), April 6, 1918

The Ruby Loyal League, with banners and flags flying, paraded the streets of Ruby this afternoon at the opening gun in the Third Liberty Loan Campaign and to show where Ruby stands on the anniversary of our entrance into the war. It was a huge success. If you are a good American you'll want to be in the next one.

## DISCHARGE THE DISLOYAL

*Anchorage Weekly Times*, May 30, 1918

The *Times* is informed that an employee of the Alaska Engineering Commission has been discharged for refusing to make a small contribution to the Red Cross fund during the drive which comes to an end tonight. This man has been employed throughout the winter, when many loyal men have been out of employment. We heartily approve of the discharge of this man, on the grounds stated. There may be an excuse for a man who is out of employment to decline to subscribe to this Red Cross fund, because he may not have the money. But there is absolutely no excuse for a man who has had steady employment at a good wage to refuse to give a small donation. If he refuses, it is not because he has no money; it is rather because he is not patriotic. And if this railway cannot be constructed by patriotic men, as much as we desire its construction, we should say, let it remain unbuilt rather than employ men who are disloyal. Judging by the many Red Cross tags displayed on the coat lapels of our working men, we believe there are plenty of loyal men in this community to supply, at least, the present labor demand. The disloyal, it is gratifying to say, are very largely in the minority in Anchorage.

But there are disloyal men in this community, as there are disloyal [men] in all communities. If they are Americans by birth, they should be placed in custody for substantial terms of imprisonment. If they are of foreign birth, they should be interned until the war is over, their property should be confiscated, and they should be sent, empty-handed, from whence they came. This is no time to extend mercy to those who would disrupt, if they could, this great democratic country, in which all men are free and equal, in which all men, of all nationalities, have an equal opportunity. But if people have high privileges, they likewise have some responsibilities.

The American people are in no mood now to feed the mouths of those who would betray us, if the opportunity presented itself to them. And any man, or any set of men, who think they can oppose the great Red Cross society—which is world-wide in its noble activities and which is semi-official in character—are but branding themselves as disloyal, and they should be treated as such.

## PATRIOTISM, GOOD CITIZENSHIP, AND CHRISTIAN SCIENCE

*Daily Alaskan* (Skagway), July 13, 1918

Mrs. [Mary Baker] Eddy, the Discoverer and Founder of Christian Science, has said that Christian Science "stands for the inalienable, universal rights of men"...Thus it will be found that the great majority of alert students of Christian Science are endeavoring to be good citizens, and loyal upholders of every good and righteous cause. If a student of Christian Science believes that he is not a loyal supporter of this great government, it is without doubt because he has not as yet realized that if he is loyal to the ideals of Christian Science he cannot help being loyal to the ideals of America.

## DON'T OVERLOOK THE FRENCH ORPHANS

*Anchorage Weekly Times*, September 12, 1918

Some of our residents who have adopted French war orphans are leaving for the states.[1] Some of these good people may get out of touch with the local committee in charge of the subscriptions in Anchorage, and lest they forget, the *Times* has been asked to kindly request all who intend to leave...to either make arrangements to send the monthly amount to the treasurer of the local fund...or better still...pay the entire subscription before departing....

Mrs. J. E. Robars is at the head of the local committee that is in charge of the French war orphan campaign. Herself and the members of her committee have been most unremitting in their efforts to make a good showing for this town in this worthy charity.

## STUDENT LOYALTY PLEDGE

Reproduced in the *Report of Commissioner of Education, 1918–1920*

We the pupils of the...Alaska schools, being loyal to our country, the United States of America, and knowing that our soldiers, and sailors, with their comrades, are at present fighting against those who would destroy liberty in the world and overthrow our nation, do hereby pledge ourselves to the following, in order that we may assist in this great cause and help to make the world a better place for boys and girls of all nations:

(1) We will be loyal in word and deed to the government of the United States of America, and to the territory of Alaska.

(2) We will help our parents, or those with whom we live, to save wheat, meat, fats and sugar.

(3) We will not waste food or anything else which is useful to our country.

(4) We will help to save sugar by eating not more than one-half as much candy as we have been eating.

(5) We will be careful of our shoes and clothing in order that they may be worn as long as possible.

## Chapter 5: Organizing

### ALASKAN TELLS OF FRENCH WAR DOGS

*Anchorage Weekly Times*, June 6, 1918

Graphic account of the cleverness of French war dogs, glowing pictures of the devotion and fortitude of the French women and other noncombatants of Paris, and severe denunciations of the German brutalities committed upon their prisoners of war and the women of occupied territory, characterizes the letters received by the editor of [Juneau's] *Empire*, from L. F. French, now a lieutenant-commander in the United States Navy detailed to dock and troop and supply movements in France. Major French is well known in Alaska by reason of his long residence at Nome and southwestern Alaska.

In part, Major French writes: "The French war dogs are wonderful. The sentry dogs are trained not to bark and when they scent a German, which they can do at 200 yards, long before a man could see or hear him in the dark, they poke their masters with their noses and the French soldiers have time to escape and save their posts.

"The ambulance dogs do splendid life-saving work. When a man is wounded, his first instinct is to crawl out of danger and out of sight—under a bush or into a hole. Becoming unconscious, he cannot call for help, and these dogs find him. They bring back to their masters a cap, a button, or a piece of cloth, and then guide help back to the wounded man.

"On the other hand, they will not leave a man who is not dead, as so many are mistakenly believed to be, and as the dog is never wrong. This saves many lives. Dogs also carry messages where a man would surely be shot, and sometimes they are camouflaged and painted to escape detection. Many cases are on record where dogs have been mortally wounded and have nonetheless carried their messages through and then dropped dead.

"Hate the Germans? If you were over here and could know about the atrocities they commit you would agree with me that the best thing would be to have every one of them wiped out.

"The French women do many fine things. When they see their men folk off on a train, they laugh and shout and say good-byes—until the train is out of sight. They then fall on each other's necks and give way to complete despair. I doubt if our women could refrain from weeping at the moment of departure of their loved ones.

"Don't ever forget that these . . . Germans can fight, and that we have got a fight for life over here right this minute. It is impossible to convey to you, who are on the other side of the ocean, the real and terrible strength of the German war machine. We shall beat it—but it must take time and men and more men and countless sums of money and endless munitions. Any peace which can be made within a year or more would be one which would in no degree accomplish the purpose for which we entered the war.

"The Hun is an unspeakable beast. God save the world from his much vaunted efficiency. No man can deny his bravery, but all credit for that or for any other thing is taken away by his devilish designs and his inhuman conduct. The Prussian government must be completely crushed and the German people absolutely robbed of all power for future harm to mankind."

## FIGHTING MEN COULD BE RECRUITED FROM ALASKAN ABORIGINES

*Anchorage Weekly Times*, April 11, 1918

The Alaskan aborigine is one of the best and most patriotic citizens in existence, as regards his sublime faith in "Nesike Papa," the United States government, says the *Valdez Miner*. With no knowledge of the purpose for which his money is to be spent; with no knowledge of the race of men we are fighting; with no knowledge of the geographical location of the present world conflict we are fighting, he takes all for granted and [stands with] the best-blooded American in the territory.

The Alaskan native from Tenakee [Springs] to Cape Barrow has shown the most loyal and intense patriotism in helping the government in its present crisis. They have helped knit, held meetings, and talked over the war question pro and con, and then walked forward in a body subscribing their last dollar with a magnificent devotion to a cause they know nothing of...

A splendid organization of fighting men could be recruited among the Alaskan natives. Their patriotic work in giving their time and money to the government without reservation and without question entitles them to a more generous treatment. The Alaskan native has shown that he is behind the government heart and soul, and the war has demonstrated that the American patriot is of no particular race or color.

## THEY'RE OFF

*Anchorage Weekly Times*, March 21, 1918

Brave and true, willing to face the dangers of the battlefields of Europe in defense of their ideals of good government, sixty-one Anchorage boys today departed for the front to do their share in the greatest war of history.

Anchorage is proud of her boys. At the [train] station this morning they were bid God Speed by the greatest assemblage of people ever gathered in Anchorage. There was many a wet eye as the train carrying the pride and hope of Anchorage moved away from the station, but the boys leaving, filled with courage and hope, left with high heads and brave hearts.

The war is now brought home to Anchorage. We know what it means to send the best blood of our community to face the unknown dangers of a ruthless war, and it is up to this community to bear in mind the fact...that the boys on the front look for support, and taking pattern from the brave ones who left this morning [we should] exert every effort in our power to see that they will want for nothing which will tend to make their lot as safe and comfortable as possible.

## GODSPEED

*Alaska Citizen* (Fairbanks), July 2, 1918

Today the boys who have been selected to serve in the National Army leave town for Fort Gibbon. It is with mixed feelings that we see them go. We have a feeling of pride that this town can supply such a fine lot of young men. For we are proud of them. They are a credit to us all and we feel sure that they will continue to be a credit to the town from which they hail. Then we have a deep regret and a feeling of pity for ourselves, that we have to lose them, even if only for the time being. We are selfish creatures, you know, and we hate to see the flower of our youth go out and leave the town. They will leave a hole that will be hard to fill. Then our heart goes out to them as they start for the great unknown. It is hard to tell just what is ahead of them. They do not know; we do not know. All we can do is to give them our best wishes for the future, and make them feel that our hopes go with them, and that we will stand firmly behind them here at home.

## THE REASON FOR CENSORSHIP

*McCarthy Weekly News*, June 8, 1918

"Why must my boy's letter be censored? Why can't they let him tell me where he is and what he is doing? Surely a mother has a right to know such things. Besides, he is a loyal American and could be trusted."

It would be most unnatural if American parents did not feel that way. But they forget that in the end censorship is for the safety of the men themselves.

An American officer, and this is a true story, indiscreetly mentioned, in a letter home, the name of the French village where his regiment was billeted. This slipped by the censor and the letter was published in his local newspaper. Shortly afterward the Germans launched a particularly destructive raid against that town, which before had not been attacked. The officer was a loyal American, as were the old home-folks who innocently gave his letter to the loyal little newspaper. But good American lives were needlessly jeopardized.

Soldiers will die the victims of our carelessness before we fully learn this lesson, but we are learning fast.... Remember the German object is to kill. We must not help him. Indiscreet statements are too easily translated into terms of death for Americans soldiers—perhaps your boy.

## HERE AND THERE

*McCarthy Weekly News*, August 3, 1918

Another contingent of our boys left Thursday to join the ranks. What is worrying those who have not yet been accepted is the fear that the great adventure will be over before they can be in on it.

Not idly, nor in quest of experience are the boys making every effort to get across the water, but with singleness of purpose and the longing to be identified with everything that will help to exterminate that great monster which makes no secret of wanting the Earth.

McCarthy is now well represented overseas and also from Florida to [Alaska].

In the meantime we who are left behind must keep our end up. So many ways, so much to do. Are you carrying your share of the weight?

## KILLED IN ACTION

*Nenana Daily News*, August 28, 1918

Carter Koon, who is the first Nenanaite to be killed in action, was very widely known and popular in the North, and was much liked for his sterling qualities by all who knew him. He counted a great many friends among Nenanaites who greatly regret his end, while being proud to know at the same time that he gave up his life in the cause of humanity, justice and freedom.

## AGAINST SLACKERS

*Alaska Citizen* (Fairbanks), September 30, 1918

Whereas the Ruby District has supported the Government in the present war to the fullest extent; oversubscribing the Liberty loans; more than filling our quotas of the Red Cross subscription; filling our quotas in the Selective Draft and furnishing many volunteers,

And Whereas FRED NEILSON and THEODORE SVINDLUND, both [from neutral countries], but having previously declared their intentions to become citizens of this country, have availed themselves of their privilege to decline military service, when called in their regular turns,

And Whereas, such action of said Neilson and Svindlund is a blot upon the general reputation and patriotism of this community.

THEREFORE, BE IT RESOLVED, that this Loyal League hereby goes on record as follows:

That said Neilson and Svindlund are unpatriotic, undesirable residents of this community and territory, and that this league will use its every effort to lawfully clear this district of the presence of the aforesaid undesirables—and this league will use its best efforts to lawfully force the said Neilson and Svindlund from the community and cause them to lose all rights to exploit the natural resources of the public domain.

## Chapter 6: Aftermath

### WHY ARE PEOPLE LEAVING ALASKA?

*Record-Citizen* (Ruby), April 6, 1918

Report reached us the other day that 1,700 people on their way to the Outside from the interior of Alaska had registered their names at one of the Roadhouses between Fairbanks and the coast up to March 1st.

The question now arises: Why are Alaskans leaving the country? It is true that during the winter months the chances for work in Alaska are fewer than in the summer, and the report from the outside says there is plenty of work for everybody. However, late arrivals have another story to tell.

It is true that skilled mechanics are in demand, but unskilled labor has just as hard a time of it, as before the war. Another thing, the wages for common labor are not so high that they average up to the high cost of living. Furthermore, if a man is lucky enough to get a job he doesn't know how long it is going to last. He may lose it any time on account of material not arriving in time, or he may be called out on strike, and we know that one month on strike will take a year to make up. In communities where shipbuilding is going on and in munitions centers, there is demand for labor, but it is usually skilled labor that is required, and in most parts of the country there is a surplus of unskilled labor. A laboring man in Alaska is much better off than his brother on the outside. A workingman in Alaska makes in most instances, enough in summer time so that he can take it easy and live comfortably during the winter months, without that restless search for work of the workingman on the outside. All over the East and even in New York, so the arrivals from the outside tell us, is a surplus of unskilled labor. And letters from the outside tell us that most of the men leaving here last fall will be glad to get back in the spring. We advise everyone who intends to go outside looking for a job to think twice before going.

### BOUND FOR THE OUTSIDE

*Record-Citizen* (Ruby), July 27, 1918

[A] number of old time Rubyites are bound for the outside.... Ruby is certainly beginning to feel the effect of the war.... People are leaving on every boat and it begins to look like there won't be even a corporal's guard left here for the winter. Plenty of work outside with the prospect of high wages is the lure that is attracting Alaskans to the states. Of course the fact that every commodity has advanced in price, with the exception of gold, is having something to do with the exodus of the population from Interior Alaska.

## MANY WILL COME TO ALASKA

*Anchorage Weekly Times*, August 1, 1918

Many of our soldier boys now fighting the battle of freedom in the old world will come to Alaska, after a glorious victory shall have been gained over the Huns—and that won't take long now, according to the encouraging [news] from the fighting front. As the veterans of the Mexican war, after a restoration of peace settled in large numbers in California, Texas, Arizona, and other southwestern states, so will the veterans of the European war stampede to the last great frontier of the United States—Alaska. It is natural that they should do so.

Many of our soldier boys fighting "over there" are away from their home localities for the first time in their lives. They will be filled with a love for adventure; they will be filled with the spirit of conquest. Alaska will have no terrors for them now. After strenuous days on the firing line, they will be capable of "making good" anywhere. They will be especially adapted for the pioneer life in a new country. They will be seeking an opportunity to better their financial condition, and they will hope to find it in the only remaining undeveloped frontier country that is a possession of the United States—Alaska.

That this is not an idle dream or a vain vagary may be substantiated by a letter received by a local citizen from a "Sergeant from New York" in expressing thanks for receiving a liberal quantity of real American tobacco, the appreciated gift of the aforesaid citizen. That part of the missive that deals with the subject under discussion says: "We do not know much more about Alaska than we do about France, but there is a party of us coming to visit you at the close of the war." These boys will come, and they will remain. They will receive a hearty welcome, for they will make our best citizens. They will like Alaska, and they will like Alaskans.

## ALL PUBLIC PLACES ARE CLOSED

*Anchorage Weekly Times*, October 31, 1918

The local board of health has issued an order closing the public schools, theatres, pool halls, public resorts, churches, Sunday schools, etc. The Anchorage Council of Defense met at 2 o'clock this afternoon and passed a set of resolutions . . . calling upon all citizens to willingly obey the mandate of the board of health. Dances, parties and the like come under the ban, and those scheduled after tonight are cancelled. No violations of the board's orders will be tolerated. The order was made in the interest of the public and will be backed by a strong public sentiment. The epidemic of the [influenza] now prevailing is not in violent form, but it is the part of wisdom to prevent its spread as much as possible.

## A BIG JOB YET

*Alaska Citizen* (Fairbanks), November 18, 1918

There is quite apt to be the impression in the minds of people that, now that the war is practically over, the American soldiers in France and other parts of Europe will immediately return home. As a matter of fact this is not true for a number of reasons.

In the first place consider the number of soldiers in France alone. Remember how long it took to get them all there, shipping them at a tremendous rate across the sea. It will take as long at least to get them back, probably longer, because there will not be the pressing need for haste that there was when they were sent. Then there are considerable numbers of the Yankee doughboys in other parts of the world, in Italy, and in Siberia and Russia. In all the number reaches the magnificent total of over two million, two hundred thousand. The very strength of the fighting forces will stand in the way of a speedy return to their home stores.

Then there is the fact that is coming to light, as talk of peace becomes more and more rife, that there is a tremendous job yet remaining for Uncle Sam's soldier boys up to the time that peace is signed and afterwards. There will be a sort of wholesale policing needed to keep order until the countries that are now suffering from civil wars and revolutions become settled down to their life in the family of nations. . . .

America, the greatest and most successful of all nations of present time, will furnish the necessary force to keep the light of liberty and justice shinning all over the world. The United States is giving proof that she is worthy of the trust and faith of all nations, and it is this characteristic that is winning her the position of arbiter for all peoples and nations.

The war is over as far as fighting is concerned, but there is a big job still awaiting our soldiers and sailors before they will be able to return to civil life.

## HAPPY NEW YEAR

*Nenana Daily News*, December 31, 1918

The end of the year 1918 finds Nenana, at the tender age of thirty months, well established among the towns of Interior Alaska, and populated by prosperous and contented Alaskans whose number is increasing steadily and who have an abiding faith in the permanence and continued prosperity of the community. Nenana has a record of growth of which those responsible for it need not blush. It stands as a monument to the indomitable spirit of Nenanaites, who have built well and persistently, very often in the face of discouragements not frequently encountered in town building.

But those days of depression have ended with the war. The new year will dawn upon a new era for Nenana. With the restoration of peace has come the conviction that travel will start Alaskawards and that much of the capital earned during the war period will be released for investment in Northern properties, promising early development in all sections of the territory. . . .

The future of Nenana looks good to the *News* and we feel sure every resident of the town and every prospector in the adjacent hills shares our optimistic views. We welcome the new year full of confidence that it will not be long ere development of worthwhile proportions begins, fostered and encouraged by our government and stimulated by private activities.

## BRING MORE PEOPLE TO ALASKA

*McCarthy Weekly News*, January 11, 1919

It is now time to take up the cause of the many people who might be populating the vast expanse of unoccupied Alaskan Territory and enjoying the benefits of the untold resources of the country.

There should be great pleasure in re-awakening the good old pioneering instinct, which lay dormant during the period of the war.

When such a handful of people as we, who have such a territory as this, lose the craving to see it full of cities, farms, and factories, we are either aging too rapidly, or something has "got our goat."

APPENDIX II

# A Snapshot of Alaska in 1918

## *A Letter from Governor Strong*

*In early January 1918, Governor John Strong wrote a letter to a woman in Georgia. There is no evidence that the governor knew the woman. Given the many responsibilities that pressed on him, including the organization of the military draft, it is notable that the governor spent the time to write a letter of this length to a private citizen in a far-away state.*

*Governor Strong's letter presents an insider's overview of Alaska at the time of the First World War.*

January 4, 1918
Mrs. Irvin Sims
520 45th Street, East
Savannah, Georgia

Dear Madam:

I beg to acknowledge receipt of your letter of November 26, which I have deferred answering simply because of the pressure of official business.

Permit me to say that it affords me much pleasure to give you such information with regard to this Territory as it may be possible for me to do. In the first place, Alaska is not a state, but a territory, having been granted a territorial legislature by act of Congress in 1912. Its legislature is composed of two houses, the House of Representatives and the Senate, and consists of 24 members: 8 senators and 16 representatives. The Governor is appointed by the President and confirmed by the United States Senate. Alaska is represented in Congress by a delegate, who has a voice but no vote.

Both the Republican and Democratic parties are represented in Alaska, but there is a large independent vote, and I do not believe that either of the old parties has a majority, politics being controlled, as intimated, by independent vote.

Alaska was first given a delegate in Congress in 1906 and all the delegates have been elected on the Independent ticket except the present [Charles Sulzer], who ran on the Democratic ticket, but his election is being now contested [by James Wickersham] in the House of Representatives in Washington.

Alaska became "dry" on January 1 of this year, the matter of prohibiting the importation and sale of intoxicating liquors having been submitted to a referendum of the people in the election of November 1916, and the referendum having been carried by a heavy majority. So, since January 1, Alaska has been in the dry column, and this fact is considered remarkable in some states of the Union, because Alaska is a frontier country where, to quote Kipling, "No law of God or man runs north of fifty-three." Whether Kipling was right in respect to other countries north of fifty-three, I cannot say, but certainly, as far as Alaska is concerned, he was very much mistaken. Alaska is probably one of the best law-observing possessions of the United States.

We have churches of nearly every denomination in every town in Alaska; and this leads to the thought that the churches, in my opinion, might effect a consolidation [by merging] with great benefits to themselves and the communities in which they are established, thus relieving the economic pressure and accomplishing the same results in the service of God.

Alaska's quota for the National Army has not yet been completed, but [at this time] it is 696, and I have no doubt that when we are ready for the draft in Alaska, the enlistments will have been so many that no draft will be required. So much for the patriotic spirit of Alaska.

You refer [in your letter] to Sitka, and ask whether [the women] are knitting and working for the Red Cross. I assume that you associate Sitka in your mind as the capital of Alaska. In this, you are mistaken. Sitka was the ancient Russian capital of Alaska and it was the capital under American rule until 1906, when it was removed to Juneau. Yes, all the ladies, all over Alaska, in every town, hamlet and in every remote mining camp are doing their best to assist the Red Cross work; and besides the Red Cross, we have a patriotic league, with branches in the various towns, also doing splendid work. Among this work was the raising of money for the equipping of hospital beds at Neuilly, France for the care of Alaskan soldiers when wounded.

To reach Alaska, one must go by water, it being a sea voyage all the way to any Alaska port. The chief point of embarkation for Alaska is Seattle, and what is called the "Inside Passage" to Alaska is one of the grandest in the world, scenically and for safety, especially during the summer season.

We have three railroads operating in Alaska—one is called the White Pass, which runs from Skagway on the coast to White Horse, the head of navigation on the Yukon River; another the Copper River & Northwestern Railroad, with its coast terminus at Cordova. It penetrates the Copper River Valley for a distance of 196 miles to Chitina. This railroad handles the immense copper output of the Kennecott Copper Corporation at Kennecott. The third railroad is that now being constructed by the United States Government from Seward on the north Pacific coast to Fairbanks in the interior, a distance of approximately 400 miles. About 150 miles of this railroad has been completed and in operation.

Personally, I may say that I have been a resident of Alaska since 1897 and was appointed Governor in 1913. I was raised in New England, but I have lived on the Pacific coast for over 35 years, and I call myself a Westerner, having lived long enough and having come to the West early enough to absorb the spirit of what is sometimes called the "free and boundless West."[1]

Mail for Alaska is carried from Seattle and Tacoma by steamers, several steamship companies being engaged in the Alaska business, and during the summer-season southeastern Alaska has a steamer arrival practically every day and some days two or three. These steamers carry mail for all the coastal towns and the interior. During the summer, mail to interior points, such as Fairbanks, is carried by auto stage and distributed through the interior by the same means and by steamers which ply the different rivers, including the Yukon, one of the greatest rivers on the North American Continent. During the winter, mail to the interior is carried by both dog and horse teams, some of the mail routes being hundreds of miles in length. For instance, Nome in northwestern Alaska, on the Bering Sea, has a biweekly mail carried by horse teams to Fairbanks and thence by horse teams to Chitina, the interior terminus of the Copper River and Northwestern Railroad, and thence by rail to Cordova, from whence it reaches Seattle for distributing to its various destinations.

The people of Alaska subscribed about $1,250,000 to the second issue of the Liberty bonds, the city of Juneau having subscribed $330,000 alone.

Alaska has a splendid school system, from common schools to high schools. The Agricultural College and School of Mines, to be located at Fairbanks, was authorized by the last session of the legislature in 1917 and work will be begun on the buildings this year.[2]

The Holy Trinity Cathedral is the Episcopal Church in [Juneau], the dean being the Rev. G. D. Christias.

Not all the [religious] work in Alaska is done by Roman Catholics, although they maintain missions at various points. Missionary work is carried on by both the Episcopalians and Presbyterians, not only for the benefits of the whites, but for the Indians and Eskimos as well. Many of the Indians belong to the Russian-Greek Orthodox Church. Others are Roman Catholics, Presbyterian, Episcopalian, Baptist, and Quakers or Friends.

There has been a great exodus from Alaska since the beginning of the war, due to the demands for labor and the higher wages paid in many of the mining states and those which have yards which are building ships for the American merchant marine. As a consequence, Alaska's population in the past two years has decreased rather than increased.

As to agricultural possibilities, there are something like 100 farms in the Tanana Valley and as many more in the Matanuska Valley, on Cook Inlet, where the Government railroad is now being built. This railroad will tap the Matanuska coal fields, and another coal field now being developed, is called the Bering River coal field.

Alaska does not produce enough foodstuffs to support its population. The cultivation of potatoes and other vegetables is increasing each year, and it is possible that in time Alaska may produce wheat, rye and other cereals, but it is not strictly a farming country, although I believe it offers great possibilities for stock raising in a limited way.

I trust that I have answered your questions intelligently and with as much detail as possible. Under separate cover I am forwarding to your address a number of pamphlets containing further information about the Territory, prepared by the Alaska Publicity Bureau.

In conclusion, I may say that it affords me pleasure to have the opportunity of writing you this letter; and with best wishes for yourself, I am,

Cordially yours,

Governor Strong

# ENDNOTES

## Notes to the Preface

1. Steven C. Levi, *The Great Red Scare in World War One Alaska: Elite Panic, Government Hysteria, Suppression of Civil Liberties, Union-Breaking and Germanophobia* (Palo Alto, CA: Academica Press, 2010), 90.
2. The topic is very briefly raised in a letter from the Territorial Council of Defense in Ketchikan to Governor J. F. A. Strong, January 28, 1918; General Correspondence of Alaska Territorial Governors (GCATG), 1909–1958; file 99, roll 54; Alaska State Library, Juneau.
3. Levi, *The Great Red Scare in World War One Alaska*, 39.
4. Ibid., 38.
5. Ibid.
6. Katharine Carson Crittenden, *Get Mears! Frederick Mears: Builder of the Alaska Railroad* (Portland, OR: Binford & Mort, 2002), 134.
7. Finnegan to local boards, November 14, 1918; Files of the Alaska Territorial Governors (FATG); roll 42; Alaska State Library, Juneau.
8. Jeanette Paddock Nichols, *Alaska: A History of Its Administration, Exploitation, and Industrial Development during Its First Half Century under the Rule of the United States* (Cleveland: Arthur H. Clark Company, 1924), 407–8.
9. John Strong to Charles C. Murrah, March 28, 1918; FATG; roll 29.
10. John J. Underwood, *Alaska: An Empire in the Making* (New York: Dodd, Mead and Company, 1913), 343.
11. Ibid., 140.
12. Ibid., 209–10.
13. Albert P. Niblack, "Naval Defenses of the United States," unpublished manuscript, c. 1915; Alaska Railroad records, box 66, file 138.1; National Archives and Records Administration-Pacific-Alaska Region (NARA-PAR), Anchorage, Alaska.

## Notes to Chapter 1

1. Frank Foster to J. F. A. Strong, August 17, 1917; GCATG; file 99, roll 46.
2. Underwood, *Alaska*, 132.
3. Ibid., xi.
4. Strong to John G. Murphy, March 23, 1918; FATG; roll 29.
5. *Daily Alaskan* (Skagway), February 28, 1898, and May 4, 1899. Also see the *Skaguay* [*sic*] *News*, July 1, 1898.
6. *The Dyea Trail*, April 2, 1898.
7. *Teller News*, April 11, 1901; *Nome Gold Digger*, January 24, 1900.
8. Charlotte Cameron, A *Cheechako in Alaska and Yukon* (London: Frederick A. Stokes, Co., 1920), 160–61, 170.

9. Hudson Stuck, *The Alaskan Missions of the Episcopal Church* (New York: Domestic and Foreign Mission Society, 1920), 151.
10. *Cook Inlet Pioneer*, June 5, 1915.
11. *Seward Gateway* article reprinted in the *Daily Alaska Dispatch* (Juneau), August 24, 1915.
12. *Fort Worth Star-Telegram*, February 12, 1914; and "Keys to Alaska's Wealth," *Outlook* (June 7, 1913), 267–8.
13. Charles R. Tuttle, *Alaska: Its Meaning to the World* (Seattle: Franklin Shuey, 1914), 27.
14. Finnegan to Riggs, September 28, 1918; FATG; roll 42.
15. *Daily Alaskan* (Skagway), December 31, 1917.
16. *Forty-Ninth Star* (Anchorage), July 30, 1916.
17. Ibid., January 28, 1917.
18. For the case of Anchorage, see Preston Jones, *City for Empire: An Anchorage History, 1914–1941* (Fairbanks: University of Alaska Press, 2010), 80–83, 96–104, and 127–37.
19. T.C. Carlson to Helen Van Campen, April 17, 1917; Helen Van Campen Photo Album, University of Alaska Fairbanks archives.
20. *Alaska Citizen* (Fairbanks), January 15, 1917.
21. *Anchorage Weekly Times*, May 30, 1918.
22. Underwood, *Alaska*, 71, 72–4.
23. Strong to Frederick Bentley, October 25, 1917, and January 17, 1918; FATG; roll 29.
24. Strong to Ralph Young, March 19, 1918; FATG; roll 29.
25. Strong letter of recommendation, April 10, 1918; FATG; roll 29.
26. Strong to R.K. Ludy, November 6, 1917; FATG; roll 29.
27. Strong to Ella D. Carr, January 22, 1918; FATG; roll 29.
28. Strong to D.J. Waggoner, November 17, 1917; FATG; roll 29.
29. Lopp quoted in "Eskimos Help Red Cross," *Kansas City Star*, May 5, 1918.
30. Strong to Charles Ondonotk, February 19, 1918; FATG; roll 29.
31. Frank Waskey to Governor Riggs, October 18, 1918; GCATG; roll 54.
32. Helen Kreps, "The Eskimo of Alaska," *The Aurora* (Nome High School, 1915), 5–6.
33. *Daily Miner* (Ketchikan), November 4, 1907.
34. *Nome Nugget*, April 7, 1917.
35. *Nome Gold Digger*, February 7 and 28, 1900. Also see the *Nome News*, April 17, 1903.
36. Elizabeth Wood Albums, 1902–1914, box 2; Alaska and Polar Regions Archives, University of Alaska Fairbanks.
37. David Gove, "Educating the Alaska Natives," *Overland Monthly and Out West Magazine* (March 1917), 17.
38. *Nome Daily Gold Digger*, October 31, 1906.
39. Kreps, "Eskimo of Alaska," 5.
40. *Alaska Citizen* (Fairbanks), January 29, 1917.
41. The phrase is Donald Craig Mitchell's, *Sold American: The True Story of Alaska's Natives and Their Land*, 1867–1919 (Hanover, NH: University Press of New England, 1997), 101.
42. Underwood, *Alaska*, 302.
43. *Anchorage Weekly Times*, April 11, 1918.
44. Cameron, *Cheechako in Alaska and Yukon*, 163.
45. Ibid., 174.
46. *Daily Alaskan* (Skagway), July 6, 1917.
47. *Wrangell Sentinel*, April 26, 1917.

48. *Daily Alaska Dispatch*, August 22, 1915.
49. Strong to Ernest H. Cherrington, March 14, 1918; FATG; roll 29.
50. Strong to Arthur Shoup, December 14, 1917, and March 12, 1918; FATG; roll 29. Strong also referred to his political adversaries as Bolsheviks.
51. *Alaska Daily Empire* (Juneau), April 13, 1918.
52. James Wickersham diary, August 23, 1919; Alaska State Library, Juneau.
53. James Wickersham diary, August 24, 1919. For an overview of the episode, see Evangeline Atwood, *Frontier Politics: Alaska's James Wickersham* (Portland, OR: Binford and Mort, 1979), 325–9.
54. Olga McCullough vs. Fred D. McCullough, U.S. District Courts Alaska (Anchorage), Civil Case Files, 1915–1960, box 1, case no. A00023; NARA-PAR.
55. Cameron, *Cheechako in Alaska and Yukon*, 164.
56. *Daily Alaska Dispatch*, May 13, 1915.
57. Strong to S. B. Lockwood, March 23, 1918; FATG; roll 29.
58. Strong to Mrs. W. D. Moorhead, November 24, 1917; FATG; roll 29.
59. Strong to Jacob Otness, November 28, 1917.
60. *Anchorage Weekly Times*, November 15, 1917.
61. James Wickersham diary, July 9, 1917. In the original, the sentence ends with an exclamation point.
62. *Record-Citizen* (Ruby), April 21, 1917.
63. William B. Stephenson, *The Land of Tomorrow* (New York: George H. Doran Company, 1919), 205–6.
64. *Alaska Citizen* (Fairbanks), January 29, 1917.
65. Fernand du Journal to Governor Strong, November 3, 1917; GCATG; roll 47.
66. Agnes Rush Burr, *Alaska—Our Beautiful Northland of Opportunity* (Boston: Page Company, 1919), 388.
67. Joe Mitchell Chapple, "Discovering Alaska with President Harding," *McClure's Magazine* (October 1923), 16 and 22.
68. Cameron, *Cheechako in Alaska and Yukon*, 162.
69. *Alaska Citizen* (Fairbanks), January 29, 1917.
70. Underwood, *Alaska*, 309.
71. *Daily Alaska Dispatch* (Juneau), May 6, 1915.
72. *Ruby Record*, March 10, 1917.
73. Nome High School, *Aurora* (1915), 41.
74. Underwood, *Alaska*, ix; *Boston Alaskan*, December 1906.
75. Burr, *Alaska—Our Beautiful Northland of Opportunity*, 6–7.
76. *Daily Alaska Dispatch* (Juneau), August 22, 1915.
77. Ibid., August 24, 1915.
78. J. L. Hughes to Governor Strong, May 10, 1917; GCATG; roll 46.
79. James Willis to Governor Strong, July 28, 1917; GCATG; roll 47.
80. H. D. Reynolds to Governor Strong, June 21, 1917; GCATG; roll 54.
81. *Boston Alaskan*, August 1906.
82. *Alaska Evening Post* (Seward) January 8, 1917.
83. *Knik News*, March 6 and 27, 1915.
84. *Cook Inlet Pioneer*, June 26, 1915.
85. Federal Commissioners of Conciliation to Frederick Mears, May 2, 1916, "Labor-Wages" file, Records of the Alaska Railroad, Accession no. 322-69-0966, box 63; NARA-PAR.

86. Franklin K. Lane, "Freeing Alaska from Red-Tape," *North American Review* (June 1915), 892.
87. *Alaska Evening Post*, January 8, 1917.
88. *Boston Alaskan*, January 1907.
89. David Kennedy et al., *The American Pageant* (New York: Houghton Mifflin, 2002), 496.
90. Keith Wheeler, *The Alaskans* (Alexandria, VA: Time-Life Books, 1977), 56.
91. Sarah Palin, *Going Rogue: An American Life* (New York: HarperCollins, 2009), 12–13.
92. *Daily State Gazette* (Trenton, NJ), December 11, 1867.
93. New York newspapers quoted in Wheeler, *The Alaskans*, 56.
94. *Daily Evening Bulletin* (San Francisco), July 3, 1867.
95. *Flake's Bulletin* (Galveston, TX), December 8, 1867.
96. *Nome Nugget*, July 1, 1905.
97. Sam C. Dunham, *The Goldsmith of Nome* (Washington, DC: The Neale Publishing Co., 1901), 37.
98. *Alaska Evening Post*, January 8, 1917.
99. *Record-Citizen* (Ruby), July 28, 1917; March 8, 1918.
100. *Forty-Ninth Star* (Anchorage), July 30, 1916.

## Notes to Chapter 2

1. The most comprehensive study on the Alaska Purchase is N.N. Bolkhovitinov, *Russian-American Relations and the Sale of Alaska, 1834–1867* (Fairbanks: Limestone Press, 1996).
2. Charles Sumner, *The Cession of Russian America to the United States* (Washington, DC: Congressional Globe Office, 1867), 11–12.
3. *Evening Bulletin* (San Francisco), April 1, 1867.
4. Ibid.
5. The *Times* reproduced in ibid., May 17, 1867.
6. *Times-Picayune* (New Orleans), November 11, 1867.
7. Ibid., December 8, 1867.
8. Lester D. Henderson, *Report of the Commissioner of Education for the Years Ending June 30, 1918, June 30, 1919, and June 30, 1920* (Juneau: Juneau Daily Capital, 1920), 39.
9. Quoted in Mitchell, *Sold American*, 112–4.
10. Quoted in ibid., 156–7.
11. R.M. Johnston, "The Imperial Future of the United States," *Infantry Journal* x:3 (November–December), 314 and 317.
12. Tuttle, *Alaska*, 27.
13. Thomas Paine, *Rights of Man* and *Common Sense* (New York: Knopf, 1994), 269.
14. For an overview of these conflicts, see Max Boot, *Savage Wars of Peace: Small Wars and the Rise of American Power* (New York: Basic Books, 2002).
15. *Daily Alaska Dispatch* (Juneau), February 2, 1915.
16. Ibid., February 3, 1917.
17. Ibid., February 4, 1915.
18. *Daily Alaska Dispatch* (Juneau), June 4, 1914.
19. Ibid., July 21, 1915.
20. Ibid., June 4, 1915.
21. Ibid., July 21, 1915.
22. James Wickersham diary, February 2, 1917. Italics added.

23. The figures are given in Edmund Morris, *Colonel Roosevelt* (New York: Random House, 2010), 421.
24. Thomas White to Governor Strong, January 1, 1918; GCATG; file 99, roll 54.
25. *Daily Alaska Dispatch* (Juneau), June 4, 1915.
26. Ibid.
27. James Wickersham diary, March 19, 1917.
28. Ibid., February 4, 1915.
29. Ibid., May 12, 1915.
30. *Alaska Evening Post* (Seward), January 4, 1917.
31. James Wickersham diary, March 3 and April 16, 1917. Italics added.
32. Ibid., August 28, 1917. Emphasis in the original.
33. Ibid., March 10, 1917.
34. *Stop the War! Set the Example of Mutual Concessions!; Alaska Panhandle—Its Proposed Cession to Canada* (Washington, DC: Judd and Detweiler, 1915), 3–11.
35. Ibid., 70.
36. *Morning Oregonian*, May 9, 1914,
37. William B. Stephenson, *The Land of Tomorrow* (New York: George H. Doran Company, 1919), 213.
38. *Oregonian* (Portland), November 12, 1914. The figures on trade with the belligerent powers is taken from William Bruce Wheeler and Susan D. Becker, *Discovering the American Past*, vol. II (New York: Houghton Mifflin Company, 1998), 134.
39. Nome High School, *Aurora* (1915), 37
40. *Weekly Alaskan* (Anchorage), May 13, 1916.
41. *Forty-Ninth Star* (Anchorage), January 28, 1917.
42. *Cordova Daily World*, October 8, 1918.
43. *Record-Citizen* (Ruby), March 10, 1917.
44. E. S. Harrison, *Nome and Seward Peninsula*, quoted in Preston Jones, *Empire's Edge: American Society in Nome, Alaska, 1898–1934* (Fairbanks: University of Alaska Press, 2007), 20.
45. Woodrow Wilson, "Address to Congress on War with Germany," in *American Speeches: Political Oratory from Abraham Lincoln to Bill Clinton*, ed. Ted Widmer (New York: Library of America, 2006), 238–46.
46. *Ruby Record*, April 7, 1917. The year is incorrectly typed in the newspaper as 1916.
47. James Wickersham diary, August 30, 1917.
48. James Wickersham diary, July 24, 1918.
49. Governor Strong to President Wilson, April 5, 1917; GCATG; roll 47.

## Notes to Chapter 3

1. David Kennedy, *Over Here: The First World War and American Society* (New York: Oxford University Press, 1980), 74.
2. Ellis W. Hawley, *The Great War and the Search for a Modern Order* (New York: St. Martin's Press, 1992), 41.
3. George Brown Tindall and David Emory Shi, *America: A Narrative History* (New York: W. W. Norton & Co., 2010), 1002.
4. Arthur Link quoted by Hawley, *The Great War*, 24; and *Alaska Citizen* (Fairbanks), April 9, 1917.
5. James Wickersham diary, April 28, 1917.

6. Unaddressed letter from D. B. Lewkesbury, September 28, 1918; Alaska Railroad Records, box 66, file 138.1; NARA-PAR; Treasury Department to Governor Riggs, October 30, 1918; GCATG; file 99, roll 54.
7. *Daily Alaska Dispatch* (Juneau), February 2, 1915.
8. Ibid., May 6, 1915.
9. *Seward Gateway*, March 16, 1917.
10. *Alaska Citizen* (Fairbanks), April 2, 1917.
11. *Daily Alaskan* (Skagway), April 16, 1917.
12. Ibid., April 26, 1917.
13. *Record-Citizen* (Ruby), April 14, 1917.
14. *Daily Alaskan* (Skagway), July 20, 1917.
15. This summary is drawn from Hawley, *The Great War*, 18.
16. This summary draws on Kennedy, *Over Here*, 80.
17. *Daily Alaskan* (Skagway), September 14, 1917.
18. Ibid., April 4, 1917.
19. *Alaska Citizen* (Fairbanks), June 23, 1918.
20. William R. Hunt, *Distant Justice: Policing the Alaska Frontier* (Norman: University of Oklahoma Press, 1987), 224–5.
21. *Forty-Ninth Star* (Anchorage), November 12, 1916.
22. *Record-Citizen* (Ruby), March 28, 1918.
23. Ibid., April 6, 1918.
24. United States versus William N. C. Waddleton (June 1917); U.S. Commissioner's Court, Juneau, Alaska. Copy of the case records in the author's possession.
25. *Record-Citizen*, March 30, 1918.
26. Edward Bernays, *Propaganda* (New York: Ig Publishing, 2005 [orig. pub. 1928]), 9–11.
27. *Daily Alaskan* (Skagway), April 9, 1917.
28. *Record-Citizen* (Ruby), March 23, 1918.
29. *Nenana Daily News*, November 11, 1918.
30. *Daily Alaskan* (Skagway), February 13, 1918. Concerns about sinister German and Japanese agents were widespread and not completely without foundation. See Friedrich E. Schuler, *Secret Wars and Secret Policies in the Americas, 1842–1929* (Albuquerque: University of New Mexico Press, 2010).
31. See Governor Strong to B. B. Whitney, November 25, 1917; GCATG; roll 47.
32. Chris Peterson to Governor Strong, December 14, 1917; GCATG; roll 47.
33. *Daily Alaskan* (Skagway), July 8, 1918.
34. Ibid., February 16, 1918.
35. Ibid., April 14, 1917.
36. Levi, *The Great Red Scare in World War One Alaska*, 94 and 196.
37. John T. Hunt to Provost Marshal, April 27, 1918; FATG; roll 30.
38. Governor's office to Provost Marshal General, April 5, 1918; FATG; roll 31.
39. A memo on Britt noted that he had announced himself as a candidate for the state senate on the Democratic ticket. See Governor's office to Provost Marshal General, c. April 25, 1918; FATG; roll 30.
40. *Alaska Daily Empire* (Juneau), April 13, 1918.
41. Governor's office to Jacob Johnson, April 6, 1918; and Governor's office to A. M. Jones, April 18, 1918; FATG; roll 30.
42. Frank G. Carpenter, *Alaska: Our Northern Wonderland* (New York: Doubleday, Page and Co., 1925), 67.

43. Governor to James S. Truitt, April 13, 1918; FATG; roll 30; and Governor's office to Commanding Officer, Camp Lewis, June 11, 1918; FATG; roll 31.
44. Hunt to Crower, April 19, 1918; FATG; roll 30.
45. Hunt to Smiser, April 23, 1918; FATG; roll 30.
46. *Alaska Daily Empire*, April 27, 1918.
47. Levi, *The Great Red Scare in World War One Alaska*, 100.
48. *Alaska Daily Empire*, September 1, 1917.
49. *Duluth News-Tribune* (Minnesota), June 6, 1917.
50. *Nenana Daily News*, September 26, 1918.
51. *Anchorage Weekly News*, September 5, 1918.
52. *Daily Alaskan* (Skagway), October 26, 1917.
53. Ibid., September 20, 1917.
54. *Record-Citizen* (Ruby), April 14, 1917; *Alaska Citizen* (Fairbanks), April 9, 1917.
55. *Wrangell Sentinel*, April 12, 1917.
56. *Alaska Daily Empire* (Juneau), April 17, 1918.
57. Governor Strong to Territorial Council of Defense, Seward, January 31, 1918; GCATG; roll 54.
58. Frank Waskey to Governor Riggs, October 8, 1918; GCATG; roll 54.
59. *Daily Alaskan* (Skagway), July 18, 1918.
60. Anchorage criminal case files, 1902–1960 (no. 716-743), file no. 726; record group 21 (U.S. district courts), box 38; NARA-PAR.
61. Anchorage criminal case files, 1902–1960 (no. 716-743), file no. 725; record group 21 (U.S. district courts), box 38; NARA-PAR.
62. *Alaska Citizen* (Fairbanks), July 1, 1918.
63. *Anchorage Weekly Times*, October 24, 1918.
64. James Wickersham diary, October 19, 1918. The incident is described in the *Cordova Daily Herald*, October 9, 1918.
65. Governor's office to Jacob Johnson, February 19, 1918; FATG; roll 30.
66. Memo from U.S. Attorney Steve Ragan, June 1, 1918; GCATG; file 99, roll 54.
67. Strong to John W. Dunn, December 24, 1917; FATG; roll 30.
68. *Anchorage Weekly Times*, September 5, 1918.
69. Governor Strong to To Whom It May Concern, May 21, 1917; GCATG; roll 47.

## Notes to Chapter 4

1. John M. Tatum, "A Spell on the Yukon," *Coast Artillery Journal* (January–February 1937), 32.
2. Lyman Woodman, *Duty Station Northwest: The U.S. Army in Alaska and Canada*, vol. I (Anchorage: Alaska Historical Society, 1996), 307.
3. *Nome Gold Digger*, November 16, 1907.
4. Governor Strong to Newton B. Baker, June 12, 1916; FATG; roll 25.
5. Albert P. Niblack, "Naval Defenses of the United States," unpublished manuscript; Alaska Railroad records, box 66, file 138.1; NARA-PAR.
6. Quoted in Woodman, *Duty Station Northwest*, vol. I, 286.
7. Tatum, "Spell on the Yukon," 35.
8. James Wickersham diary, May 17, 1918.
9. *Daily Alaskan* (Skagway), April 21, 1917.
10. Ibid., April 23, 1917.
11. *Alaska Citizen* (Fairbanks), September 10, 1917.

12. *Anchorage Weekly Times*, October 3, 1917.
13. Carl J. Lomen diaries, May 1917; Alaska and Polar Regions Collections, University of Alaska Fairbanks.
14. Strong to Albert Smith, December 28, 1917; FATG; roll 30.
15. *Wrangell Sentinel*, April 12, 1917.
16. *Daily Alaskan* (Skagway), May 11, 1917.
17. James Wickersham diary, January 17, 1918.
18. Paul P. Kern to C. H. Cosgrove, January 26, 1918; GCATG; file 99, roll 54.
19. *Daily Alaskan* (Skagway), December 4, 1917.
20. Strong to Fred M. Brown, December 7, 1917; FATG; roll 30.
21. Memo from the Governor's office, January 16, 1918, FATG; roll 30.
22. Finnegan to Riggs, December 14, 1918; FATG; roll 42.
23. *Daily Alaskan* (Skagway), December 6, 1917.
24. *Alaska Citizen* (Fairbanks), April 9, 1917.
25. *Alaska Railroad Record*, May 7, 1918.
26. *Daily Alaskan* (Skagway), December 8, 1917.
27. Ibid., August 27, 1917.
28. *Record-Citizen* (Ruby), March 30, 1918.
29. *Anchorage Weekly Times*, October 3, 1917.
30. *Anchorage Weekly Times*, September 26, 1918.
31. *McCarthy Weekly News*, August 17, 1918.
32. Unsigned, unaddressed, undated memo; Alaska Railroad records, box 66, file 138.1; NARA-PAR.
33. *Aberdeen Daily News* (South Dakota), February 22, 1918.
34. C. G. McClure, letter to the editor, *McClure's Magazine* (August 1918), 36.
35. James Wickersham diary, April 6, 1918.
36. Ibid., April 25, 1918.
37. *Tri-Weekly Nome Industrial Worker*, May 4, 1918.
38. Candle Council of National Defense to Governor Riggs, date unavailable; GCATG; roll 54.
39. *Alaska Railroad Record*, April 9, 1918.
40. *Alaska Citizen* (Fairbanks), October 22, 1917.
41. *Anchorage Weekly Times*, August 22, 1918.
42. Mitchell, *Sold American*, 214. All Alaska Natives were granted citizenship in 1924.
43. *Nenana Daily News*, September 30, 1918.
44. *Daily Alaskan* (Skagway), November 28, 1917.
45. Ibid., August 1, 1917.
46. *Alaska Railroad Record*, November 27, 1917.
47. *Record-Citizen* (Ruby), June 22, 1918.
48. *Wrangell Sentinel*, January 2, 1918.
49. *Anchorage Weekly Times*, June 6, 1918.
50. *Daily Alaskan* (Skagway), August 27, 1917.
51. *McCarthy Weekly News*, November 10, 1917.
52. *Nenana Daily News*, September 26, 1918.
53. Cameron, *Cheechako in Alaska and Yukon*, 162.
54. Ibid, 163.
55. A copy of Adleman's Water-Front Pass is in the author's possession. The original is held by the Tongass Historical Museum, Ketchikan, Alaska.

56. James Wickersham diary, December 29, 1917.
57. Celia Malone Kingsbury, *For Home and Country: World War I Propaganda on the Home Front* (Lincoln: University of Nebraska Press, 2010), 34.
58. *Tri-Weekly Nome Industrial Worker,* July 11, 1918, 2.
59. Ibid., May 7, 1917.
60. *Alaska Citizen* (Fairbanks), April 9, 1917.
61. *Anchorage Weekly Times,* January 24, 1918.
62. *Tri-Weekly Nome Industrial Worker,* July 27, 1918, 2; and *Daily Alaskan,* February 13, 1918.
63. *Alaska Railroad Record,* January 15, 1918.
64. Ibid., April 30, 1918.
65. Ibid., March 12, 1918.
66. Ibid., April 23, 1918.
67. Ibid., June 25, 1918.
68. *Record-Citizen* (Ruby), March 30, 1918; *Alaska Railroad Record,* February 5, 1918; and Pearl James, ed., *Picture This: World War I Posters and Visual Culture* (Lincoln: University of Nebraska Press, 2009), 10.
69. *Alaska Railroad Record,* April 16, 1918.
70. Strong to A. G. Shoup, October 15, 1917; FATG; roll 29.
71. *Alaska Railroad Record,* July 9, 1918.
72. At the time of writing Kahiltna Birchworks in Palmer and the Alaska Birch Syrup Company in Talkeetna and Wasilla were active in this industry.
73. James, *Picture This,* 7.
74. Anchorage Territorial Council of Defense to Governor Strong, February 11, 1918; GCATG; roll 54.
75. *Alaska Railroad Record,* October 29, 1918.
76. Ibid., January 15, 1918.
77. Ibid., October 29, 1918.
78. *McCarthy Weekly News,* December 29, 1917.
79. *Alaska Railroad Record,* February 5, 1918
80. *Seward Gateway,* April 4, 1917.
81. *Daily Alaskan* (Skagway), September 21, 1917.
82. John A. Strong to Chief of Military Bureau, January 4, 1917; FATG; roll 29.
83. *Daily Alaskan* (Skagway), September 21, 1917.
84. Ibid., May 29, 1917.
85. Ibid., October 19, 1917.
86. *Record-Citizen* (Ruby), May 11, 1918.
87. *Daily Alaskan* (Skagway), July 16, 1918.
88. A short article in the *Grand Forks Herald* (North Dakota) reported that French children with rickets and tuberculosis were treated by American nurses at this hospital.
89. In the original Smith uses the traditional pronoun "he," but since she is referring to herself, I have changed the pronoun to the feminine.
90. There is no evidence that Germans targeted hospitals as a matter of practice or policy.

## Notes to Chapter 5

1. Strong to Thomas Riggs, April 11, 1918; FATG; roll 29.
2. Strong to A. G. Shoup, March 12, 1918; FATG; roll 29.

3. See correspondence from Governor Strong in 1917: August 16, 24, 30; October 23, 25, 27, 31; and November 10. In 1918: January 4 and 8; March 3; FATG; roll 29. On "All Hail America," see *Dallas Morning News*, July 7 and December 20, 1917.
4. Secretary to the Governor to Charles P. Sheffner, March 20, 1918; FATG; roll 29.
5. Unsigned, undated memo, GCATG; file 99, roll 54.
6. George Johnson to Adjutant General, August 16, 1917; Justrite Manufacturing Company to Adjutant General, June 28, 1917; and Smith Worthington Company to Adjutant General, May 15, 1917; GCATG; roll 46.
7. Edgar J. Banks to the Alaska Historical Museum, May 29, 1918; GCATG; roll 54.
8. William Pallister to Governor Strong, August 16, 1917; GCATG; roll 47.
9. Governor Strong to Secretary of War, September 11, 1917; GCATG; roll 47.
10. Strong to Henry Burson, Curtis Welch, and William Ramsay, December 7, 1917; FATG; roll 30.
11. Governor's office to Ernest Blue, June 12, 1918; FATG; roll 31.
12. Strong to Captain Wills, January 5, 1918; FATG; roll 30.
13. Hunt to Heilig, April 17, 1918; FATG; roll 30.
14. Levi, *The Great Red Scare in World War One Alaska*, 172.
15. Governor's office to J. W. Martin, July 29, 1918; FATG; roll 32.
16. Governor's office to Local Board No. 4, June 14, 1918; FATG; roll 31.
17. Governor's office to Commanding officer, Fort William H. Seward, July 29, 1918; FATG; roll 32.
18. Governor's office to Simmons, August 2, 1918; FATG.
19. Final List of Delinquents and Deserters, Cordova, March 1, 1919; and Final List of Delinquents and Deserters, Nenana, June 10, 1919; FATG, roll 42.
20. Leander James to Thomas Riggs, May 31, 1918; GCATG; file 99, roll 54.
21. *Alaska Railroad Record*, July 9, 1918.
22. The other quota figures given in the *Alaska Railroad Record* (May 14, 1918) were: Douglas, 20; Eagle, 2; Haines, 3; Iditarod, 13; Ketchikan, 83; McCarthy, 27; Nome, 26; Petersburg, 14; Ruby, 7; Seward, 51; Sitka, 16; Skagway, 9; Tanana, 4; Valdez, 31; and Wrangell, 10.
23. Strong to Rathbun, December 21, 1917; Governor's office to Henry Suzzallo, December 24, 1917; and Strong to Reames, January 11, 1918; FATG; roll 30.
24. Governor's office to Jacob Johnson, April 10, 1918; FATG; roll 30.
25. Governor's office to Commanding officer, Camp Lewis, July 31, 1918; and Governor's office to Commanding officer, Fort William H. Seward, undated; FATG; roll 32.
26. *Nenana Daily News*, August 29, 1918.
27. Governor's office to Commanding officer, Camp Lewis; FATG; roll 32.
28. Governor's office to D. W. Figgins, September 12, 1918; FATG; roll 32.
29. Governor's office to Local Board no. 6, June 11, 1918; FATG; roll 31.
30. Governor's office to Local Board No. 4, June 14, 1918; FATG; roll 31.
31. Governor's office to F. M. Boyle, August 19, 1918; FATG; roll 32.
32. Governor's office to Commanding officer, Fort Seward, April 25, 1919; FATG; roll 32.
33. A. A. "Scotty" Allan, *Gold, Men and Dogs* (New York: G. P. Putnam's Sons, 1931), 234, 238.
34. Ibid., 237.
35. *Duluth News-Tribune* (Minnesota), September 25, 1915.
36. *Daily Herald* (Biloxi, MS), October 13, 1915.

37. Esther Birdsall Darling, *Baldy of Nome* (Philadelphia: Penn Publishing Company, 1917), 300–1.
38. Allan, *Gold, Men and Dogs*, 267.
39. Reported in the *Kansas City Star* (Missouri), December 20, 1916.
40. U.S. Congressmen quoted in Archie Shiels, *The Purchase of Alaska* (College: University of Alaska Press, 1967), 180, 192.
41. *Daily Alaskan* (Skagway), May 23, 1917.
42. Ibid., February 26, 1918.
43. William Wood to Governor Strong, April 10, 1917; GCATG; file 99, roll 47.
44. Charles Fowler to Governor Strong, April 1, 1917; GCATG; roll 47.
45. *Anchorage Daily Times*, November 1, 1917.
46. Serbian National Defense Committee to Governor Strong, January 7, 1918; GCATG; roll 54.
47. James Wickersham diary, August 17, 1918.
48. Strong to Matheson, February 19, 1918; FATG; roll 30.
49. Governor's office to W. B Stout, July 5, 1918; FATG; roll 32.
50. Governor's office to J.W. Stoft, July 16, 1918; and Governor's office to All Local Boards, July 22, 1918; FATG; roll 32.
51. Governor's office to Arthur Lang, July 9, 1917; GCATG; roll 46.
52. Councilmen of Wrangell to Governor Strong, September 6, 1917; GCATG; roll 46.
53. Undated registration cards; GCATG; rolls 46 and 47..
54. Governor's office to Ernest Blue, February 20, 1918; FATG; roll 30.
55. Finnegan to A. H. Proctor, October 3, 1918; FATG; roll 42.
56. *Wrangell Sentinel*, October 17, 1918.
57. *Alaska Citizen* (Fairbanks), September 30, 1918.
58. Ibid., October 7, 1918.
59. Ibid., July 1, 1918.
60. *Cordova Daily Herald*, September 27 and 28, 1918.
61. Ibid., September 27, 1918.
62. *Alaska Citizen* (Fairbanks), October 7, 1918.
63. *Daily Alaskan* (Skagway), April 6, 1917.
64. Ibid., October 15, 1917.
65. James Wickersham diary, July 24 and August 18, 1918.
66. James Wickersham diary, January 24, 1918. The title Wickersham writes is simply *En Alaska*.
67. *Alaska Citizen* (Fairbanks), April 1, 1918.
68. *Nenana Daily News*, September 26, 1918.
69. Ibid., August 30, 1918.
70. *Alaska Citizen* (Fairbanks), September 30, 1918.
71. *Wrangell Sentinel*, May 16, 1918.
72. *Alaska Railroad Record*, July 2, 1918.
73. Ibid., January 2, 1919.
74. James Wickersham diary March 28 and 31, 1918. The author has slightly edited these entries.
75. James Wickersham diary, May 16, 1918.
76. *Alaska Railroad Record*, October 1, 1918.
77. Letter to the *Empire* excerpted in *Anchorage Weekly News*, June 6, 1918.
78. Department of Public Health to Governor Strong, January 8, 1918; GCATG; roll 54.

79. *Anchorage Weekly Times*, January 31, 1918
80. William C. Harvey and Eric T. Harvey, eds., *Letters from Verdun: Frontline Experiences of an American Volunteer in World War I France* (Philadelphia: Casemate, 2009), 54.
81. *Aberdeen Daily News* (South Dakota), August 29, 1914.
82. *Charlotte Observer* (North Carolina), August 29, 1914.
83. *Philadelphia Inquirer*, June 13, 1918; *Wilkes-Barre Times*, October 17, 1917.
84. *Miami Herald*, May 8, 1917.
85. *Cordova Daily Herald*, September 22, 1918.
86. Governor Riggs to Crowder, September 2, 1918; FATG; roll 42.
87. Finnegan to Shaw, October 3, 1918; FATG; roll 42. The surname is difficult to read; its correct spelling may be Wimpo.
88. *Daily Progressive Miner* (Ketchikan), September 27, 1918.
89. A letter from Beasley to the National Association for the Advancement of Colored People is cited in Alvin B. Tillery, *Between Homeland and Motherland: Africa, U.S. Foreign Policy, and Black Leadership in America* (Ithaca, NY: Cornell University Press, 2011), 52 and 172. Beasley's letter was sent in January 1921 from Ketchikan.
90. *Anchorage Weekly Times*, February 28 and July 11, 1918.
91. Strong, October 23, 1917; FATG; roll 29; and see *Fairbanks Daily News-Miner*, November 11, 1917.
92. *Anchorage Weekly Times*, April 11, 1918.
93. *Wrangell Sentinel*, April 12, 1917.
94. *Lexington Herald* (Kentucky), October 6, 1918.
95. *Anchorage Weekly Times*, February 28, 1918
96. *Daily Herald* (Biloxi, MS), August 7, 1917.
97. *Anchorage Weekly Times*, February 14, 1918.
98. Undated memo of the Executive Board of the Council of National Defense, Juneau; GCATG; roll 54..
99. John Stewart, "The Alaskan Home Front during World War I," unpublished manuscript (1984), 22. Manuscript provided to the author.
100. Minutes of the Alaska Council on National Defense, undated (circa August 19, 1918); GCATG; roll 54.
101. *Anchorage Weekly Times*, September 26, 1918.
102. James Wickersham diary, October 14, 1918.

## Notes to Chapter 6

1. *Nenana Daily News*, September 26, 1918.
2. *Wrangell Sentinel*, December 26, 1918.
3. *Nenana Daily News*, November 13, 1918.
4. William B. Stephenson, *The Land of Tomorrow* (New York: George H. Doran Company, 1919), ix.
5. *Alaska Evening Post* (Seward), January 13, 1917.
6. *Seward Gateway*, April 7, 1917.
7. *Times-Picayune* (New Orleans) reproduced in *Daily Herald* (Biloxi, MS), January 11, 1918.
8. Secretary to the governor to Captain McMahon, December 23, 1918; GCATG; file 99, roll 54.
9. Acting governor Davidson to Governor Riggs, December 27, 1918; GCATG; roll 54.

10. James Wickersham diary, December 31, 1918.
11. Ibid., December 17 and 26, 1918; January 30, 1919.
12. Ibid., December 21 and 30, 1918.
13. Ibid., May 23, 1919.
14. *Idaho Statesman*, January 22, 1918.
15. See Jones, *Empire's Edge*, 83–91.
16. *Wyoming State Tribune*, August 30, 1918.
17. Woodman, *Duty Station Northwest*, 15
18. *Nome Nugget*, 19 June 1920.
19. *Alaska Dispatch* (Skagway), June 25, 1920, 1.
20. Carl J. Lomen, *Fifty Years in Alaska* New (York: David McKay Co., 1954), 163–7.
21. *Nome Nugget*, 26 June 1920, 4.
22. Cameron, *Cheechako in Alaska and Yukon*, 5.
23. Ibid., 17, 19.
24. G.C. Martin et al., *Mineral Resources of Alaska: Report on Progress of Investigations in 1918* (Washington, DC: Government Printing Office, 1920), 1.
25. Theodore Chapin and George L. Harrington, *Mining in Fairbanks, Ruby, Hot Springs, and Tolstoi Districts, Alaska* (Washington, DC: Government Printing Office, 1919), 321.
26. Illegible name to Thomas Riggs, August 24, 1918; GCATG; roll 54.
27. G. Campbell, July 1, 1918; GCATG; roll 54.
28. Allan quoted in *Duluth News-Tribune* (Minnesota), November 30, 1918.
29. *Record-Citizen* (Ruby), July 20, 1918.
30. Ibid., July 27, 1918.
31. Ibid., August 3, 1918.
32. *Anchorage Weekly Times*, June 13, 1918.
33. "Labor Mass Meeting" (unsigned record of labor meeting at Labor Temple, Anchorage, August 7, 1918), "Wages," file, Records of the Alaska Railroad, accession no. 322-69-0966, box 68; NARA-PAR.
34. Illegible name to Governor Riggs, December 28, 1918; GCATG; roll 54.
35. *McCarthy Weekly News*, September 29, 1918.
36. *Alaska Citizen* (Fairbanks), July 1, 1918.
37. *Alaska Railroad Record*, October 1, 1918.
38. Ibid., January 5, 1920.
39. Ibid., April 8, 1918.
40. *Anchorage Weekly News*, November 23, 1918.
41. *Alaska Citizen* (Fairbanks), January 26, 1920.
42. Ibid., January 19, 1920.
43. Nichols, *Alaska*, 33.
44. Thomas Riggs, "Report of the Governor of Alaska," in *Reports of the Department of the Interior for the Fiscal Year Ended June 30, 1919*, vol. II (Washington, DC: Government Printing Office, 1920), 405.
45. Wilds P. Richardson, "Alaska," *Atlantic Monthly* (January 1928), 111 and 113.
46. *Alaska Citizen* (Fairbanks), January 12, 1920.
47. James Wickersham diary, October 29, 1918.
48. Ibid., November 12, 1918
49. Ibid., December 22, 1918.
50. Moa's letter is reproduced in the *Daily Progressive Miner* (Ketchikan), October 18, 1918.

51. *Nenana Daily News*, December 24, 1918.
52. Ibid., November 13, 1918.
53. *McCarthy Weekly News*, January 4, 1917.
54. Riggs, "Report," 407–9.
55. Nichols, *Alaska*, 409.
56. *Record-Citizen* (Ruby), July 14, 1917.
57. Ibid., August 25, 1917.
58. Strong to William H. Short, April 5, 1918; FATG; roll 29.
59. Thomas Riggs, unpublished manuscript; University of Alaska Fairbanks library; accession no. 16,715; unpaginated and undated.
60. Frank G. Carpenter, *Alaska, Our Northern Wonderland* (New York: Doubleday, Page & Co., 1925), 1, 2, and 65.
61. In Nichols, *Alaska*, 34.

## Notes to Appendix I

1. Adoption here refers to paying for the care of the orphan in France, not to making the orphan a literal son or daughter.

## Notes to Appendix II

1. Strong was born and raised in New Brunswick, Canada, and therefore was not a U.S. citizen. Discovery of this later in 1918 led President Wilson to remove Strong from office.
2. This was the future University of Alaska Fairbanks.

# BIBLIOGRAPHY


## Archival Sources

Alaska File of the Special Agents Division of the Department of the Treasury, publication number M802. National Archives and Records Administration, Pacific-Alaska Region, Anchorage (NARA-PAR).

Anchorage Criminal Case Files, 1902–1960, record group 21, box 38. NARA-PAR.

Anchorage school, *The Anchor* (1917). Anchorage Municipal Library.

Files of the Alaska Territorial Governors, 1917–1919; microfilm rolls 22, 29, 30–33, 40, 42; Alaska State Library, Juneau.

General Correspondence of the Alaska Territorial Governors, 1917–1918; microfilm rolls 46, 47, 54; Alaska State Library, Juneau.

Ron Inouye, interviewer and editor. "Alaska's Japanese Pioneers Research Project" (1991), unpublished manuscript, Archives and Special Collections, University of Alaska Anchorage.

Carl J. Lomen diary. Alaska and Polar Regions Collections, University of Alaska Fairbanks (APRC).

Niblack, Albert P. "Naval Defenses of the United States," unpublished manuscript (c. 1915). Alaska Railroad records, box 66, file 138.1 NARA-PAR.

Nome High School. *The Aurora* (1907, 1907, 1908, 1910, 1914). Carrie M. McClain Memorial Museum, Nome, Alaska.

Records of the Alaska Railroad, Accession no. 322-69-0966, boxes 63 and 68. NARA-PAR.

Records of the Selective Service System, record group 163. NARA-PAR.

Riggs, Thomas. "Autobiographical Memoir," manuscript. University of Alaska Fairbanks library, accession no. MSS 16, 715.

Helen Van Campen photo album. APRC.

Elizabeth Wood albums, 1902–1914, box 2. APRC.

Water-Front Pass for Stephen Adleman (1918). Held by Resurrection Bay Historical Society; copy in the author's possession.

James Wickersham Diary, 1917–1918. Alaska State Library.

## Alaska Newspapers

*Alaska Citizen* (Fairbanks)

*Alaska Daily Empire* (Juneau)

*Alaska Evening Post* (Seward)

*Alaska Labor News* (Anchorage)

*Alaska Railroad Record* (Anchorage)

*Anchorage Daily Times*
*Anchorage Weekly Times*
*Cook Inlet Pioneer*
*Daily Alaska Dispatch* (Juneau)
*Daily Alaskan* (Skagway)
*Daily Progressive Miner* (Ketchikan)
*Dyea Trail*
*Forty-Ninth Star* (Anchorage)
*McCarthy Weekly News*
*Nenana Daily News*
*Nome Gold Digger*
*Nome Industrial Worker*
*Nome News*
*Nome Nugget*
*Record-Citizen* (Ruby)
*Seward Gateway*
*Skaguay [sic] News*
*Teller News*
*Tri-Weekly Nome Industrial Worker*
*Weekly Alaskan* (Anchorage)
*Wrangell Sentinel*

## Outside Newspapers

*Aberdeen Daily News* (South Dakota)
*Boston Alaskan* (Boston)
*Charlotte Observer* (North Carolina)
*Daily Evening Bulletin* (San Francisco)
*Daily Herald* (Biloxi, Mississippi)
*Daily State Gazette* (Trenton, New Jersey)
*Duluth News-Tribune* (Minnesota)
*Flake's Bulletin* (Galveston, Texas)
*Fort Worth Star-Telegram*
*Grand Forks Herald* (North Dakota)
*Kansas City Star* (Missouri)
*Lexington Herald* (Kentucky)
*Miami Herald* (Florida)
*Morning Oregonian*
*Philadelphia Inquirer*
*San Jose Mercury News* (California)
*The Sun* (Baltimore)
*Times-Picayune* (New Orleans)
*Trenton Star Gazette* (New Jersey)
*Wilkes-Barre Times* (Pennsylvania)

## Primary Sources

"A United World," *Outlook* (July 27, 1912): 684–5.

"Alaska Railway Problem," *Outlook* (January 20, 1912): 114.

"Alaska's Resources Neglected," *The Independent* (August 21, 1913): 425.

Allan, A. A. *Gold, Men and Dogs*. New York: G. P. Putnam's Sons, 1931.

Austin, Harry Albert. "The United States Unprepared for War," *Forum* (April 1914): 526–34.

Burr, Agnes Rush. *Alaska—Our Beautiful Northland of Opportunity*. Boston: Page Company, 1919.

Cameron, Charlotte. *A Cheechako in Alaska and Yukon*. London: Frederick A. Stokes, Co., 1920.

Chapple, Joe Mitchell. "Discovering Alaska with President Harding," *McClure's Magazine* (October 1923): 8.

Carpenter, Frank G. *Alaska, Our Northern Wonderland*. New York: Doubleday, Page and Co., 1925.

Chapin, Theodore, and George L. Harrington. *Mining in Fairbanks, Ruby, Hot Springs, and Tolstoi Districts, Alaska*. Washington, DC: Government Printing Office, 1919.

Darling, Esther Birdsall. *Baldy of Nome*. Philadelphia: Penn Publishing Company, 1917.

"Developing the Nation's Treasure House in Alaska," *Current Opinion* (February 1914): 95–6.

Dunham, Sam C. *The Goldsmith of Nome*. Washington, DC: The Neale Publishing Co., 1901.

Gove, David. "Educating the Alaska Natives," *Overland Monthly and Out West Magazine* (March 1917): 9–17.

Henderson, Lester D. *Report of the Commissioner of Education for the Years Ending June 30, 1918, June 30, 1919 and June 30, 1920*. Juneau: Juneau Daily Capital, 1920.

Hill, Grace A. "Along the Alaska Coast," *Overland Monthly and Out West Magazine* (September 1917): 6–17.

Johnston, R. M. "The Imperial Future of the United States," *Infantry Journal* (Nov.–Dec. 1913): 311–17.

"Keys to Alaska's Wealth," *Outlook* (June 7, 1913): 267–8.

Lacouture, Onésime. *Mon sejour en Alaska, 1910–1913*. Quebec: n.p., 1978.

Lane, Franklin K. "Freeing Alaska from Red-Tape," *North American Review* (June 1915): 841–52.

Lautaret, Ronald, ed. *Alaskan Historical Documents since 1867*. Jefferson, NC: Mcfarland & Company, 1989.

Lomen, Carl J. *Fifty Years in Alaska*. New York: David McKay Co., 1954.

Madsen, Charles. *Arctic Trader*. New York: Dodd, Mead and Co., 1957.

Martin, G. C., et al., *Mineral Resources of Alaska: Report on Progress of Investigations in 1918*. Washington, DC: Government Printing Office, 1920.

Martin, Louise Anita. *North to Nome*. Chicago: Albert Whitman Co., 1939.

Nichols, Jeanette Paddock. *Alaska: A History of Its Administration, Exploitation, and Industrial Development during Its First Half Century under the Rule of the United States.* Cleveland: Arthur H. Clark Company, 1924.

Redfield, William C. "Rebuilding Our Foreign Trade," *Forum* (January 1919): 35–43.

Reed, Irving McKenny. *Boyhood in the Nome Gold Camp.* College, AK: Mineral Industry Research Laboratory, 1969.

Richardson, Wilds P. "Alaska," *Atlantic Monthly* (January 1928): 111–20.

Riggs, Thomas. "Report of the Governor of Alaska." In *Reports of the Department of the Interior for the Fiscal Year Ended June 30, 1919*, vol. II. Washington, DC: Government Printing Office, 1920.

"Self-Government for Alaska," *Outlook* (June 15, 1912): 320–1.

Stephenson, William B. *The Land of Tomorrow.* New York: George H. Doran Company, 1919.

*Stop the War! Set the Example of Mutual Concessions!; Alaska Panhandle—Its Proposed Cession to Canada.* Washington, DC: Judd and Detweiler, 1915.

Stuck, Hudson. *The Alaskan Missions of the Episcopal Church.* New York: Domestic and Foreign Mission Society, 1920.

Sumner, Charles. *The Cession of Russian America to the United States.* Washington, DC: Congressional Globe Office, 1867.

Tarr, Ralph S. "The Alaskan Problem," *North American Review* (January 1912): 40–56.

Tatum, John M. "A Spell on the Yukon," *Coast Artillery Journal* (January–February 1937): 32–5.

Tuttle, Charles R. *Alaska: Its Meaning to the World.* Seattle: Franklin Shuey & Co., 1914.

Underwood, John J. *Alaska: An Empire in the Making.* New York: Dodd, Mead and Company, 1913.

Weems, Carrington. "Government Railroads in Alaska," *The North American Review* (April 1914): 573–84.

Wickersham, James. *Old Yukon: Tales-Trails-and Trials.* Washington, DC: Washington Law Book Company, 1938.

Wilford, C. G. Letter to the editor, *McClure's Magazine* 50, no. 10 (August 1918): 36.

Wilson, Woodrow. "Address to Congress on war with Germany." In *American Speeches: Political Oratory from Abraham Lincoln to Bill Clinton*, ed. Ted Widmer. New York: Library of America, 2006.

## Secondary Sources

Atwood, Evangeline. *Anchorage: All-American City.* Portland, OR: Binford and Mort, 1957.

——. *Frontier Politics: Alaska's James Wickersham.* Portland, OR: Binford and Mort, 1979.

Axel, Alan. *Selling the Great War: The Making of American Propaganda.* New York: Palgrave, 2007.

Bernays, Edward. *Propaganda.* New York: Ig Publishing, 2005. First published 1928.

Bolkhovitinov, N. N. *Russian-American Relations and the Sale of Alaska, 1834–1867.* Fairbanks: Limestone Press, 1996.
Boot, Max. *Savage Wars of Peace: Small Wars and the Rise of American Power.* New York: Basic Books, 2002.
Borneman, Walter R. *Alaska: Saga of a Bold Land.* New York: HarperCollins, 2003.
Crittenden, Katherine Carson. *Get Mears! Frederick Mears: Builder of the Alaska Railroad.* Portland, OR: Binford and Mort, 2002.
Gavin, Letty. *American Women in World War I: They Also Served.* Niwot: University of Colorado Press, 1997.
Grayzel, Susan R. *Women and the First World War.* New York: Longman, 2002.
Harvey, William C., and Eric T. Harvey, eds. *Letters from Verdun: Frontline Experiences of an American Volunteer in World War I France.* Philadelphia: Casemate, 2009.
Hawley, Ellis W. *The Great War and the Search for a Modern Order.* New York: St. Martin's Press, 1992.
Hayman, Neil M. *Daily Life during World War I.* Westport, CT: Greenwood Press, 2002.
Horne, John, and Alan Kramer. *German Atrocities, 1914: A History of Denial.* New Haven: Yale University Press, 2001.
Hunt, William R. *Distant Justice: Policing the Alaska Frontier.* Norman: University of Oklahoma Press, 1987.
James, Pearl, ed. *Picture This: World War I Posters and Visual Culture.* Lincoln: University of Nebraska Press, 2009.
Jones, Preston. *City for Empire: An Anchorage History, 1914–1941.* Fairbanks: University of Alaska Press, 2010.
——. "Loyalty and Civic Culture on the Farthest Frontier: Anchorage and the Great War, 1917–1919," *Alaska History* 25, no. 1 (Spring 2010): 23–37.
——. "Struggle" and "War." In *Empire's Edge: American Society in Nome, Alaska, 1898–1934.* Fairbanks: University of Alaska Press, 2007.
——. "Yankees in Parkas: Native Influence at Nome, 1900–1920," *Alaska History* 20, no. 2 (Fall 2005): 43–58.
Kennedy, David. *Over Here: The First World War and American Society.* New York: Oxford University Press, 1980.
——., et al., *The American Pageant.* New York: Houghton Mifflin, 2002.
Kingsbury, Celia Malone. *For Home and Country: World War I Propaganda on the Home Front.* Lincoln: University of Nebraska Press, 2010.
Krug, John W., and Caryl Sale Krug. *One Dog Short: The Odyssey and Collection of a Family in Alaska during the Gold Rush.* Juneau: Alaska Department of Education, 1998.
Lasswell, Harold D. *Propaganda Technique in World War I.* Cambridge, MA: MIT Press, 1927.
Levi, Stephen C. *The Great Red Scare in World War One Alaska: Elite Panic, Government Hysteria, Suppression of Civil Liberties, Union-Breaking and Germanophobia.* Palo Alto, CA: Academica Press, 2010.

Mitchell, Donald Craig. *Sold American: The True Story of Alaska's Natives and Their Land, 1867–1919.* Hanover, NH: University Press of New England, 1997.
Morris, Edmund. *Colonel Roosevelt.* New York: Random House, 2010.
Ponsonby, Arthur. *Falsehood in War-Time.* New York: E.P. Dutton, 1928.
Shiels, Archie. *The Purchase of Alaska.* College: University of Alaska Press, 1967.
Stewart, John. "The Alaskan Home Front during World War I." Unpublished manuscript, 1984.
Studley. George M. *History of the 31st Railway Engineer of the* A.E.F. Berkeley, CA: n.p., 1941.
Tindall, George Brown, and David Emory Shi. *America: A Narrative History.* New York: W.W. Norton & Co., 2010.
Westwood, John. "Railways in the First World War." In *Railways at War.* San Diego: Howell North Books, 1980.
Wheeler, Keith. *The Alaskans.* Alexandria, VA: Time-Life Books, 1977.
Woodman, Lyman L. *Duty Station Northwest: The U.S. Army in Alaska and Canada,* vols. I and II. Anchorage: Alaska Historical Society, 1996.
Zeiger, Susan. "Mobilizing Women for War." In *In Uncle Sam's Service: Women Workers with the American Expeditionary Force, 1917–1919.* Ithaca, NY: Cornell University Press, 1999.

# INDEX


active duty
  Canadians in, 95–97
  casualties, 111–113, *114–115f*, 116, *117–118f*, 119–120
  discharges, 124, 126, 136, 160
  dogs role in, 95, 153–154
  draft registration, 92–95
  France
    letters from, 25, 43–44, 59–62, 85–90, 121–122
    photos from, *26f*, *60–62f*, *114–115f*
  governor's role, 91–95
  military service
    Africans and African Americans, 108–111
    men, 97–107
    women, 111–116
  political cartoons, *98f*, *99f*
  send-offs, 102, 155–157
Ade, George, 83
Adelman, Stephen, 78
adoption of orphans, 181n1(App1)
Africans/African Americans on active duty, 108–109, *110f*
aftermath
  economic downturn, 127–132, 137
  influenza (1918), 134–135
  military discharges, 124, 126, 136, 160
  post-war mood, 132–134
  Siberia, turmoil in, 126–127
  victory, 123–124, *125f*
  World War II foreshadowed, 136–137
Agricultural College and School of Mines, x, 166, 181n2(App2)
Alaska
  agriculture in, 166
  border dispute, 30, 96
  as empire/territory, xiii–xiv
  opportunities in, 139–140, 142
  Outside compared with, 1–2
  population decline, xii–xiii, 128, 166
  snapshot (1918), 163–166
  statehood, 1, 23, 140
  strategic location of, 27–28
  vulnerability of, 63–66, 148–149
Alaska: An Empire in the Making, 124
Alaska Birch Syrup Company, 176n72
*Alaska Citizen. See under* Fairbanks
Alaska Council of Defense, 76, 77
Alaska Council of National Defense, 119
*Alaska Daily Empire. See under* Juneau
*Alaska Daily Mail*, 52
Alaska Engineering Commission
  Armenian and Syrian Relief Fund, 70–71
  food conservation by, 81–82
  hospital beds, *70f*
  naval base proposal, 65
  property, guarding, 63
  Red Cross donations, 75
  women at, 116
  workforce decline, 127–128
*Alaska Evening Post. See under* Seward
"Alaska for Alaskans," 23, *24f*
*Alaska: Its Meaning to the World* (Tuttle), 4
*Alaska Labor News*, as English-only publication, 55
Alaska Loyal League, 76

Alaska Native Brotherhood, 8, 10, 100
Alaska Natives. *See* Natives
Alaska Pacific Herring Company, draft exemptions for, 94
Alaska Panhandle cession proposal, 36–37
Alaska Publicity Bureau, *130f*, 131
Alaska purchase
  arguments in favor of, 96
  support for, 21–22, 27–28
  in U.S. global presence, 31
Alaska Railroad, ix, xii, 3–4, 139–140, 165
*Alaska Railroad Record*
  on AEC workforce decline, 127–128
  on food bases, 80
  letter from France, 43
  on restaurant food conservation, 81
  on transient workers' draft registration, 93
Alaska Women's Patriotic League, 76
Alaska–British Columbia boundary dispute, 30, 96
Alaskans
  cultural setting of, 12–15
  distinctness of, 18–19
  educational level of, 15–18
  government role for, 19–23
  immigrants. *See* immigrants
  Natives. *See* Natives
  outlook of, 1–4, 6–7, *24f*
  war casualties, 111–113, *114–115f*, 116, *117–118f*, 119–120
*Alaska—Our Beautiful Northland of Opportunity* (Burr), 142
Albrecht, H.W.L., 58
Aleutian chain naval base proposal, 65
*Algonquin* (American), sinking of, 35
All-Alaska Sweepstakes dogsled race, cancellation of, 128
Allan, Scotty, 95, 128
Allen, Coe, 25
allied nations military, Americans serving with, 93
ambulance dogs, 153–154
*America as a World Power* (Latané), 30
American merchant ships, sinking of, 33
American Revolution, 83
Anchorage
  *Anchorage Weekly Times*
    on Alaska attractions, 159
    on anarchists, *133f*
    on battlefront nursing, 113, *114–115f*, 116
    on French war orphans, 152
    on German extermination as justifiable, 58
    on German surrender, 55
    on influenza quarantine, 159–160
    letter from France, 25
    on Natives, 100, 102, 141–142, 154–155
    on send-offs, 155
    on war dogs, 153–154
  bootlegging in, 13
  education in, 18
  founding of, ix, xii, 3–4
  government role in, 19–20
  Home Guards, 91
  inductees, *103f*
  *Knik News*, 19–20
  Rifle Company, 91
  Socialism in, 48
  *Weekly Alaskan*, 38
Anchorage's Fatherless Children of France Fund, 70
Anchorage's Woman Patriotic League, 69
Anderson, Olgat, 102
Anderson, Oscar, 53
anti-Canadian feeling, 96
Anti-Saloon League, 91
anti-sedition laws, 47–48, 49
*Arabic* (British ship), sinking of, 34
Arctic Brotherhood, contributions of, 66
arms sales. *See* defense industry
army presence, skeletal, 63–66
Army Signal Corps, 63–64
arts and crafts, Native, 141
Ashley, Burnett, recommendation for, 91–92
Austria-Hungary, U.S. declaration of war on, x

Austrian-Hungarian immigrants
fishing restrictions, 58
number of, 55–56
proclamation on, 148
scrutiny of, 6, 51

bakeries, food conservation, 80
Balls, A. G., 119
Banks, Edgar, Babylonian tablet sales, 92
Beasley, Charles, 111
"bellicose psychosis," 32
Benedictus XV, peace communication, 36
Bennett, Mrs. L. G., 96–97
birch sap syrup, 81, 176n72
birds, legal protection change proposals, 92
Bland, Corbett, 126
Blee, Robert, 119
Blue, Ernest, 93
Bogan, James, 124
Bolsheviks
Alaskans' battle with, 126
revolution, 49
Strong's political adversaries as, 169n50
"Bone Dry" Law. *See* prohibition laws
bootlegging, 13
Bopp, Franz, 54
Brady, John, 30, 96
*Bray Head* (British), sinking of, 35
Britain
North American holdings, 28
Russia vs., 27
U.S. and, 37, 96
Britt, William
as Democratic legislative candidate, 173n39
media defense of, 56
as vice consul for Norway, 51–53
Brooks, Alfred H., 104
Brotherson, Fred, 102
build-up to war
inevitability of, 33–36
Natives, 29–30
noninvolvement sentiment, 31, 36
peace proposals, 36–37
preceding wars/conflict, 30–32
territorial expansion, 27–28
war entry, 37–42
Burr, Agnes Rush
*Alaska—Our Beautiful Northland of Opportunity*, 142
Bylund, Albert, 102

Cameron, Charlotte
on Alaska, 127
on Alaskans' literacy, 17
*A Cheechako in Alaska and Yukon* (1920), 142–143
on crime-free setting, 14
on Fairbanks, 3
on Nenana, 12
Canada
boundary dispute, 30, 96
Panhandle cession, support for, 37
Canadian forces, 93, 95–97
Carpenter, Frank, 137
Case, Kenneth, 120
Case, T. J., 106
casualties, 111–113, *114–115f*, 116, *117–118f*, 119–120
Caswell, Mrs. W. H., 85

censorship
of letters home, 106, 107, 156
of newspapers, 46–47, 52
*A Cheechako in Alaska and Yukon* (Cameron), 142–143
Cherrington, Ernest, 12
children at play, integration of, 10
*Chitina Leader*, letter from France, 121
Christensen, Andrew, 106
Christian Science, patriotism and, 152
Christias, G. D., 166
churches, war views of, 67
citizenship
cancellation of, 147
denial of, 73
draft registration and, 102, 157
Natives and, 100

civil liberties of Natives, 29
Civil War, 83, 109
clergy, war views of, 67
coal
  access challenges, xii
  local use of, 82
  opportunities with, 139–140
  post-war production, 127–128
  as potential enemy target, 66
  sources of, 166
coastline vulnerability, 148–149
cod fishing, 28
collaboration, U.S./Canada, 96
Collier, Richard, 67
colonial forces, 108–109, *110f*
commercial sector war benefits, 42, 46–47, 145
Commissioner of Education, Report, 152–153
Committee on Public Information (CPI), 47
communist revolution in Russia, 126
community, sense of, 46
conformity of public outlook/opinion, 49–51, 136
conscription. *See* draft
constitutionally protected free speech, 46–47, 50
convictions for sedition, 48, 57
*Cook Inlet Pioneer*, 20
Cooney Hotel, 3, *6f*
Copper River & Northwestern Railroad, 165
*Cordova Daily Herald*
  letters from France, 59, 85
  on send-offs, 102
CPI (Committee on Public Information), 47
Cratts, Jacob, 55
Crimean War as driver for Alaska purchase, 27

*Daily Alaska Dispatch*. *See under* Juneau
*Daily Alaskan*. *See under* Skagway
*Daily Herald*. See *Cordova Daily Herald*
Darling, C.E., 37–38
Davis, Cedric, recommendation for, 91–92
de Journal, Robert, recommendation for, 91–92
deeds
  vulnerability and, 63–66
  service contributions, 66–71
  Liberty Bonds, 71–73
  Red Cross, 74–76
  additional donations, 76–78
  resource conservation, 78–82
  summary, 82–84
defense industry
  fatalities, 51
  profits, 33, 143
  U.S. noncombat ships for transport, 33
de-Germanization, case for, 54–55
Del Piero, Grachino, 95
delinquencies, draft registration and, 94–95
DeLong, Walter, 131
DeVane, Thomas, 15
development, government role in, 19–23
diet, xiii, 79, 141
disloyalty as grounds for termination, 151–152
Diven, Lucille, 123
Divin, Robert, 12
divorces, 14
Dobrovolsky, Peter, *101f*
dock access requirements, 78
dogs on active duty, 95, 153–154
Douglas, public schools in, 29
draft
  Alaska as leading in, xii
  evasion, 52–53
  quotas, 94, 97, 164
  registration, 5, 67, 68, 92–95
  Selective Service Law, 45, 52
Dunham, Sam C., 22
Dyea, aspirations for, 3

Eagles Club contributions, 66
Eastman, H.B., 96, 106
economic downturn, post-war, xii–xiii, 127–132, 158–159

economic reasons, draft exemptions for, 94
Eddystone munitions plant explosion, 51
Edmund, Carl, 102
education
of Alaskans, ix, 15–18, 142–143, 166
loyalty pledges and, 152–153
of Natives, 8–9, 10, 29
eight-hour workday
creating, ix
suspending, 129
Einnes, Conrad Mauritz Olson, 147
Elks Club
contributions of, 66
German language ban, 55
Emergency Italian Refugees Committee, 70
emergency preparedness, 149
enemy nations, immigrants from, 6
English-only sentiment, 55
enlistments for military service, 150
Episcopal Mission schools matron, age-difference marriage, 99
Eska War Relief Club, 75
Espionage Act (1917)
about, 47–48
Britt's "violation" of, 52
convictions under, 57
essential industries, draft exemptions for, 94
ethnic/racial interaction, 5–6

Fairbanks
about, 142–143
*Alaska Citizen*
on abnormality of war era, 45
on Alaska merits, 66, 139–140
on draft evaders, 157
on German Americans, 56, 146
on immigration, 133–134, 146
on military discharges, 160
publication policy changes, 46
on send-offs, 102, 155–156
on war burdens, 2
German flag removal, 146
inductees, *103f*
railroad connections, 3
*Falaba* (British ship), sinking of, 34
Falk, William, 93
*Falsehood in War-Time*, 136
farming, 166
Faulkner, H. L., 93
Fawcett, George, 120
Filbin, J. J.
death of, 50
reader response to, 46–47
on U.S. policy inconsistencies, 42
on war entry, 41
"fires of patriotism," 49, 58
First Amendments rights, 46–47, 50
Fisher, Irving, 37
fishing licenses/limitations, 58, 78
*Flake's Bulletin* (Galveston), on Alaska's resources, 22
Flower, J. H., 106
Flynn, E. H., 83
food conservation, 68–69, 78–80
foreign languages, antipathy toward, 55
Fort Davis, postwar closing of, 127
forts as war departure points, 104
*Forty-Ninth Star* (Valdez), 38
Foster, Frank, 2
Fraisure, Roy, 39
France
colonial forces, 108–109, *110f*
hospital at Corbeil, 85, 176n88
lifestyle, 108
U.S. and, 84
war orphans, 152
*See also* active duty
free speech, 46–47, 50
freight transport, sled dogs and, 95
French, L. F., 107, 153
fur trade decline, 37–38

Galvin, Thomas, 123
Garner, James, 25
Garvey, Marcus, 111
George, Walker, 93
George Thomas Library, closing of, 128
Gerig, William, 80, 82

German agents, concerns about, 173n30
German Americans, 54–58, 146
German Kaiser, as Beast, 149
Germany
  hospitals as targets, 88, 176n90
  invasion threat, 63
  Mexico, alliance offer to, x, 38–39
  passenger ship warning notices, 34, 35
  racial prejudice in, 109, 111
  U.S. break with, 33
  U.S. declaration of war on, x
Gilbertson, Sigurd, 106
global presence, U.S., 31
gold, 28, 129
*Gold Digger* (Nome), 10
Good, Dr., 48–49
governance, Native, 142
government
  overview, ix, 163–164
  criticism of, 46, 50
  role of, 19–23
  war controls, 78
Graham, Mrs. R., 149
Grand Forks Herald (North Dakota), on French hospital at Corbeil, 176n90
Green, Richard, 93
Griffith, George, 55
Grigg, W. H., 97
*Gulflight* (American ship), damage to, 34

hair donations, 71
Halvorsen, Magnus, draft exemptions for, 94
Hatch, Nick, 100
Hatcher, Cornelia, 13
Hawkesworth, Charles, 100
Hayakawa, Soichi, 93
Henderson, Lester, 29
Henry, G. Hinton, 57
Henry, Jack, 119
Hettel, Bernard, 57
Hogan, James, recommendation for, 92
Holy Trinity Cathedral, 166
honor rolls
  of Liberty Bond purchasers, 71, 73
  of Red Cross donors, 75–76

hospital beds, *70f*, 111, 149
humor, loss of, 45
Hunt, John, 13–14, 52
hysteria, 45, 49

"imbecile children," care of, 91
immigrants
  acceptance of, 5–6
  Austrian-Hungarian. *See* Austrian-Hungarian immigrants
  draft and, 102, 108, 157
  eastern European, 29
  German Americans, 54–58, 146
inductees
  Alaska as leading in, xii
  mood of, 102, 104
  photos of, *103–104f*
  *See also* draft
*Industrial Worker*, 48
Industrial Workers of the World, 48, 53–54
influenza (1918)
  overview, 134–135
  battlefront deaths from, 113, 119
  quarantines and, 159–160
infrastructure limitations, xii
Ingersoll, C. F., 106
"Inside Passage" to Alaska, 165
integration of public schools, 29
interest rates, Liberty Bonds, 73
interpreters, draft registration and, 93
interracial mixing, 11
isolation as protection, 2
isolationist sentiment, 31–32, 133

James, Leander, 93
Japanese agents, concerns about, 173n30
Japanese Americans, Liberty Bond purchases, 73
Japanese threat, 64–65
Jaslin, Zoleon, 34
Johnson, Albert, 91
Johnson, Raymond, 97
Jones, Preston, on Anderson's death, 53

Juneau
  *Alaska Daily Empire*
    broadsides against Strong, 13–14, 52
    defense of Britt, 56
    letter from the front, 107
  as capitol, 164
  *Daily Alaska Dispatch*
    Adam Smith, excerpt from, 17
    on *Lusitania* sinking, 34, *35f*
    on military preparation, 35
    on noninvolvement, 32
    photo, *16f*
    publication policy changes, 46
    on religion, 12
    on statehood, 140
    on war, 143
  early days of, *4f*
  predictions for, 3, 4
  Treasure and Trinket Fund, 70
  *Weekly Mining Record*, 31
Jusserand, Jean, 84

Kah-du-shan, 30
Kahiltna Birchworks, 176n72
Kalissoff, Alek, draft exemption for, 94
Kaska, Newton, 100
Katzenstein, Selma, 91
Keely, L. C., 59–62
Kehoe, John, 131
Kellum, Mrs. Leon, 123
Kennelly, Martin, 48, 49
Kern, Paul, 67
Keys, George, 106
Keys, Ralph, 106
kilts, worn in battle, 121
Kinninook, Paul Albert, 100
*Knik News. See under* Anchorage
Kodiak, inductees from, *101f*
Koon, Carter, 119, 157
Krause, Edward, 51, 53
Kremmer, Theodore, 56
Kreps, Helen, 10–11

Lane, Franklin, 4, 131
Latané, John
  *America as a World Power*, 30
Latin American alignment with U.S., 66
law enforcement problems, 14
lawsuits, 14
Leacock, Stephen, 37
League of Nations, 133
Lester, E. G., 97
Lewis, Lena Morrow, 48
Lewkesbury, D. B., 45
Liberty Bonds
  about, 71, *72f*, 73
  Alaska response to, 132
  press coverage of, 150–151
  total contributions to, 165
Liberty Gardens, 79
literacy levels, 16–17
local produce, 81–82
Lomen, Alfred, 17
Lomen, Carl, 11, 68, 127, 134
London *Times*, on Alaska purchase, 28
Longfellow, Lyman, 105
Lopp, William T., 9
Lott, Harry, 97
Loyal League (Fairbanks), 102
Loyal League (Ruby), 49, 102, 157
loyalty of German Americans, 56
loyalty pledges, 152–153
Lumpkin, H. H., 102
*Lusitania* (British ship), sinking of, x, 34, 42, 46–47, 145
Lynch, D. M., 81
lynch law proposal, 53
Lynell, Gus, 50

Mackeever, Sanford, 4
mail service
  about, 165
  draft registration and, 93
Mare Island naval yard explosion, 51
*Mariposa*, sinking of, 51
Martin, William, draft exemption for, 94
materiel transport, sled dogs and, 95
McCarthy
  draftee lists, 109
  *Weekly News*
    aspirations for, 161
    on censorship of letters, 156

draftee lists, *109f*
on send-offs, 156–157
on victory, *125f*
wartime donations, 75, 82
*McClure's Magazine*, 16–17
McCullough, Olga, 14
McEwan, John, 93
McGoun, Archibald, 37
McMasters, B. D., 59
Mears, Frederick, 43, 59, 63, 97, 106, 119
meatless days, 79
medical exams, inductees, 92
Meechan, James, 119
merchants, patriotic promotions, 73–74
messengers, dogs as, 154
Mexico, German alliance offer, x, 38
*Miami Herald Record*, on Alaska, 22
Mikoff (Bolshevik leader), 127
military presence in Alaska, 63–66
military registration. *See* draft
military service. *See* active duty
Milne, Charles, 100
mineral resources, 20–21
mining productivity decline, 127–128
mission schools matron, age-difference marriage, 99
missionary work, 166
Moa, Arthur, 134
Moody, Paul, 100
morality of war, 83
munitions. *See* defense industry

Natives
about, 6–11
cultural influence of, 7–8, 9–10
draft registration, 67, 100
in economic downturn, 129
hair donations, 71
influenza (1918), 134–135
Liberty Bonds/Red Cross donations, 73, 76
lifestyle, 141–142
Outside impact on, 29–30
recruiting, 154–155
natural resources
access challenges, xii
Natives' loss of, 29, 30
as potential enemy target, 66
richness of, 20–21
Neilson, Fred, 102, 157
Nenana
about, 142
founding of, ix, xii, 3, *3f*
government role in, 20
*Nenana Daily News*
aspirations for, 161
on Carter Koon, 157
on Griffith, 55
letter from France, 105
on Nenana, 142
on victory celebration, 50
neutrality sentiment, 33, 145–146
*New York Tribune*, on Alaska purchase, 21–22
newspapers
overview, xiv–xv
censorship of, 46–47, 52
See also *specific newspapers*
Nome
aspirations for, 3
education in, 17–18
inductees, *104f*
Natives in, 9
*Nome Nugget*
on Fort Davis closing, 127
on Japanese threat, 64
population decline, 128
public schools in, 29
Siberian trade disruptions, 126–127
noncombat ships, munitions transport, 33–34
noninvolvement sentiment, 31, 32–33, 36
*North American Review*, on Alaska red-tape, 20
nursing homes, food conservation, 81
Nussbaumer, Wagoner, 123

orphans, adoption of, 181n1(App1)
Outside
Alaska compared with, 1–2
Natives' draft registration and, 100

war-related economic boom, 130–131
Overaa, Rangwald, draft exemption for, 94
*Overland Monthly*, on Native education, 10
over-reaction of public outlook/opinion, 48, 51–54

Pacific regions
power balance shift in, 30–31
vulnerability of, 65–66
Pallister, William, 92
Palmer, Merlin, 119
paper conservation, 82
patriotic song, promotion of, 91
Paul, Louis, 100
Paul, William, 10, 100
peace proposals, 36–37
Pershing, John
armistice prediction, 123
on casualties, 116
Mexico, withdrawal from, 38
on military training, 132
photo of, *39f*
physical disabilities, draft exemptions for, 94
Pigg, J.W., 97
poison gas attacks, 108, *113f*
politics
combative, 13–14
dissent, 133
imprisonment/deportation for, 133
political correctness, 47
See also *specific politicians*
porkless days, 79
Porter, C.J., 123
power balance shift, Pacific, 30–31
prohibition laws
overview, 12–13, 164
opposition to, 52
passage of, x
propaganda, negative connotations of, 136
*Propaganda Technique in World War I*, 136
*Providence Journal* (RI), on natural resources, 124
public outlook/opinion
conformity, 49–51
German Americans, 54–58
over-reaction of, 48, 49, 51–54
Socialists, 48–49
transformation of, 45–48
public schools, integration/segregation of, 29
Pullen, Daniel B., 97
Pyne, Charles, 57

Quandra Cannery, draft exemptions for, 94
quarantine, influenza and, 134, 159–160
Quirk, L.M., 126
quotas for draft registration, 94, 97, 164

racial/ethnic interaction, 5–6
radio stations, guarding, 66–67
railroads
about, 165
Alaska Railroad, ix, xii, 3–4, 139–140, 165
government control of, 78
See also *Alaska Railroad Record*
Ray, Henry, 91
recipes for food conservation, 78–79
*Record-Citizen. See under* Ruby
Red Cross
about, 74–76
Alaska response to, 132, 164–165
Anchorage workers, *74f*
battlefront nursing, 111–113, 116
donations to, 9, 73, 151–152
Nome workers, *76f*
on victory, *125f*
Reed, Constance, 36
registration for military service. *See* draft
registration of German Americans, 57
Reinert, Albert, 73–74, *75f*
religious options, 12, *13f*, 164, 166
religious views of war, 67
resource conservation, 78–82
"return to normalcy," 133–134
Revelation (Biblical book), 149

Reynolds, H. D., 19
Richardson, Wilds P., 132
Riggs, Thomas
appointment of, x, 23, 91
Britt as supporter of, 51–52
on economic downturn, 128
on federal neglect, 132
on influenza deaths, 135
law and order, assurance of, 45–46
on military discharges, 124, 126
on Native Red Cross contributions, 9
on post-war world, 136–137
proclamation of support, 150
sedition claims, 56
Siberian turmoil communications, 126
Rocky Mountain Club–Hoover Fund for Relief in Belgium, 91
Rogers, Bruce, 48
Rolston, Howard, 42
Roosevelt, Theodore
on development, 21
on military preparation, 35, 39
*Record-Citizen* on, 36
Ruby
decline of, 129
*Record-Citizen*
on air raids, 136
benefit for a hospital bed, 149
on Britain as international pest, 37
on censorship of speech, 147
demise of, 129
on Dr. Good, 48–49
on economic downturn, 158–159
on German destructiveness, 17
on neutrality sentiment, 145–146
photo, *41f*
on "prejudiced race hatred," 56
publication policy changes, 46–47, 50
on Roosevelt's outlook, 36
self-description, 23
on U.S. policy inconsistencies, 144–145
on war entry, 39, 41–42
on Wilson, 144
Russell, Howard H., 91
Russia
Britain vs., 27
threat from, 65
turmoil in, 126
Russian flag, permission for, 91
Ryan, Jimmy, 15
Rydholm, H. M., 106
sacrifice comparisons, 78
Salem Indian School, draft registration at, 100
"San Diego Plan," 38
San Francisco *Evening Bulletin*, on Alaska purchase, 28
Saville, M. A., 97
Scandinavians, draft evasion and, 52–53
Schafer, Henry, draft exemption for, 94
schizophrenia, draft exemption for, 94
Schmidt, John, 56–57
schools. *See* education
Schott, Raymond C., 43–44
Scidmore, Eliza Ruhama, on Tlingits, 29–30
Second Battle of the Somme, 107
Second Organic Act (1912), ix
Sedition Act (1918), 47–48, 57
segregation
of Natives, 9
of public schools, 29
U.S., 108
Selby, Hal, 14
Selby, Tom, 14
Selective Service Law, 45, 52
*See also* draft
sentry dogs, 153
Serbian National Defense Committee, 98–99
service organizations, contributions, 66, 69
Seward
*Alaska Evening Post*
on government role, 19
on mineral resources, 20
on natural resources, 124
railroad connections, 3
Seward day, 146
*Seward Gateway*

on active duty, *98f, 99f, 101f*
coercive editorials, 69
on forced patriotism, 46
on natural resources, 124
political cartoons, *69f*
population predictions, 4
on war entry, *39f*
Seward, William, 21
"Seward's Folly" myth, 21, 23
Shaffer, Luella, 123
Shea, Arthur, 93
sheep poisoning in California, 51
Sheppard, Fred, 97
Sheppard, R. J., 97
ships
renaming of, 55
submarine warfare on, 33–34, 38, 40
wrecks off Alaska coast, 51
See also *specific ships*
Siberia, trade disruptions, 126
Sitka, 164
Skagway
about, 140–141
anti-Canadian feeling, 96
aspirations for, 3
*Daily Alaskan*
on coastline vulnerability, 148–149
emergency preparedness, 149
on Espionage Act enforcement, 48
on German flag removal, 146
on Liberty Bonds, *72f, 77f*, 150
on Skagway, 140–141
on survival rates, 97
tobacco for soldiers, 150
on war entry/end date, 147, 149
World War I comparisons, 83
*Skagway Alaskan*, on Russian threat, 65
sled dogs on active duty, 95
Smith, Frank, 36–37
Smith, Middleton, 37
Smith, Molly, 74, 85–90
Socialists, 48–49, 52
Somme, Battle of, 107
Spanish-American War (1898), 28, 83, 109
Spinoza, Carlos, 102
*Spokane*, sinking of, 51
sponsored beds for casualties, 111
St. James Methodist Church (Fairbanks), closing of, 128
Starving Armenians Fund, 70
statehood, Alaska, 1, 140
Stimson, Henry, 65
strategic locations, guarding, 66–67
Strong, John (governor)
Alaska overview, xiii, 163–166
defense board nominees, 34
on development, 2
draft board compensation and, 68
on fires of patriotism, 49, 58
on German American tolerance, 148
on Japanese threat, 64–65
Natives and, 8, 100
personal comments, 165
on post-war world, 136
proclamation of support, 147
on prohibition laws, 12, 14–15
removal from office, x, 13–14, 91, 181n1(App2)
Serbian National Defense Committee, communication from, 98–99
swearing in, ix
wartime duties, 91–95
Wilson, support for, 42
Strong, John (soldier), 107
Strong, Mrs. J. F. A., 149
submarine warfare by Germans, x, 33–34, 38, 40, 63
Sulzer, Charles, 57, 164
Sumerlin, Grady, 120
Summers, Clem, 119
Sumner, Charles, 27
Sunday, Billy, 67
Svindlund, Theodore, 102, 157

Tanana, public schools in, 29
Tatum, John, 64, 65
telegraph stations, guarding, 66–67
Teller, aspirations for, 3

territorial ambitions, 27–28
Thomas, Charles, draft exemption for, 94
Thrift Stamps, 150
*Through Siberia: The Land of the Future*, 126
*Times Picayune*
 on cod fishing, 28
 on natural resources, 124
tobacco for soldiers, 150
tourism, Native income from, 29–30
towns, renaming of, 55
trade decline, 37–38
train depots, guarding, 66–67
transient workers, draft registration and, 93
travel restrictions on German Americans, 57, 58
Treatafelopealos, Christ, 94
Troy, John, 13
Tuttle, Charles
 *Alaska: Its Meaning to the World*, 4
Twain, Mark, 82

Underwood, John
 on Alaska's promise, xiii
 on Natives, 6–7, 11
university faculty, sacking of, 48
University of Alaska Fairbanks, x, 181n2(App2)
urbanization, hopes for, 2–4
U.S.
 border disputes/hostilities
  Alaska–British Columbia, 30, 96
  Mexico, 38–39, 46–47, 145
 break with Germany, 33
 Britain and, 37, 96
 France and, 84
 government war controls, 78
 as international policeman, 31
 Latin American alignment with, 66
 policy inconsistencies, 42, 46–47, 144–145
 political dissent in, 133
 Russian threat, 65
 territorial ambitions, 27–28
U.S. Food Administration, 80
USS *Housatonic*, sinking of, 38

*Valdez Miner*, letter from France, 85
"victory bread," 79, 80
*Vigilancia* (American), sinking of, 35
Villa, Pancho (Francisco Villa), 38

Waddleton, William, 49
wages, Alaska vs. Outside, 129, 158–159
Wagner, E. L., 81
Wall Street war benefits, 42, 46–47, 145
WAMCATS, 63–64
war deprivation fatigue, 82
war opportunists, 92
War Savings, 150
wartime contributions. *See* deeds
Washington-Alaska Military Cable and Telegraph System. *See* WAMCATS
weather as draft registration impediment, 100
*Weekly Alaskan*. *See under* Anchorage
*Weekly Mining Record*. *See under* Juneau
*Weekly News*. *See under* McCarthy
*Weekly Times*. *See under* Anchorage
wheatless days, 79
White Pass and Yukon Railway, 96
White Pass Railroad, 165
Wickersham, Frank, 107
Wickersham, James
 on Alaska defenses, 65
 on Alaskans, 137
 assault injuries of, 14
 on Billy Sunday, 67
 on bureaucracy, 132
 campaign rhetoric, 57
 on draftees, 104
 on economic revitalization possibilities, 131
 election of, 164
 on government control of railroads, 78
 on letter from France, 104
 on Liberty Bonds, 71
 on military discharges, 126

on mission schools matron, age-difference marriage, 99
Native culture studies, 10
on quarantine, 134
on returning veterans, 120
on Rolston, 42
on statehood, 23
on a suicide, 15
on U.S. break with Germany, 33
on war, 36, 45, 107
Wilford, C.G., 71
Willis, James, 19
Wilson, Woodrow
break with Germany, 34
criticism of, 133, 147
on draft registration, 97
election of, x
German pamphlet deriding, 106
letters to, 56
Pope Benedictus XV, peace communication, 36
qualities of, 144
Strong's termination, 14, 91, 181n1(App2)
on war entry, 39–41
Wimpe, Abe, 111
Windmueller, Dick, 57
winter dress, Native clothing, 9–10
Wobblies. *See* Industrial Workers of the World
women
on active duty, 111–113, *114–115f*, 116
in positions formerly held by men, 116
suffrage, ix
Women's Christian Temperance Union, 77
Wood, Elizabeth, 10
*World* (New York), 22
World War I
beginning of, ix, x, 23, 147
conclusion of, x, 123–124, *125f*
conflicts/wars, preceding, 1, 30–32, 83, 102, 104, 109
end date prophesy, 149
influenza (1918), 134
military discharges, 124, 126, 136
post-war turmoil, 132
proclamation of support, 147
*See also* active duty
World War II, as follow-on, 136
Wrangell
draftee lists, 109
public schools in, 29
*Wrangell Sentinel*
on criticism of government, 46
on ethnic mix, 67
on German-American loyalty, 56
inductees, *109f*
on Natives' active duty, 100
on patriotism, 148
on poison gas attacks, *113f*

YMCA, 106, 111, 116
Young, Ralph, 8

Zimmermann telegram, x, 38
Zoraeff, Gene, 98